Reflect: the Portishead branch

Mike Vincent

Oxford Publishing Co.

Typesetting by Aquarius Typesetting Services, New Milton,
Hants.

Printed in Great Britain by
S & S Press, Abingdon, Oxon.

Published by:
Oxford Publishing Co.,
Link House,
West Street,
POOLE, Dorset.

CONTENTS

The book is divided into two main sections. The first of these, chapters one to eight inclusive, examines the planning, construction, development and eventual decline of the Bristol to Portishead Railway of the former Great Western Railway. The second section comprises chapters nine and ten and these recount the history of the Bristol (Temple Meads) to Wapping Wharf, and Bristol (Temple Meads) to Canon's Marsh goods line, respectively. Appendices included examine motive power at PBA (Portishead), together with tunnelling and signalling matters on the three lines outlined above.

A typical scene at Portishead (Old) Station.

DEDICATION

This book is very sincerely dedicated to my parents, with thanks for all their help and support.

ACKNOWLEDGEMENTS

Many people have helped in the preparation of this book. I am grateful to them all. Very special thanks must go to: Henry Arberry, Roy Ball, G. Bevan, A. E. Brewer, Terry Dart, Doug Evans, Ron Gardner, Fred Gibson, Hy Goodhind, Don Harwood, Roger Hateley, Cyril Hayman, Paul Holley, J. W. Mann, A. Morgan, R. E. Morgan, Mrs Elsie Moore, Ivor Phillips, Tom Pugsley, John Rich, S. C. T. Rich, Philip and Gordon Smith, D. Stoyel, Garfield Trudgian, L. F. Tucker, Mrs Barbara Voisey, Colin Weekes, Stan Wiltshire and George Woodland.

Sincere thanks must also go to: L. Bennett, Mr Ching, R. F. Cook, M. Dudman, D. J. Fleming, C. Gingell, K. Hurley, Terry Lyons, Colin Maggs, P. Marshall, Jan Murray (CEGB), R. Nelson, George Pryer, C. Redwood, R. C. Riley and Michael Wyatt.

The following organizations have also contributed a great deal to this book: Albright & Wilson, British Rail, both at Bristol and Paddington, Freightliners Limited, Local History Library, Taunton (D. Bromwich), Public Record Offices (Bristol and Kew), Reference Libraries (Bath and Bristol), Signalling Record Society, (J. D. Francis, G. Pryer, J. Morris), South West Gas and Strachan & Henshaw (D. Evans).

Finally, I would like to gratefully express my thanks to the following, for their photographic contributions: Roy Ball, Hugh Ballantyne, L. A. G. Bennett, Bristol City Museum, H. C. Casserley, CEGB, C. R. L. Coles, Terry Dart, Arthur Day, M. E. J. Deane, G. Farr, Cyril Hayman, B. Hill, Grenville Hounsell, the late R. J. Leonard, Mrs Elsie Moore, National Railway Museum (T. J. Edgington), B. J. Nicolle, D. J. Pollard, Port of Bristol Authority, Martin Smith, Steven Smith, Mike Tozer and Mrs Barbara Voisey.

Particular thanks are due to all those who have helped at the Port of Bristol Authority, to Mike Tozer for the tremendous amount of specialist photographic work undertaken, to Steven Smith for handling the photographs of the tickets and handbills, and to J. W. Mann at BR for his help with official railway plans and his constructive comments.

Passengers and pace varied according to the time of day and season, with rushes as children went to school and returned in the afternoon, more people and a festive mood on market days, less travel and more tension as harvest time approached, especially if the weather was bad, and special noisy roistering on that institution, the Saturday night extra. Right down to the 1950s, probably half Britain's branch lines closed later on Saturdays, with gangs of teenage boys, courting couples, perfume and fish and chips percolating into the scene. A happy person with an uncertain gait would arrive from the nearest hostelry just before departure time and produce a roar as he asked the guard if he knew where he was going and did he require any help.

Photograph National Railway Museum and Text David St. John Thomas

The GWR around Bristol, 1932.

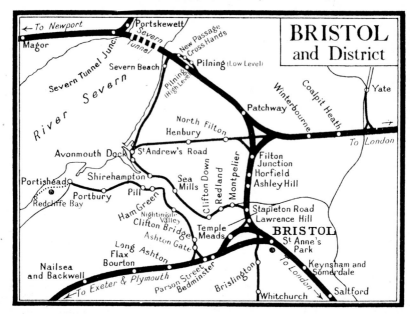

The River Avon and Sea Walls, Bristol, looking towards Avonmouth.
On the left is the line to Portishead, while on the right is the Port & Pier
line from Hotwells, with the CER line from Clifton Down emerging
from Clifton Down Tunnel in the middle foreground. The Portway
road now runs through the Avon Gorge on the site of the Port & Pier
line.

Author's Collection

experience of travelling on the Portishead line. 'During the late 1930s, I travelled over the line about six times a year when I was at school in Portishead. At that time there used to be one of those steam railcars plus a one coach trailer that covered some of the passenger train requirements. However, not all trains were of this formation. Others had either a 'Dean Goods' or one of the 2301 series or one of the many pannier tanks. Tickets were collected at Portbury on trains going to Portishead. On trains from Portishead, tickets were collected at Bedminster. One thing I can always remember was that as the train approached Portishead from Portbury, near the junction where the line into the docks split with those going into the station, the engines always gave a long whistle as if to say 'we will be there in a moment or two' . . .'

Photograph and text C. R. L. Coles

GWR

Portishead Branch

Summary

Distances in miles and chains from London (Paddington)

Parson Street Junction, 120 miles 26¼ chains (formerly Portishead Junction, 120 miles 27 chains)

Parson Street (or Portishead) West Loop:
West Loop Junction, 120 miles 68 chains (Main Line)

West Loop North Junction, 120 miles 50 chains

Ashton Junction, 121 miles 19¼ chains (Junction for lines to Wapping Wharf and Canon's Marsh)

ASHTON GATE PLATFORM, 121 miles 30 chains

Clifton Bridge Sidings, 121 miles 40 chains

CLIFTON BRIDGE, 121 miles 40 chains

No. 1 Tunnel, 59 yards in length

NIGHTINGALE VALLEY HALT, 122 miles 37 chains

No. 2 Tunnel, 232 yards in length

No. 3 (Sandstone) Tunnel, 88 yards in length

Oakwood, 124 miles 40 chains

HAM GREEN HALT, 125 miles 26 chains

Pill Tunnel, 665 yards in length

Pill Viaduct

PILL, 126 miles 12 chains

Portbury Shipyard, 127 miles 30 chains

PORTBURY, 127 miles 77 chains

PORTISHEAD Junction for line to new station, 129 miles 43 chains: New Station, 129 miles 64¾ chains

Junction with Light Railway, 129 miles 71½ chains

PORTISHEAD, 129 miles 75 chains

Portishead Pier, 130 miles 29 chains

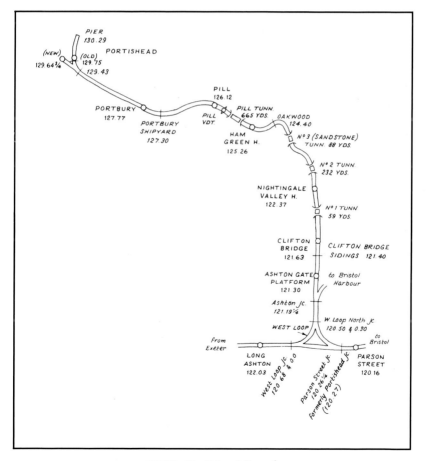

GWR : Portishead Branch.

GWR

Portishead Branch

General Information

Constructed under Bristol & Portishead Pier & Railway Act, 1863.
Opened from Portishead Junction to Portishead Pier, 18th April 1867.
Converted from broad to narrow gauge, 24th-27th January 1880.
Doubled as far as Clifton Bridge in 1883.
Vested in GWR by GWR & Portishead Railway Act, 1884.
Closed to passengers, 7th September 1964.
Cement traffic ceased, 3rd April 1981.

Portishead West Loop — Constructed under GWR (General Powers) Act, 1898. Opened 4th October 1906.
Also opened 4th October 1906:

Wapping Wharf Branch:	Ashton Junction to Wapping Wharf Junction (1 mile 26 chains)
Canon's Marsh Branch:	Ashton Swing Bridge Junction to Canon's Marsh (G) (1 mile 7 chains)
Corporation Lines:	Canon's Marsh (15 chains)

Portishead branch was originally maintained by the Divisional Engineer at Taunton and transferred to Bristol Division on change of boundaries, probably following the opening of the Castle Cary to Langport Line, in 1906.

Ashton Gate Platform
Opened 23rd May 1926. Closed to all traffic 7th September 1964.
Photo (1950) L&GRP 24965

Private Sidings (including sidings on the Wapping Wharf branch)
Ashton Vale Colliery
Ashton Vale Iron Co.
J. Giles & Sons
Ashton Containers Ltd.   (previously Ashton Saw Mills Ltd)
F. Braby & Co. Ltd.
Shell Mex
Bristol Tramways & Carriage Co. Ltd.
S.P.D. Ltd.
Strachan & Henshaw Ltd.

Clifton Bridge (later Clifton Bridge Halt)
Opened 18th April 1867. Unstaffed from 29th October 1962.
Closed 7th September 1964 (P), 5th July 1965 (G)

Quarry Workings adjacent to the railway
United Alkali Co.,
P. J. W. & W. H. H. Mills; Leigh Court Estate
T. Wethered & Woolsley

Nightingale Valley Halt
Opened 9th July 1928. Closed 11th September 1932

Ham Green Halt
Opened 23rd December 1926. Closed 7th September 1964.
Photo (1948) L&GRP 13893

Quarry Workings adjacent to the railway
W. Cowlin & Son; Leigh Court Estate

Portbury Shipyard
Opened 16th September 1918. Closed 26th March 1923.
(Passenger traffic only). Shipyard not used and abandoned
before completion.

Portbury
Opened 18th April 1867. Closed to all traffic 30th April 1962.
Photo L&GRP 15449

Portishead
Old station opened 18th April 1867. Closed to all traffic 4th
January 1954. Photos L&GRP 15448 (1948) and 11943 (date
unknown). New station opened 1954. Closed 7th September
1964 (P) 1st May 1967 (G).

Private Sidings
Bristol Corporation
Malt & Milling Co.,
Bailey & Son Ltd.
Gas Company
W. Cowlin & Son (temporary sidings for new generating station)
Severn Kraft Mills (1928) Ltd.
Ministry of Power
CEGB

Portishead Pier
Sold to Bristol Corporation 31st December 1962.

PORTISHEAD BRANCH
GRADIENTS

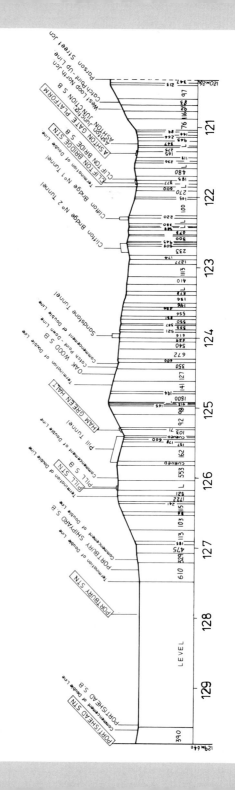

INTRODUCTION

'. . . The transformation of the (Portishead) Pill into a floating dock was the very climax to much planning. Deep water piers had been proposed in 1832 and again in 1839 but the first Portishead Dock scheme was suggested by C. F. Thomas in 1853 with a highly complicated and ambitious plan. Eventually the Portishead Dock was built, as a sort of expensive spite, by a group of Bristol merchants who opposed the excavating of docks at Avonmouth. . . . The struggles between Portishead Dock and Avonmouth Docks and the Bristol City Docks were bitter but stopped on 1st September 1884 when the Bristol Corporation assumed control of all three.'

Text: *Somerset Harbours* — G. Farr

The first railway to arrive at the quiet mid-nineteenth century hamlet of Portishead was the 9 mile 49 chain Bristol & Portishead Pier & Railway Company's line. Broad gauge and single throughout, it left the Bristol & Exeter main line near Telegraph Inn Bridge, Bedminster. At its opening, on 18th April 1867, the impoverished line had stations at Clifton Bridge, Pill, Portbury and Portishead. Although the line had been built, and was maintained by, the B&PP&RCo., it was worked by the Bristol & Exeter Company. Until 1880, the line had no crossing places, but in that year a passing loop was installed at Clifton Bridge.

In 1871 the company obtained an Act to build a dock at Portishead and, after various serious mishaps during the construction period, this was eventually opened on 28th June 1879. In 1880 the line was converted from broad to narrow gauge, while in 1883 the section from Clifton Bridge Station to the line's junction with the GWR was doubled. In 1884 Portishead Dock and its competitors at Avonmouth and the City Docks in Bristol were all taken over by Bristol Corporation, the railway and pier having passed into the hands of the GWR earlier in the year on 1st July.

In retrospect, it can clearly be seen that the dock's construction was a mistake, and the years up until the turn of the twentieth century would appear to have been lean ones. However, new developments at Portishead during the Edwardian period, up to World War I, gave rise to some optimism, although the opening of the Royal Edward Dock at Avonmouth, in 1908, was clearly pointing out the direction in which the tide was going to be running in the long term.

On 7th August 1907, and without fuss or ceremony, another impoverished railway entered the annals of Portishead's railway history. This was the Portishead extension of the Weston, Clevedon & Portishead Light Railway (the WC&PLR), one of the West Country's few light railways. A detailed history of this line is not within the scope of this particular book, but mention will be made of it whenever its history becomes intimately entwined with that of the GWR branch.

Meanwhile, on the latter railway, World War I saw new developments taking place along its length, the main one being the construction of a Government shipyard near Portbury. This yard was rail connected and, where it joined the GWR, a loop, some sidings, a signal box and a small passenger station were all constructed. The shipyard project was never successful and the rail facilities, likewise, withered, although later in the line's history some reinstatement took place.

During the 1920s the GWR developed the passenger traffic, particularly that of the 'day tripper', and new halts at Ham Green (1926) and Nightingale Valley (1928) were opened. Ashton Gate Platform was also reopened in 1926, having previously been in operation from 1906 to 1917 while a second passenger platform was provided, in 1930, at Portishead. Further industrial developments took place at Portishead in the fading years of the 1920s but, in spite of all the projects, by 1938 the Port of Bristol was actually considering closing the other partner in the B&PP&R Co., for the dock had fallen on very hard times.

The GWR branch was very busy during World War II, but the war years saw the inevitable disappearance of the WC&PLR. Closed in May 1940, it was subsequently purchased by the GWR. The line was lifted during late 1942, work continuing into 1943. Post-war, major demolition work also occurred at Portishead where, due to the construction of a second power station, (Portishead 'B'), the old railway station had to be demolished. Rebuilt on a site nearer the town, the new station had, as its location, a site on which it had originally been proposed to build the branch terminus way back in the plans of 1862. The new station was opened in January 1954.

Ten years later, there had been a complete turn around in the line's fortunes, with the branch losing its passenger services after a period of deliberate running down by the railway authorities. The line remained open for freight, essentially woodpulp, containers and cement traffic, until 3rd April 1981 when the last cement train left the few remaining sidings at Portishead. Only a few years before, these sidings had been part of a new and bustling railway centre.

The future of the line today (1983) is uncertain. At the time of writing no traffic at all runs along its rusting metals. Future traffic could include stone for Foster Yeoman, or passengers for the proposed Avon Metro, if the latter is ever built. The line has always had a very chequered career. There have been times when the branch has been very busy indeed, times such as World War I, the 1920s and the 1950s, for example, but there have also been other periods when the future has looked very bleak indeed. The present time, unfortunately, is one of these periods.

However, in spite of its current precarious position, it is still true to say that the branch, and the remnants of the City Docks system, are still lines full of contrast and interest. They pass near the centre of a great city, rubbing shoulders with industries old and new. They were once thriving, throbbing arteries of trade, now they are quiet ageing capillaries, thinned but not yet completely deprived of life. From the city outskirts to the depths of Leigh Woods, under the Avon Suspension Bridge and over the viaduct at Pill, across farmland which once provided the line with milk traffic, passing two of Bristol's hopes for the future, the Royal Portbury Dock and the motorway, we arrive at Portishead itself, now changed beyond belief from those early days of the 1860s and 1870s. Is it really surprising that the line still has an attraction?

Mike Vincent
Bath
1983

Chapter One

Docks and railways seem naturally to go together. This book is about a number of docks and railways developing, growing and, unfortunately, dying together. In this chapter I want to look at some of the plans and proposals put forward in the early and mid-nineteenth century that eventually led to the building and opening, in April 1867, of the Bristol & Portishead Pier & Railway Company's broad gauge line, from Bristol Temple Meads to the then quiet hamlet of Portishead.

In the first few years of the 1800s the only major docks in use in the area were those in the centre of Bristol. However, certain individuals in the city believed that the only place that the port could really develop was at the mouth of the Avon where it joined the River Severn. The debate about whether to extend the City Docks system by widening the River Avon between the city and its mouth, or by building river-mouth docks, occupied businessmen, local councillors, politicians and many others right up to the turn of the twentieth century and, of course, allied with this debate was the development of the railway network in the area.

In order to set the background for the Portishead area's railway development, let us go back to the first visions and ideas that led to port improvements in and around Bristol in the nineteenth and twentieth centuries. For that we will, indeed, have to go back quite a long way, to the year of 1800 when a Bristol colliery owner, a certain Mr Grace, planned the building of a railway from his collieries to his Portishead Wharf. The railway was to have been built on a gradient so that the empty wagons would be drawn up by descending full ones. However, like many of the projects we are about to examine, this one never got started. In 1832, more plans were put forward by Mr Milne. He suggested that a pier should be built at Portishead. It would have been 800 ft. long and would have provided three landing stages. Again, nothing happened.

In a report dated 26th December 1839, Isambard Kingdom Brunel added weight to the debate by making the following suggestions about the dock accommodation at the port of Bristol. He put forward the following three proposals:

1) A lock large enough to take large vessels into the Floating Harbour (the name for the Inner City Docks) could be built. In addition, he also felt that the channel from the City Docks to the mouth of the River Avon could be straightened and widened.

2) Secondly, docks could be constructed some way down the river nearer the sea. From the docks to the sea the channel could be wider and deeper.

3) Finally, a pier could be built at Portishead. Along with this proposal was the suggestion that a railway be built to join the Bristol & Exeter railway some three miles from its Bristol terminus. Nearly thirty years later, this was, in fact, what happened.

In 1842, another plan for a pier at Portishead emerged, although, this time, a railway was not part of the overall plan. The scheme was put forward by Mr (afterwards Sir) John McNeil and matters went as far as the acquisition of an Act of Parliament in July 1841. However, due to design problems the project proved impossible to carry out.

Further plans flowed and, in May 1845, Brunel propounded yet another scheme, this time for a floating pier near Portbury, with a railway, working on Brunel's (in)famous atmospheric principle, through to Bristol. The Portbury Pier & Railway Company was formed, with a capital of £200,000 in £50 shares, to carry out this proposal. An Act was obtained in 1946 (9 & 10 Vic c 344) but, in spite of the fact that the promoters tried desperately hard to get funding for the project, they were unsuccessful. This was essentially due to the problems following on from the 'railway mania' of the mid-1840s. The exercise was abandoned, and the company was wound up.

Meanwhile, at Portishead itself, a small stone pier had been built in 1849. This was situated below the Royal Hotel at Portishead Point and, after that time, packet steamers usually unloaded passengers there. However, at high tides the packets could steam right up the Pill to the Old Wharf. Plans, rather than more positive results, continued to be put forward. In 1852 a certain Mr Rendel put forward very important proposals in November of that year, and for what was believed to be the first time, it was suggested that docks should be constructed at the actual mouth of the Avon. In addition, it was also suggested that the docks, this time on the Gloucestershire side of the river, should be connected to the GWR at Bristol by a railway. History tells us, in hindsight, that this scheme was really the forerunner of the 1864 Bristol Port & Channel Dock project and the Bristol Port Railway & Pier Company's 1862 proposal to serve that dock. However, more of these schemes later.

In 1853 Mr Croome produced a scheme for two gigantic docks, each of fifty acres, with a canal to Pill to connect the dock to the Avon at that village. This plan also envisaged the use of a railway from the dock to Bristol. In the same year, a rival plan for a dock in Portishead Pill, virtually the same plan as the one adopted twenty years later, was produced by Mr W. R. Neale. The plans are, at long last, starting to get closer to the reality that later grew

PORTBURY FLOATING PIER, LANDING PLACE, & STEAM PACKET HARBOUR,
IN THE CHANNEL 8 MILES BELOW **BRISTOL**, IN CONTINUATION OF THE LINE OF THE **GREAT WESTERN RAILWAY** & IN THE PROPERTY OF **JAMES ADAM GORDON** Esq.[re]

ENGINEER I. K. BRUNEL Esq[re]

Pub.[d] by George Davey, Liberal, & Bristol.

Brunel's proposed floating pier, the landing place and steam packet harbour at Portbury.

up. The flood of schemes continued and, later in the decade in 1858, Mr Thornton prepared an elaborate plan for dockising the River Avon. 'Dockisation', one of the key alternatives in the development of the nineteenth century Port of Bristol, was the arrangement whereby the whole course of the tidal Avon, from its mouth right up to the City Docks, would be turned into a series of docks. In order to keep high water levels in the river, a dam would have been built, precisely where Royal Portbury Dock is today, so that ships could travel up and down river at all times. However, one major problem with the dockisation alternative was that ships were getting larger all the time and they were finding it increasingly difficult to navigate the river. Indeed, many foundered on the mudbanks and, later in the book, we will see how this problem remained until well after the Portishead branch had been built.

Mr Thornton's name appears in another plan released in 1860. At this time he proposed the construction of a small quay and facilities on the Gloucestershire (northern) side of the Avon. This dock was intended for ocean-going steamships and, by now, things were starting to 'hot up' in the battle between those who supported the development of the City Docks and those who felt that entirely new docks should be constructed at the mouth of the river. These latter supporters were again split into two camps, namely, those who supported the developments on the Gloucestershire side, at what was, later, to become Avonmouth, and those who felt that money could be more wisely spent on developing the land on the Somerset side, the subject of this story, the land later to become Portishead Dock.

From the early 1860s onwards, in the City Council, and out of it, there followed a long series of debates and discussions concerning the development of the Port of Bristol. These debates became known as 'the battle of the docks'. Looking back, one thing that is very easy to forget is the amount of very bad feeling that was created by the various factions involved in the debates over the siting and building of Bristol's docks. Today, the arguments are academic. At the time, however, the infighting was most unpleasant. The *Bristol Times* of 7th May 1864 said that the debate had been:

'. . . a sort of nightmare on the society of the city. Worse than politics, because more bitterly fought, it has cooled, if not quite destroyed, many friendships, and certainly broken up many associations. (The debate had been) . . . of a character to break up old acquaintances, to chill conviviality, to make men look pale and spiteful at one another when it was introduced at table . . .'

This was strong stuff, indeed!

Bristol Corporation owned a good deal of land at Portishead and several members of the council favoured the development of dock facilities on this side of the river rather than on the Gloucestershire side. In 1861 the corporation went to Parliament with plans for the widening and general improvement of the river, while an independent company, the Bristol Port Railway & Pier Company, sought powers to build a railway along the north bank of the Avon, from Clifton, under the, then, unfinished Suspension Bridge, to Avonmouth, where a deep water pier was to be built. Opposed, both plans were unsuccessful. In the following year the promoters of the Port & Pier Bill were once more faced with opposition, but this time, this did not include opposition from the corporation. The Bill received the Royal Assent in July 1862 (25 & 26 Vic). Work on the railway began in 1863. It continued through 1864, when the Suspension Bridge was opened, until, in March 1865, the line opened quietly for business. The pier was opened in June of the same year and the battle of the river-mouth docks began to take shape. (For further information on the Bristol Port Railway & Pier Company's development and, indeed, for a history of many of the other Bristol—Severnside railways, please see the author's companion book, *Lines to Avonmouth*, published by OPC).

Just before the Port & Pier line was finished, another company was formed. This was almost entirely made up of members of the Port & Pier Company and its aim was to develop a dock at Avonmouth, the Bristol Port & Channel Dock. When this happened, however, their opponents, who wanted to develop a dock on the Portishead side, got together to form the Bristol & Portishead Pier & Railway Company. Made up of influential Bristolians, the Portishead Company had, as its chairman, Alderman James Ford, a director of both the Taff Vale Railway and the Clifton Suspension Bridge Companies. Fellow directors included other Bristol notables such as Michael Castle, Thomas Canning, Richard Fry, Richard Fuidge and Richard Robinson.

The company's proposed pier was intended to be much about the same size as that put forward in Brunel's 1845 plan, while the railway was to run from a junction with the main Bristol & Exeter Railway line to Taunton, in the parish of Bedminster, to a pier beginning on the sea wall in the parish of Portbury. Interestingly, Portishead was to be served by a branch which would diverge from the main Portbury line at a point close to Shipway Gate Farm.

Strangely enough, particularly when one considers the amount of competition there then was for dock and railway projects at the mouth of the Avon, the Portishead Company's Bill, authorizing

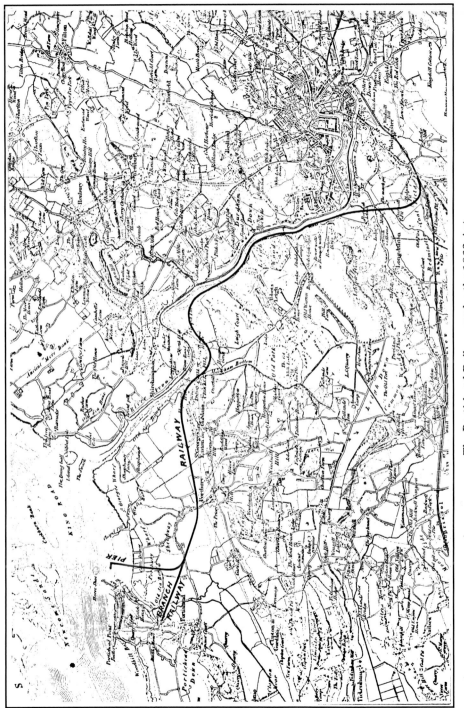

The Portishead Railway under the 1863 Act.

the works, met with little serious opposition and the Act received the Royal Assent on 29th June 1863 (26 & 27 Vic c 107). This Act authorized a capital of £200,000 with £66,600 in borrowing powers. Construction of the line began just before Easter of the following year.

Although the Bill's passage was reasonably easy, some complaints were received. The first area of protest was raised by some early conservationists who were worried about the possible damage that the construction of the railway would cause as it ran along the foot of the beautiful Leigh Woods. Alderman Ford responded by saying that:

'. . . no better security could be taken for the preservation of the beauty of the woods than the construction of the railway, as it would put a stop to the quarrying and blasting which had much damaged them . . . '

Ford was wrong. The blasting and quarrying continued well into the twentieth century and even a special Avon Gorge Committee of the corporation in the early years of the present century, failed to stop the destruction.

One other unpopular consequence of the line being built was the demolition of two or three dwellings in the Avon Gorge, nearly under the Suspension Bridge, opposite the Hotwell. These so-called 'chocolate houses' (because they served chocolate, tea, etc.) were very popular with the working classes during the summer months, and when they had to be pulled down to make way for the line, large sums were demanded from the railway company as compensation. Unlike the 'chocolate houses', the Suspension Bridge nearby was to be protected from the railway which was to run under the west abutment of the bridge. Clauses in the 1863 Act ensured that the tunnel concerned, the 59 yard long No. 1 Tunnel, was built to the satisfaction of the Bridge Company's engineer.

At the first half-yearly meeting of the company, held on 27th February 1864, it was reported that good progress was being made in the acquisition of land for the line. In addition the following engineers' report was read out and discussed:

'Gentlemen
The line has been resurveyed and set out since the passing of the Act, and property plans prepared for the land throughout.
The contract drawings and specifications are completed, and the works are ready to be let to a contractor as soon as sufficient land is obtained to enable him to proceed with the works.
Some delay occurred in consequence of a deviation having been

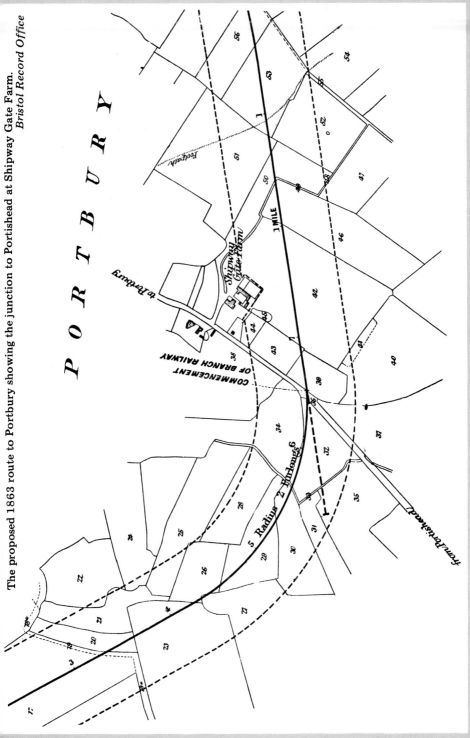

The proposed 1863 route to Portbury showing the junction to Portishead at Shipway Gate Farm.
Bristol Record Office

23

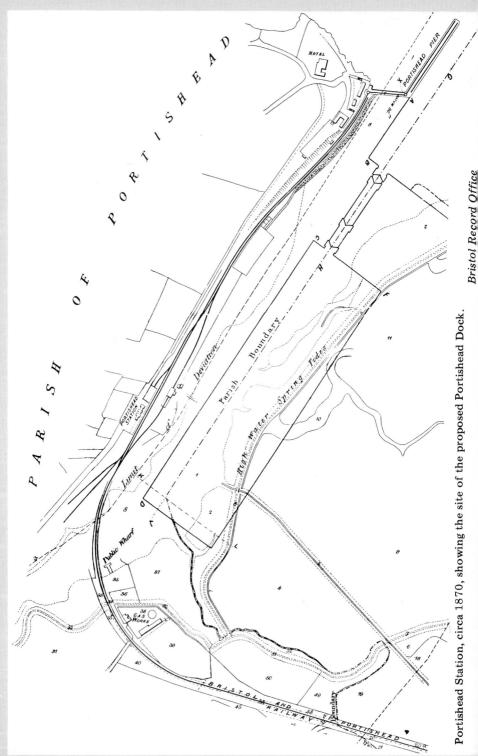

Portishead Station, circa 1870, showing the site of the proposed Portishead Dock.

surveyed through Leigh Court, which would have been beneficial to the public; but as it was not agreed to, the Line within the Parliamentary limits had to be set out again, and new property plans prepared.

We are, Gentlemen, your obedient Servants
McCLEAN & STILEMAN

By the second half-yearly meeting, held on 3rd September 1864, a contractor, Mr William Tredwell of Handsworth, had been found and work on the line had well and truly started.

It would appear that work had begun very quickly after the first meeting in February and that the traditional Victorian engineering ceremony of 'cutting the first sod' was dispensed with, possibly because of financial difficulties or, perhaps, because of the pace at which events were moving on the other side of the river on the Port & Pier.

By September 1864, arrangements had been made for the completion, early in 1865, of the section between the proposed station at Rownham (Clifton Bridge) and the line's junction with the Bristol & Exeter's main line near Telegraph Inn Bridge, Bedminster. It was then to be brought into immediate use, so that as Ford himself said to the September 1864 meeting of the Board:

'. . . at that very early period, a portion of your property will be in useful employment.'

Subscriptions, etc., by June 1864 had reached £37,600 whilst expenditure, up to the same date, had reached just over £33,700. At the same meeting the retirement of Mr M. Castle was announced. His place on the Board was to be taken up by Mr L. Fry.

Further along the line towards Portishead, the track was to go into more tunnels, past Sir William Miles' Ham Green Estate, in order to maintain its rural appearance. However, as we have seen, changes came about which led to the replacement of the tunnel at the Bristol end of the estate by a deep cutting. This was the first of many changes to the line's proposed 1863 route. The branch from Shipway Gate Farm to Portishead became the main line, while the section of track from the same farm to Portbury and the Pier was abandoned. In addition, at Portishead itself there were to be more changes. In the line's new routeing it swung northwards, in a long curve, to run alongside a quay, and finishing its course at a newly proposed pier, just alongside and below the Royal Hotel.

For these changes the company obtained a new Act in 1866 (29 Vic c 88). This allowed the changes, outlined above, to take place

This photograph shows the Avon Gorge in May 1864. The slopes are well wooded and in the middle distance can be seen one of the tea houses that was about to be demolished for the route of the Portishead line. On the right can be seen the 73 yard long No. 1 Tunnel of the Bristol Port Railway & Pier Company (as then unopened), rival to the Portishead scheme.

'The tea gardens, with silvan nooks and bowers beneath the hanging woods of Leigh, were crowded with gay holiday-makers, while omnibuses, running every quarter of an hour, (before the advent of trams), conveyed hundred to the Gay Promenade on the west side of the old lock of the basin. But the construction of the Portishead Railway destroyed one of the most accessible means of outdoor enjoyment people had within reach.'

M. J. Tozer Collection

This view shows the same spot a year later, in 1865. The house has been demolished and some of the woods cleared. Preparations are under way to cut the No. 1 Tunnel on the Portishead line which was to run through the rock beneath the high tower of the Suspension Bridge. A couple of contractor's railway trucks can be seen in the distance, the contractor for this project being William Tredwell.

M. J. Tozer Collection

and also to give the company permission to raise additional capital to the tune of £66,000 in shares and £20,000 by borrowing. Fortified by this new injection of cash, construction proceeded apace. At a point when railway construction was having a difficult time, the financial achievements of the company, in getting the line completed, were quite impressive. The *Western Daily Press*, writing about the Portishead branch just after its opening in April 1867, had this to say:

'It is an idea, if not an axiom, of the commercial world that the best time to begin business is when business is bad. If so, and without pausing to analyse the saying, we must conclude the Bristol & Portishead Railway, which was opened on Thursday last (18th April 1867) has inaugurated its career under favourable auspices: for we suppose the locomotive interest has never known a time when it lacked sunshine so much . . . '

So, from the beginning, it appeared that life was going to have more than its fair share of difficult times for the B & PP & R.

As well as financial problems, the line also had its constructional difficulties. There was a good deal of tunnelling to be done. There were embankments to be built while, at the approach to Portishead Station, there was to be a long, curving, wooden viaduct sweeping around past Parish Wharf and over the Pill itself, here about 15 ft. deep in its deepest part. Once built, this viaduct, a timber structure, had 23 spans. Of these, the two at the Portishead end appeared to have been added as an afterthought. The bridge was supported on trestles, 25 ft. apart. The underside of the structure was about 5 ft. above the water-line. The crossing of this Pill was just one of the difficulties which the engineers, Messrs McClean and Stileman of Great George Street, Westminster, and the navvies employed to build the line, had to overcome.

For the engineering work, 400 navvies came into the Pill area to work on the railway. They had the difficult task of building the railway through the environs of Pill with its cuttings, tunnels and viaduct. They were employed in digging out the very deep excavations required for the foundations of the viaduct and, according to a local writer of the time, these had to be made strong with bags of cement because of the shifting sand. The gangers lived, with their families, in huts on the site of the Monmouth Road, while the horses were stabled at Heywood Hall, the site of the vicarage. The rest of the men were billeted in the village, the

Construction work takes place alongside the New Inn near Clifton Bridge Station. All seems fairly quiet. Perhaps everyone was having a tea break?
Bristol City Museum

Clifton Bridge Station, circa 1867, with a Down train at the platform hauled by a 2-2-2WT. Note the construction materials beside the line in the foreground. Note, too, the beautiful silvan setting of the station.
M. J. Tozer Collection

masons in the better houses, the labourers in the poorer ones.

The navvies, with nicknames such as Derbyshire Sam, Lancashire Tom, Somersetshire Jack, Cornish Joe and Monmouth Bill, proved popular with the ladies of the parish. This in turn led, on Whit Monday 1863, to a fight between the local lads and the navvies in Pump Square. The village bobby was conveniently on patrol between Pill and Portbury. It was quite a fight by all accounts, but there seems to be no record of who actually won. PC Fry stopped the fight, which had started around 2.00 p.m., at 4.30 p.m.! Once the railway was finished, the navvies moved on, although a few of the navvies married local girls and stayed, bringing new names to the village.

With problems virtually solved and the line nearly built, it was inspected, on 12th April 1867, by a Board of Trade Inspector, Colonel Yolland, who assessed its ability to carry passenger traffic. Yolland's report was very full and provided a good picture of the line in its almost completed state. Single throughout, it was built to the broad gauge of 7 ft. 0¼ in. It had stations at Clifton Bridge, Pill, Portbury and Portishead, with a siding at Ashton Vale Works. The line of the B&PP&RCo. was 9 miles 11½ chains in length with an additional 48½ chains of track on the pier at Portishead. The trackwork, itself, had rails that were fixed directly to the sleepers using screw bolts and fang nuts. Chairs were not used. There were engine turntables at Portishead Station and at the Bristol & Exeter Station at Temple Meads so as to allow engines to be turned at both ends of the journey. At the time of Yolland's inspection, the station at Portishead had not been completed.

On the civil engineering side, Yolland notes that there were 11 over and 10 underbridges, 3 viaducts and 4 tunnels. The over and underbridges and viaducts were all, with the exception of three or four which had cast-iron platforms to carry the roadways, constructed of stone and brick. In all, he seems to have been reasonably impressed with the quality of the work. He does, however, make special comment of the fact that the line differed very much indeed from the 1863 plans, particularly with regard to the curves, gradients and tunnels. The line, as built, was, he felt, in no way as good, from an engineering standpoint, as that proposed in the 1863 Act.

Although all was generally well constructed, there were one or two points that Yolland insisted should be dealt with before he allowed it to be opened to traffic. Some were fairly minor: for example, some of the fencing allowed cattle and sheep to stray on the track and Yolland insisted that more intermediate fencing posts should be added. Others were more important. Signalling matters had to be attended to at the junction with the Bristol & Exeter and at Ashton Vale siding. In addition, the line was too close to two of the overbridges and the retaining walls had to be cut back. This was also true of No. 2 Tunnel, in that open carriage doors fouled the tunnel wall. An underbridge, eight miles between Portbury and Portishead needed strengthening. Finally, and rather importantly, at Portbury Station, Yolland asked that the siding on the east of the station's platform should be made to join the Up line, rather than the Down as it then did. This would do away with an unnecessary facing point. In addition, he wanted the company to install an additional platform for Up trains.

Once the report had been received by the company, they lost no time at all in carrying out the recommendations that Colonel Yolland had made, and, in a letter, to Colonel Yolland, dated 16th April 1867, from the company's offices in Clare Street, Bristol, the B & PP & R Co. informed the Inspector that his suggestions had been carried out. In particular, the line's engineer had cut back the stone and rock faces of the bridges and tunnels, while at Clifton Bridge Station the rails had been removed in the siding at the arrival end of the Down platform. They would be reinstated as soon as the points had been interlocked with the main line signal. At Portbury Station the point leading into the siding there had been removed, while the loop line had been disconnected at one end. It would seem, from this statement, that originally Portbury would have been a passing place but, due to changes brought about by Yolland's report, this never happened. Finally, it was very reassuring to know that the company was installing manholes in Pill Viaduct! These changes having been made, the Portishead Railway was ready to be opened, and open it did, on Thursday, 18th April 1867.

This photograph shows celestine being loaded into barges at Miles Dock ▷ around 1910, some two years before operations here ceased. Celestine was formerly worked in the grounds of Leigh Court near Abbots Leigh, where there was a tramway, over half a mile in length from the workings along Paradise Bottom to Miles Dock on the Avon. The dock, which is still visible, was originally built for unloading stone used in the construction of Leigh Court, the latter being completed in 1814. It was not used for handling celestine until late in the nineteenth century when a Mr R. B. Withers, of Pill, worked the mineral. Celestine is the main source of strontium salts and these are used in the making of signal flares, tracer bullets, rockets and fireworks.
Bristol City Museum

The original plans, showing the construction of the wooden viaduct that ▷ crossed the Pill at Portishead. Note the elevated rail to ease the trains around the right hand curve into the B & PP & R Company's station at Portishead.
BR/Author's Collection

THE OPENING OF THE RAILWAY TO PORTISHEAD
18th APRIL 1867

'Without any ceremony the new line from Bristol to Portishead was ... opened for traffic. It is nearly three years ago that the railway was commenced, and taking into consideration the amount of tunnelling, excavating, and embankment-making which has been necessary, the time occupied does not seem long. Starting from the Bristol & Exeter terminus the passenger traverses a couple of miles of the main line of that company, and at the extremity of Bedminster breaks off into the permanent way of the Portishead line. . . . There are three stations between the termini, viz: Clifton Bridge, Pill and Portbury. The first of these is about four miles from Temple Meads, and is, properly speaking, at Rownham, only a road connecting with the Bridge, has led to the latter designation being employed. This road has been made at the joint expense of the Portishead Railway, Leigh Woods Land, and Suspension Bridge Companies, the object of it being to accommodate persons who may prefer going to Clifton that way to doing so via the ferry, and the long dusty Hotwell Road.

Pill Station is a conspicuous object, standing on a portion of the line raised considerably above the surrounding level. The little inlet of water called the 'Pill' is crossed by a viaduct consisting of seven piers, built upon very firm artificial foundations. Two miles from Pill is situated the Portbury Station; and two miles further on we get to Portishead, the station of which is situated about half a mile from the village.

There is a deep cutting at the junction, a cutting just before the Suspension Bridge, a tunnel in the rock under the Bridge, a tunnel through Coffee House Point, an embankment in Greenland Quarry, and short tunnel beyond, a high level at the 'dock' (*), a long cutting in Leigh Park Farm, a viaduct at Chapel Pill, a tunnel 600 yards long under Ham Green, a viaduct over Pill, and other features of a similar character. The cost of the nine and a half miles of railway, including stations, etc., has been close upon £200,000.

The ride through Leigh Woods, and by the channel side will, in the summer months, be a very delightful one. Equally beautiful is the scenery around Portishead, to which hundreds of passengers will no doubt be attracted. A goodly number of passengers went to and fro (at the opening), and the villagers of Portishead exhibited signs of rejoicing at the completion of the undertaking. It is intended shortly to commence a pier, which is expected to occupy about two years in erection.'

(*) The dock mentioned here is the Miles Dock

Lens of Sutton

table, the goods yard and, in the left distance, the dock itself.

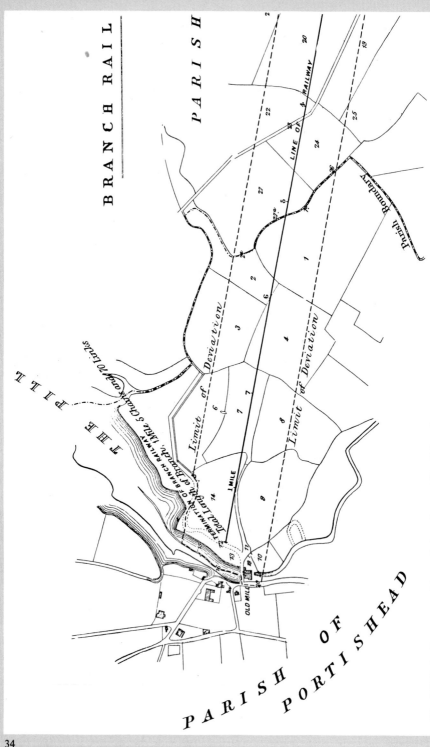

The 1863 Act's proposed branch terminus at Portishead.

Bristol Record Office.

Chapter Two

Even at its opening, the line's financial problems became apparent. It could not afford a decent banquet and celebration to get the new railway well and truly launched:

> 'Another somewhat singular circumstance in connection with the concern is that it is opened without a banquet; that not a champagne cork has been popped off or a cannon fired, a shilling expended for wine or for powder (save so far as the latter was required for blasting the Leigh rocks) from the turning of the first sod to the starting of the first train . . . There is an Irish adage which says 'a dry christening forbodes a dull baby' and we can only hope the hospitable Bristolians will forgive the omission in this case, and that it will be no ill omen to the undertaking that its inauguration has not been renowned by even an ounce of cheese or a pint of beer . . . '

The newspaper, from which the extract was taken, the *Bristol Times & Mirror*, dated 20th April 1867, suggests that the reason for the absence of food and drink was probably due to the fact that the work on the railway started in Lent 1864!

But whatever the opening was like, the local press regarded with some importance, the opening of a second riverside railway, the Port & Pier having already opened on the river's northern bank in March 1865. It also made much of the fact that the railway to Portishead and, for that matter, the Clifton Suspension Bridge were both going to open up:

> '. . . what was, only a couple of years ago, a wilderness and the haunt of conies, but which is soon destined to become the site of a fashionably inhabited suburb; and now the railway whistle echoes in glens called after the more musical nightingale: while omnibuses will carry the 'Posset' (*) visitor to Clifton along roads for which the forest oaks have only just been cleared away, and a bustling railway station is raised under the shadow of Rownham Hill (**). Verily the movement in that once secluded side of the Avon is something marvellous.'

> *(*) 'Posset' is the local name for Portishead*

> *(**) This was, of course, Clifton Bridge Station*

Text: *Bristol Times & Mirror*, dated 20th April 1867

The timetables for the line's opening are to be found below. The company was able to open in time for the Easter holiday and ran a Sunday timetable for Good Friday, while on Easter Monday and Tuesday an extra Up train left Portishead at 7.00 p.m. This called at Clifton Bridge and Temple Meads, the line's record for handling day trippers had begun! Clifton Bridge Station was served by horse buses from Tyndall's Park Road. These ran via Clifton and the Suspension Bridge. Passengers could also reach the station by catching a horse bus at the Exchange. This brought them to Rownham Ferry, which they would then catch for the last stage of the journey across the Avon. A table showing the line's fares is shown below, but it might be useful to remember that 'volunteers in uniform' were conveyed as under:

| Bristol to Portishead and back | (1st class) | 1s 0d | (2nd class) | 9d |
| Clifton Bridge to Portishead and back | (1st class) | 9d | (2nd class) | 6d |

FARES (DOWN TRAINS)

Ordinary			Return		BRISTOL
1	2	3	1	2	
s d	s d	s d	s d	s d	
0 6	0 4	0 3	0 9	0 6	CLIFTON BRIDGE
1 3	0 10	0 7½	2 0	1 3	PILL
1 7	1 0	0 9½	2 4	1 6	PORTBURY
2 0	1 6	0 11½	3 0	2 3	PORTISHEAD

FARES (UP TRAINS)

Ordinary			Return		PORTISHEAD
1	2	3	1	2	
s d	s d	s d	s d	s d	
0 5	0 3	0 1½	0 8	0 5	PORTBURY
0 9	0 6	0 3½	1 2	0 9	PILL
1 6	1 0	0 8	2 3	1 6	CLIFTON BRIDGE
2 0	1 6	0 11½	3 0	2 3	BRISTOL

At Portishead itself, one of the facilities for running the railway was an engine shed. This was provided with the opening of the railway and was built of brick. It had a gable style, slate roof. It had the usual amenities and equipment comprising an office, stores, coal plant and water tank. The latter was supplied with a pump house underneath. Sometime around 1896 the shed was closed. At the same time, in June 1896 to be exact, the 45 ft. turntable, that had been in operation up until that time, was moved from its original position on the line that ran through the shed itself, on to a spur road that ran off the through line at the Pier end of the station. The turntable remained in this position until closure of the station in 1954. Again, around 1896, the coaling road and covering were also dismantled. The shed was officially registered as being out of use in 1901.

It is believed that the depot was handed over to the goods department in 1915 but no engine had been allocated to the shed since at least 1896. The shed's allocation remains uncertain.

Once the excitement of the railway's opening had died down, the company turned its attention to developments of a more maritime nature. We have already seen how the 1866 Act of the Bristol & Portishead Pier & Railway Company had varied the provisions of their 1863 Act, and had extended the time allowed for the completion of works. In addition, however, it gave the company some of the powers of a dock company which allowed the building of basins, quays, lock gates, etc. Some of these plans were turned into reality, in June 1868, when the tidal section of the pier at Portishead was opened, £1,500 of its cost having been subscribed by the Merchant Venturers. In April 1870, a 300 ft. low water extension was added, the total cost of the railway and the pier extensions being about £290,000 up until this point in time.

From the pier, the railway company ran steamer services to Cardiff and Newport. In the summer months there were special sailings to Ilfracombe on the North Devon coast. For these, passengers could get through rail/steamer bookings from both of the railway companies serving the Bristol area, namely the Great Western and the Midland. Here we can quite clearly see the beginnings of the line's long connection with summer sailings connecting with trains on the branch.

One maritime service that severely declined, on the other hand, with the opening of the railway, was that plied by the *Fairy Queen*, an iron screw packet built in 1850. This ship plied the river (Bristol—Portishead) until the railway opened, when she lost most of her traffic to the railway. After 1867, the ship began running to Chepstow calling at Portishead in each direction. This practice continued until 1884 when she was scrapped. After that there was no regular packet to Portishead, although pleasure steamers occasionally called at the pier as they made their way down the Bristol Channel.

TABLE No. 54.

WOOFERTON AND TENBURY.

For Trains between Tenbury and Bewdley, see page 46.

		wEEK DAYS.								WEEK DAYS.				
Miles.	DOWN TRAINS.	1 2 P	1 2 3	1 & 2	1 & 2	1 2 P		Miles.	UP TRAINS.	1 & 2	1 2 P	1 & 2	1 2 P	1
		a m	a m	a m	p m	p m				a m	a m	p m	p m	
	WOOFERTON ... dep	7 20	8 45	11 25	4 25	6 30	..		TENBURY ... dep	7 55	10 55	12 35	5 40	
2½	Easton Court ... ,,	7 27	8 55	11 32	4 31	6 37	..	2½	Easton Court ... ,,	8 5	11	12 42	5 50	7
5½	TENBURY ... arr	7 35	9 5	11 55	4 40	6 45	..	5½	WOOFERTON ... arr	8 15	11 10	12 50	6 0	

For Trains to and from Shrewsbury and Hereford, see pages 44 and 45.

TABLE No. 55.

WITNEY BRANCH.

For Main Line Trains to and from Oxford, see Tables 16 to 19.

DOWN TRAINS.		WEEK DAYS.			SUNDAYS.	UP TRAINS.		WEEK DAYS.				SUNDAYS.
Classes on Witney Line.	1 & 2	1 & 2	1 2 3	1 & 2		Classes on Witney Line.		**A**				
	P.						1 & 2	1 & 2	1 & 2	1 2 3	
	a m	a m	p m	p m			a m	a m	p m		p m
LONDON (Pad.) dep	6 0	10 0	2 20	6 20		Witney (leave for Oxford). dep	8 10	10 50	3 15		6 55
Reading ... ,,	7 30	10 54	3 20	7 12		South Leigh ... ,,	8 16	10 57	3 21		7 3
Oxford ... arr	8 15	11 31	4 5	7 50		Eynsham ... ,,	8 21	11 5	3 28		7 14
						Yarnton ... ,,	8 35	11 15	3 37		7 27
OXFORD (leave for Witney) dp.	9 15	12 0	4 35	8 35		Oxford (ar. from Witney) dep.	8 45	11 25	3 45		7 35
Yarnton ... ,,	9 30	12 10	4 45	8 45							
Eynsham ... ,,	9 43	12 20	4 53	8 53		OXFORD (for Lon.) dep.	9 5	11 55	4 0		9 3
South Leigh ... ,,	9 52	12 27	5 0	9 0		Reading ... arr	9 42	12 40	6 10		9 43
Witney ... arr	10 0	12 35	5 10	9 10		LONDON (Pad.) ,,	10 30	1 45	6 0		10 40

A 3rd Class Witney to Oxford.

TABLE No. 55a.

AYLESBURY AND BUCKINGHAM RAILWAY.

For G. W. R. Trains to and from Aylesbury, see pages 4 to 7.

DOWN TRAINS.		WEEK DAYS.		SUNDAYS.	UP TRAINS.		WEEK DAYS.		SUNDAYS.
Classes on A. & B. Line.	1 2 3	1 & 2	1 2 3		Classes on A. & B. Line.	1 2 3	1 & 2	1 2 3	
	a m	p m	p m			a m	p m	p m	
AYLESBURY ... dep	8 5	3 55	7 5		BICESTER ... dep	8 25	2 53	7 43	
Quainton Road ... ,,	8 25	4 12	7 22		BUCKINGHAM ... ,,	8 28	4 35	7 48	
Grandborough Road ,,	8 33	4 23	7 30		Winslow ... ,,	8 52	4 35		
Winslow Road ... ,,	**A**	**A**	**A**						
Verney Junction arr	8 43	4 33	7 43		Verney Junction ... ,,	9 0	4 50	8 5	
					Winslow Road ... ,,	**A**	**A**	**A**	
Winslow ...	8 50	4 50	8 7		Grandborough Road ,,	9 8	4 58	8 15	
BUCKINGHAM ... ,,	9 11	5 0	9 7		Quainton Road ... ,,	9 15	5 9	8 24	
BICESTER ... ,,	9 23	5 9	9 58		AYLESBURY ... ,,	9 30	5 26	8 40	

A All Trains will stop by Signal at Winslow Road.   **B** To call at Grandborough Road by Signal only.

Market Passengers by the 9.0 a.m. Train from Verney Junction and the 3.55 p.m. Train from Aylesbury, on Saturdays, will be taken up and set down at various places along the line.

TABLE No. 56.

PORTISHEAD RAILWAY.

FARES From BRISTOL.					DOWN TRAINS.		WEEK DAYS.							SUNDAYS.
Ordinary.			Return.				**A**	**B**	**C**					
1 cl	2 cl	3 cl	1 cl	2 cl		1 2 3	1 2 3	1 2 3	1 2 3	1 2 3	1 2 3	1 2 3		1 2 3
						a m	a m	a m	a m	p m	p m	p m		p m
0/6	0/4	0/3	0/9	0/6	BRISTOL ... dep	6 0	8 10	10 20	12 55	3 10	5 0	6 35	8 35	3 45
1/3	0/10	0/7½	2/0	1/3	Clifton Bridge ,,	6 15	8 27	10 30	1 7	3 21	5 10	6 45	8 46	3 57
1/7	1/1	0/9½	2/4	1/6	Pill ,,	6 30	8 33	10 41	1 19	3 33	5 20	..	8 58	4 11
2/0	1/6	0/11½	3/0	2/3	Portbury ,,	6 36	8 38	..	1 25	3 39	5 25	..	9 4	4 16
					Portishead ... arr	6 45	8 45	10 50	1 30	3 45	5 30	7 0	9 10	4 25

FARES From PORTISHEAD.					UP TRAINS.		WEEK DAYS.							SUNDAYS.
Ordinary.			Return.											
1 cl	2 cl	3 cl	1 cl	2 cl		1 2 3	1 2 3	1 2 3	1 2 3	1 2 3	1 2 3	1 2 3	1 2 3	1 2 3
						a m	a m	a m	p m	p m	p m	p m	p m	p m
0/5	0/3	0/1½	0/8	0/5	Portishead ... dep	7 10	9 0	11 5	1 45	4 0	5	..	7 20	9 25	8 30
0/9	0/6	0/3½	1/2	0/9	Portbury ,,	7 15	9 5	..	1 50	4 5	..	7 25	9 30	8 35
1/6	1/0	0/8	2/3	1/6	Pill ,,	7 20	9 11	11 12	..	4 10	5 52	7 30	9 36	8 40
2/0	1/6	0/11½	3/0	2/3	Clifton Bridge ,,	7 30	9 21	11 20	2 6	4 22	5 42	7 42	9 46	8 53
					BRISTOL ... arr	7 45	9 35	11 40	2 20	4 35	6 15	8 10	10 0	9 5

A B C.—Excursion Tickets at low fares are issued daily by Train C; every Monday by Train A; and every Saturday by Train B.

PERIODICAL TICKETS will be issued on the following terms :—

BETWEEN	1 Month.		2 Months.		3 Months.		6 Months.		12 Months.	
	1 Class.	2 Class.	1 Class.	2 Class.	1 Class.	3 Class.	1 Class.	2 Class.	1 Class.	3 Class.
	£ s. d.	£ s. d.	£ s. d.	£ s. d.	£ s. d.	£ s. d.	£ s. d.	£ s. d.	£ s. d.	£ s. d.
Bristol and Portishead	2 0 0	1 12 0	3 10 0	3 0 0	5 0 0	4 4 0	8 0 0	7 0 0	12 12 0	11 0 0
Clifton Bridge ,, ...	1 10 0	1 5 0	2 14 0	2 5 0	3 16 0	3 0 0	6 6 0	5 5 0	10 10 0	9 0 0

Bristol—Portishead : The 1870 Timetable.

However, we have moved forward in time with our narrative. Returning to November 1870, we find the directors of the company developing their ambitions on an even grander scale, for, in that month, they issued Parliamentary notices of a Bill that would allow them to build a dock in connection with their railway and the, then, newly constructed extensions to the pier. In 1871 the company promoted a Bill to convert the Pill at Portishead into a dock that would incorporate part of the already reconstructed pier. Naturally, the Avonmouth Company fiercely fought the plans, but they lost and the Portishead faction obtained its Act (34 & 35 Vic c 142). Interestingly enough, due to delays caused by the 1866 financial slump, the Avonmouth Company obtained its Act in the same year and so the battle to build rival river-mouth docks had begun.

Among the subscribers to the Portishead scheme were Sir J. Greville Smyth (£15,000), Messrs J. Ford, R. Fuidge and G. R. Woodward (£6,000 each) and Lewis Fry (£5,000). Various other prominent citizens put up sums ranging from £2,500 downwards. The engineers for the project were McClean and Stileman, the same two who had constructed the railway. They had prepared plans for a floating dock with an outer basin, lock, graving dock, timber pond and other works. Of the two men, McClean, who died during the dock's construction in 1873, was an engineer of high standing. The scheme was, in fact, his idea. The estimated cost of the dock was £160,000. Not unreasonably, a full set of railway sidings was an integral part of the scheme.

While all these new developments were taking place at the mouth of the Avon, important moves were afoot in the world of finance for the competing docks. In 1871, the Board of Trade named two men, Mr D. Stevenson and Mr J. Ball, to examine the then present position and future prospects of both Avonmouth and Portishead docks. Their conclusions were that both concerns could handle the growing size of shipping and that both had enough Parliamentary powers to raise sufficient capital to provide all the machinery, buildings, etc., that the docks would need. They also agreed that, while the Avonmouth faction could complete its scheme under the then existing contracts, the Portishead Company would need to increase its share capital by nearly £120,000.

The two men suggested that things would be speeded up if the corporation subscribed more share capital to both concerns. The important question of which of the two groups should get the money was brought up at special council meetings in June and July, 1872. The council's conclusions were that it should not contribute to the Avonmouth Group (33 votes to 22) while a vote of 36 to 19 ensured that £100,000 should go to the Portishead

Company. History shows us that just as the company's director, Alderman Ford, had got it wrong about quarrying in the Avon, so the council had got it wrong when it came to a decision over Avonmouth and Portishead.

An interesting incidental point here, that ties in with the development of the Bristol Harbour Railway described later in the book, is that the corporation also agreed to spend a fairly large sum in the City Docks. New works were started in 1872/3 in the Cumberland Basin, in the area of the docks near Clifton Bridge Station, where new entrance locks were built. The work was carried out to plans drawn by Mr Howard.

Back at Portishead, the contract for the building of Portishead Dock was let to Messrs Barnett & Gale for £160,000 on 20th July 1872. Shortly afterwards, the contractors took possession of the site and, by the end of October, work had got underway, men being employed to clear the ground. By January 1873 excavations had begun for the diversion of a stream which would have finished in the dock itself. Another of the preliminary works, indeed, one of the most important, was a huge coffer dam, over 500 ft. in length, which was built to keep back the cold, grey waters of the Severn. However, more problems were looming up for the company! On Sunday, 15th February 1874, a high tide in the Severn caused a portion of a dam forming a connection between the sea wall at Portbury and the coffer dam, mentioned above, to give way. Reconstruction had to take place and the work was not finished until June of the following year. The delay gave the Avonmouth Group a breathing space in the race to finish the river-mouth docks and it opened its own dock in February 1877.

For the Portishead Company, there was even more delay in the offing. It had been hoped to let water into the dock on May Day 1878, but on Monday, 18th March of that very year, part of the dock's west wall collapsed. The reconstruction work was a much more massive task than had been the case at Avonmouth in 1876, when about 130 yards of the dock's east wall had collapsed, taking with it two large warehouses each 250 ft. long. The replacement work at Portishead took nearly a year to carry out, cost an extra £30,000 and meant that it was not until 30th April 1879 that water was let (intentionally!) into the dock, by which time, of course, its competitor across the river had been open for over two years. These delays were bound to be bad news for the railway since it meant that the line's freight traffic simply could not develop. Indeed, until roughly July 1876, any goods traffic was carried by the passenger trains.

Eventually, however, the dock was finished and on Saturday morning, 28th June 1879, the company's own boat, *Lyn*, went

The *PS Taff* in Portishead Pool about 1875 during the construction of Portishead Dock. This photograph should give the reader some idea of the scene in those early days.

G. Farr

Bristol & Exeter Railway 4-4-0ST, No. 72, with an Up train at Portishead, circa 1870. The massive station building dominates the scene. The town is hidden behind the station building away to the left, while to the right of the picture, the dock would later be built, construction of this large project beginning in the autumn of 1872.

Bristol City Museum

through the lock and the dock was open. By all accounts, there were very few people there to see the event. The boat, a pleasure steamer, had been running between Ilfracombe and Portishead Pier after the latter's completion in June 1868. On the day of the opening the weather was rough but the ship had absolutely no trouble in docking.

Traffic at the dock is actually dated from Sunday, 6th July 1879 when the *SS Magdeburg* arrived with over 1,000 tons of barley. The long running grain trade at the port had begun. This particular cargo was consigned to Messrs R. & H. Adams, the majority of that cargo being put on to rail. The other partner in the Bristol & Portishead Pier & Railway was doing its share of the work as well.

One of the more interesting buildings, apparently constructed at the dock at this time, was Portishead's second station. This was the Pier Station and, as its name suggests, was located at the seaward end of the Pill below the hotel, near the pier. The evidence for its construction in the mid to late 1870s is as follows. Firstly, no mention of the station was made by Yolland in his 1867 report, and this would have been unusual and out of character as Yolland's reports and surveys were generally very detailed indeed. In his description of the line he only mentions one station at Portishead and on this he passed only one comment: it was unfinished at the time of his inspection.

Secondly, the 1870 plan, included in this book, shows no real sign of a station at the pier, and close examination of the plan reveals that there would have been very little room for a station to be sited in the Pier Station's actual, later, location before the construction of the dock had taken place, At the same time, it would seem reasonable to assume that a Pier Station would only have been justified in connection with a dock. This leads me on to surmise that the station at Portishead Pier probably went in sometime in the late 1870s. The section of line from Portishead Station itself to the Pier was only ever used for freight traffic. In a purely speculative mood, and without a doubt, this is one aspect of the line's history that deserves closer scrutiny in the future. It could be assumed that, if for any reason the occasional passenger train ever did venture to the Pier Station, this practice would almost certainly have ceased after 1884 when the regular shipping packets also ceased to call. However, the Pier Station was long lived and remained in position until the construction of the second power station at Portishead, an event that took place in the 1950s. The Pier Station's short operational life probably closely reflected the trends of poor trade and poor financial results then occurring.

Other traffic, was, however, on offer at Portishead at this time. The gas company had its own works at Portishead and, before construction of the dock had taken place, coal and other goods would come and go from the works through Parish Wharf. The construction of the dock, however, prevented ships having access to the works and so special arrangements had to be made to overcome this problem. Before the passing of the 1871 Act, incidentally, the gas and railway companies agreed that they should enter into some agreement concerning the traffic at Portishead and this they did in 1877.

The main items of interest in this agreement were as follows. Firstly, during the construction of the dock, at least from 1877 onwards, any traffic for the gasworks was unloaded at the railway company's pier and carried, by the railway, to the works itself. Certain charges were made by the gas company for this service. At the same time the gas company built a siding serving its works while the railway company laid in a connection to serve this siding. The signals controlling the connection, and the connection itself, were to be maintained at the gas company's expense, in addition to which the latter company was also responsible for the maintenance of the siding.

There were some other interesting items in that there would be free wayleave for trucks of the B&PP&R Company between their station yard and the siding itself. Last, but by no means least, the manager of the gasworks was to have one free pass over the line between Portishead and Bristol. For all this, the gas company would supply the railway company at Portishead with a ten per cent discount on the gas it used!

All these clauses appear to have remained in force until the difficult times of spring 1931 when the two companies agreed that the discount and the free pass should be discontinued. Gas production at Portishead was closed down just after World War II and by the summer of 1950 the facilities had become redundant. The siding and its associated connection were lifted in August of that year.

Returning to the 1870s, the B&PP&R was used for a rather novel experiment, on 23rd June 1874, when an arrangement was tested for communication between driver and guard and passengers and guard. Designed by a Bristol man, Reuben Lyon, the arrangement was made up of a bellows and handle attached to each compartment. The total arrangement was fixed to three coaches. It worked in the following way; by pulling down the handle, air was blown from the bellows through a pipe to the guard's box and engine, this air in turn blew whistles which were inserted into the ends of the pipes. Additionally, the handle raised a signal arm, at night, a light, to indicate the compartment in which the apparatus had been used. This arm could not be lowered while the train was moving. The pipes also provided a speaking tube between the guard's, or between a guard and the driver. It seems that the experiment was a complete success, and it is an interesting question to ask why the equipment was not used on a wider scale. It is also worth remembering that we have had to wait for the arrival of the IC125 before this kind of comprehensive communication between, driver, guard and passenger actually came about.

In 1878 the line had a royal visitor, when the then Prince of Wales visited the Royal Agricultural Society's Show which was being held on the Downs in Bristol. Arriving at Temple Meads, on a special train from London, he crossed the city in a horse and carriage, visited the show and then was driven along the Downs and over the Suspension Bridge to Clifton Bridge Station where a special train was ready to take him out of the city. One final incident in the 1870s proved Alderman Ford wrong about the effect the railway would have upon the magnificent scenery in the Gorge. In February 1879 a 21 year lease was agreed between the council and Sir Philip Miles for opening a quarry on the Somerset side of the river near the railway in the Gorge. Further industrial growth was starting to take place.

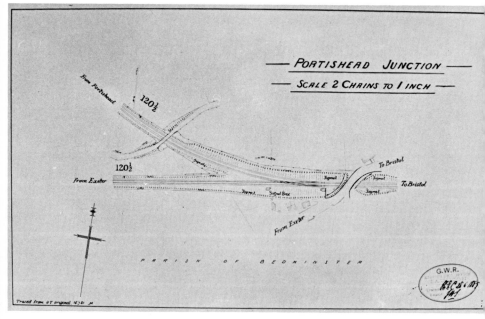

Portishead Junction, 1885.

CHAPTER lxxix.

An Act to confer further Powers on the Bristol and Portishead Pier and Railway Company ; and for other purposes.   A.D. 1877.

[12th July 1877.]

WHEREAS by " The Bristol and Portishead Pier and Railway Act, 1863," (in this Act called "the Act of 1863,") the Bristol and Portishead Pier and Railway Company, (in this Act called " the Company ") were incorporated and authorised to make a pier in the parish of Portbury, in the county of Somerset, and a railway from that pier to the Bristol and Exeter Railway at Bedminster, and a branch railway to Portishead, and for the purposes aforesaid to raise the sum of two hundred thousand pounds by shares and sixty-six thousand six hundred pounds by borrowing :   26 & 27 Vict. c. cvii.

And whereas by " The Bristol and Portishead Pier and Railway Act, 1866," (in this Act called " the Act of 1866,") the site of the said pier was altered, and the Company were authorised to construct n lieu of the said pier a pier and other works connected therewith extending along Portishead Pill into the River Severn (the time for the completion of which was limited by section fourteen to seven years from the passing of that Act), and to raise an additional capital of sixty thousand pounds in shares and twenty thousand pounds by borrowing :   29 & 30 Vict. c. lxxxviii.

And whereas by " The Portishead Docks Act, 1871," (in this Act called "the Act of 1871,") the Company were authorised to construct docks at Portishead Pill, and for that purpose to raise an additional share capital of one hundred and ninety-five thousand pounds, and to borrow an additional sum of sixty-five thousand pounds, and the mayor, aldermen, and burgesses of the city of Bristol (herein-after called " the corporation ") were empowered by that Act to subscribe to the undertaking thereby authorised, and it was provided (section sixty-two) that if the corporation should so subscribe, then the capital of such undertaking should be a separate capital (applicable only for the purposes of such undertaking), and   34 & 35 Vict. c. cxlii.

[*Local.*-79.]   A   1

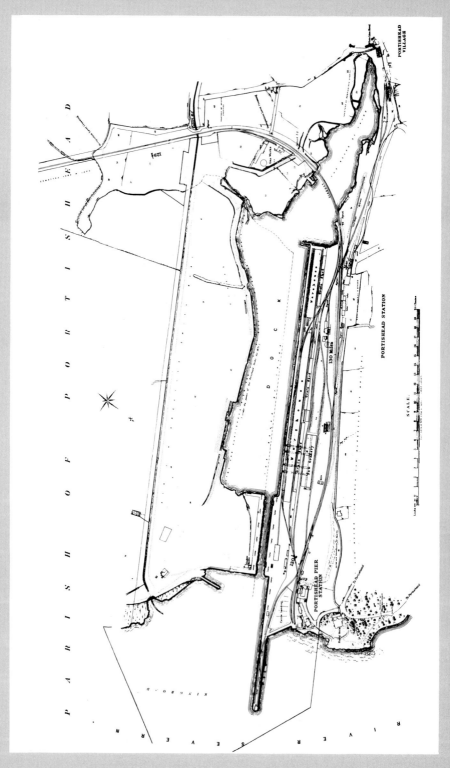

46

Chapter Three

The new decade of the 1880s started with changes for the branch. In January 1880 the platforms at Portbury and Pill were all three extended. Over the weekend of Saturday, 24th and Tuesday, 27th January more work took place when the B&PP&R Company altered its track from broad to narrow gauge. Later in the year, trackwork figured in the news again when a crossing loop was brought into use on 15th September 1880 at Clifton Bridge Station. Three years later the loop was incorporated into the doubling of the section of track between Portishead Junction and Clifton Bridge. The new section was brought into use on 2nd September 1883.

Meanwhile, by this time, further developments were taking place in connection with the dock and railway facilities at Portishead. There can be no doubt that things had not gone too well financially for the dock:

> 'In the light of subsequent events, the making of Portishead Dock appears as a blunder. But the men who made it believed the dock would attract more trade to the port and backed their belief with their purses. Mr Weston himself (the Mayor at the time of the dock's take-over by the corporation in 1884) was one of the largest supporters of the dock. Mr Lewis Fry was another. It is sometimes forgotten who were the builders of the Portishead Dock and what characters they bore. . . . It is impossible, looking calmly at the records of the men, to doubt that they were actuated by an honest desire to promote the welfare of Bristol. There were prominent Liberals and Conservatives amongst the promoters of both docks.'

Source: *C. Wells*, 1909

With the opening of the Avonmouth Dock in February 1877 and its Portishead rival in April 1879, there began an intense bout of competition between these and the City Docks further upstream in Bristol. In November 1883, the then newly re-elected Mayor, Mr Weston, conducted an investigation into the financial status of both the Avonmouth and Portishead companies. On the basis of this examination he advised the corporation to promote a Bill in order to get powers to buy the two dock companies. The council voted on the issue and his suggestion was accepted by 47 votes to 3.

However, all was not to run so smoothly. The main problem arose out of the refusal of the Portishead Company's board to sell the dock on its own; the railway and pier had to be part of the bargain as well. Mr Weston appealed to the GWR (who, by now,

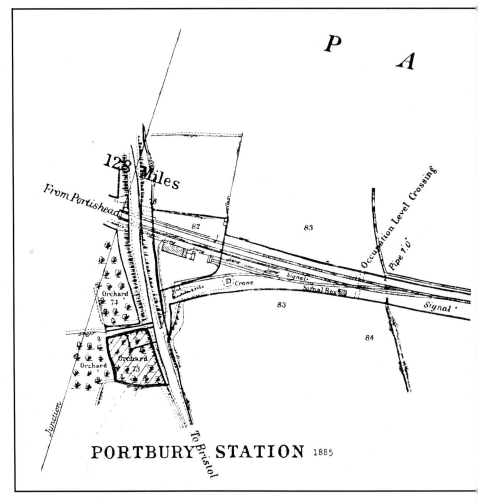

PORTBURY STATION 1885

Portbury Station, 1885.

Portishead Dock in the 1880s. The viaduct on the curve leading into the station ▷
has been markedly shortened, while close investigation reveals the position of
the station's original signal box. The engine shed can be clearly seen. It is very
interesting to see how, at this point in time, one side of the dock is totally undeveloped. In the early years of the twentieth century, the area on the right will
become the new timber wharf. In the distance can be seen *HMS Formidable*
lying at anchor. This was an old 'man o' war' which had been stationed off
Portishead at Kingroad to be used as a training ship for homeless and destitute
boys.

Port of Bristol Authority

There is a complete system of rails along the quays and warehouses, which affords exceptional facilities for the loading and quick despatch of cargoes of grain, ore, esparto grass, green fruit, sugar, etc., direct into truck from ship's side. These are connected with all parts of the kingdom, via Bristol, by the Great Western, Midland, London & North Western and other lines. There is extensive shed accommodation alongside the quays, specially provided with a thorough system of ventilation for the storage and handling of grain, rice or seed in any condition. The storage capacity is about 100,000 qrs. A granary, fitted with Armstrong's elevating machinery, and capable of storing a further 800,000 qrs of grain, has been completed, and whole and part cargoes of grain can be discharged thereinto by machinery with the greatest dispatch. There are also special appliances for washing and cleaning cargoes of Egyptian, or other, beans.

Photograph Author's Collection and Text 1886 PBA Handbook

had taken over the Bristol & Exeter's role in the proceedings) to help ease and, hopefully, solve the somewhat difficult situation. This they did and, not long after, an arrangement was agreed by which the railway and the pier would be taken into the GWR system. This actually took place under an 1884 Act (47 & 48 Vic c 256) as from 1st July 1884. The pier was used by the GWR steamer services until 1st October 1886. After that time they were discontinued, although the pier itself was used by the locally well-known pleasure steamers of P. & A. Campbell.

The details of the transaction were involved but essentially they worked out as follows. On the Avonmouth side, it was reckoned that the land, dock and warehouse, had, in all, cost £718,000. The directors agreed to take a price of £450,000. On the Portishead side, the dock and warehouses were reckoned to have cost £375,000. The sum of £250,000 was offered, £25,000 of which was to be taken in deferred bonds. These gave no interest until after the first five years. The offer was accepted.

In less high-flown circles, other agreements were being reached. On 28th April 1884, an agreement was signed between the Bristol & Portishead Railway Company and the Customs Authorities to build a Custom House on the latter's behalf. This was duly done and the Custom House was completed in 1885. The building had living quarters upstairs. The lease was £25 per annum. Other costs of interest come through in an 1885 agreement between the railway and gas companies. They agreed that the maintenance of the gasworks' siding should cost the gas company one guinea per half-year!

One area that we need to investigate more fully, in relation to the railway, is the area around Ashton Vale between the station at Clifton Bridge and the divergence of the branch at Portishead Junction. During the late 1800s there were colliery workings and an iron works here. Latterly, both of these businesses were owned by the Ashton Vale Iron Company and this firm had blast furnaces in operation by 1861. These were, in fact, blown out by 1887 but the associated forges and rolling mills continued in use into the present century.

The Ashton Vale Iron Company also owned Ashton Colliery. This firm's later shafts were in the area currently covered by Strachan & Henshaw's Works off Winterstoke Road. The abandoned railway lines, still visible in the yard, once served three closely grouped colliery shafts. It seems not unreasonable to assume that the railway could well have handled a fair amount of traffic from these coal and iron workings towards the end of the nineteenth and beginnings of the twentieth centuries.

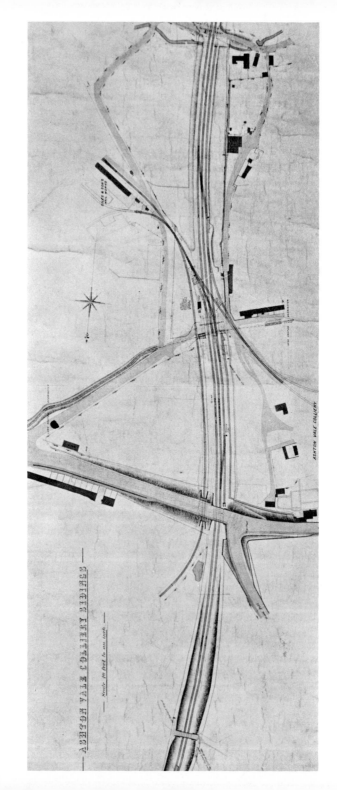

— ASHTON VALE COLLIERY SIDINGS —

Scale 70 feet to one inch

ASHTON VALE COLLIERY

GILES & SONS NAIL WORKS

Ashton Vale Colliery Sidings 1889. An interesting plan showing the sidings to Ashton Vale Colliery, to Giles & Sons' nail works and to the River Avon. This latter formed part of the route of the line that was built in the early years of the twentieth century to Canon's Marsh.

In the 1885 survey of the Portishead line, there was a signal box, shown on the Up side of the line, to control the level crossings and the sidings that ran diagonally across the double main line then in use here. This was known as Ashton Vale signal box. It seems likely that this box was installed when the line between Clifton Bridge and Portishead Junction was doubled on 2nd September 1883. This would certainly have made operational sense in that we have already seen how the colliery was in use during the 1886—1894 period, along with the iron workings.

Indeed, going back even further, this section of the branch has always commanded interest in that in Colonel Yolland's report special mention had been made, by him, about the siding which was then in existence at Ashton Vale. He had suggested, and the company had agreed, that this siding should be treated in the same way that any other junction would have been treated, namely that it should be equipped with signals that interlocked with the siding itself. In order that the opening would not be delayed, the company had promised not to use, or allow anyone else to use, the siding at Ashton Vale until these signals had been installed.

When the lines to Wapping and Canon's Marsh were opened on 4th October 1906, a new signal box was built on the Down side of the line at 121 miles 19 chains. This was called Ashton Junction signal box and it still remains in situ today. It was opened on 20th May 1906.

In an 1888 survey of the line we get further signalling information. At Clifton Bridge a signal cabin on the Up platform worked the Down loop line, six signals, five points and two facing bolt locks. At Pill, in 1888, the passing loop was in use, while at the Up end, there was a long siding that ran out on to the viaduct parallel to the Up and Down main lines.

Ticket: *Courtesy Michael Wyatt and Photography Steve Smith*

(999-1)

GREAT WESTERN RAILWAY.

From BRISTOL (Portishead Docks)

To *Redcliff Siding*

Route via

Date 7/9/ 1906. Train

Wagon No. 65326 Sheet No.

Consignee *Hannau*

(50,000—1-05.)

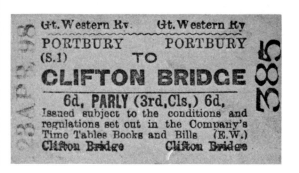

Gt. Western Ry.   Gt. Western Ry

PORTBURY   PORTBURY

(S.1)   TO

CLIFTON BRIDGE

6d, PARLY (3rd, Cls,) 6d,
Issued subject to the conditions and
regulations set out in the Company's
Time Tables Books and Bills (E.W.)
Clifton Bridge   Clifton Bridge

385

23 APR 98

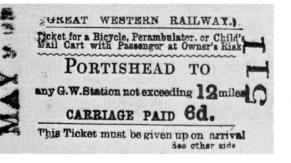

GREAT WESTERN RAILWAY.
Ticket for a Bicycle, Perambulator, or Child's
Mail Cart with Passenger at Owner's Risk

PORTISHEAD TO

any G.W.Station not exceeding 12 miles

CARRIAGE PAID 6d.

This Ticket must be given up on arrival
See other side

MAY 3 98

1115

A 00009

Great Western Railway
MONTHLY
RETURN TICKET

Ham Green Halt
TO
PORTISHEAD
AND BACK

THIRD CLASS Fare 1/1 C

Portishead
FOR CONDITIONS SEE BACK

Tickets: *Michael Wyatt and Photography Steve Smith*

54

PORTISHEAD BRANCH. Narrow Gauge.

The Line from Bristol to Clifton Bridge is double, and from Clifton Bridge to Portishead single.

The Train Staff Stations are Clifton Bridge, Pill and Portishead. Pill is the intermediate crossing place.

Section.	Shape of Staff and Ticket.	Colour of Staff and Ticket.
Clifton Bridge and Pill		White.
Pill and Portishead	Triangular. Round.	Blue.

Down Trains. — BRISTOL TO PORTISHEAD.

STATIONS.	1 Goods	2 Pass.	3 Cond'l Goods	4 Pass.	5 Cond'l Goods	6 Pass.	7 Goods	8 Pass.	9 Cond'l Goods	10 Pass.	11 Pass.	12 Cond'l Goods	13 Pass.	14 Cond'l Goods	15 Pass.	16 Pass.	17	18	Sun. 1 Pass.	Sun. 2
	A.M.	A.M.	A.M.	A.M.	A.M.	A.M.	A.M.	P.M.	P.M.	P.M.	P.M.	P.M.	P.M.	P.M.	P.M.	P.M.			P.M.	
Bristol ... dep.	5 45	6 55	7 0	7 45	9 20	10 10	10 50	12 45		2 45	3 50	4 50	5 25		7 20	8 30			3 45	
Pylle Hill ,,	—	—	RR	7 50	RR	10 15	—	—	1 30		3 55	RR		6 10	7 25	8 35			3 50	
Bedminster ,,	5 50	7 0	7 5	7 55	9 25	10 20	10 55	12 50	1 35	2 50	4 0		5 30		7 30	8 40			3 57	
Malago Siding ,,	CR		RR		CS				2X55	2 55	4X17	5X 5	5 47	RR	7X47	8X57			4 11	
Portishead Jun. ,,	6 5	7 5	7X0	8X12	CS	10 25	11X29	12X53	2X15	3 7	4X15	5 20	5 55	7X 0	7 55	9 5			4 20	
Ashton Siding ,,	6 20	7X17	CS	8 20		10 35	11 50	11 50	1 15	3 20	4 25									
Clifton Bridge ,,	6 35	7 25	8 20	8 25	10	10 45	12 5	1 20	1 20	3 20	4 30	5 30	6 0	7 15	8 0	9 10			4 25	
Pill ... ,,																				
Portbury ,,																				
Portishead ... arr.	6 45	7 30	7 55	8 25	10 50	10 50	12 5	1 20												

Up Trains. — PORTISHEAD TO BRISTOL.

STATIONS.	1 Pass.	2 Pass.	3 Pass.	4 Cond'l Goods	5 Pass.	6 Cond'l Goods	7 Pass.	8 Goods	9 Pass.	10 Cond'l Goods	11 Pass.	12 Pass.	13 Cond'l Goods	14 Pass.	15 Goods	16 Cond'l Goods	17	18	Sun. 1 Pass.	Sun. 2
	A.M.	A.M.	A.M.	A.M.	A.M.	A.M.	A.M.	P.M.	P.M.	P.M.	P.M.	P.M.	P.M.	P.M.	P.M.	P.M.			P.M.	
Portishead ... dep.	7 5	7 10	8 55	9 0	10 20	12 15	1 40	1 40	3 30	4 0	4 40	6 45	7 30	8 45	9 40	9 55			8 15	
Portbury ,,	7 10		9 0	9 7	10X38	CS	2 0	2X15	3 35	4X18	4 45	6 50	7X48	8 50	10 0	CS			8 20	
Pill ... ,,	7X17	8X16	9 17		11 17	12X50	1 48	2X15	3 42	CS	4 52	6X57	8 10	8X58	10 20	CS			8 25	
Clifton Bridge ,,	7X29	8 28	9 21		11X27		1X59	2 30	3 54	7	5X4	7		9 10					8 38	
Ashton Siding ,,	7 32	8 31	9 21	11 10			4	3 58	3 58	5 10	7 11	8 20	9 14		10 35			8 43	
Portishead Jun. ,,					11 10	RR	2 4	CR	4	5 15	7 16	RR		9 20		10 50				
Malago Siding ,,	7 37	8 36	9 25	11 15	11 37	RR	2 10		4 2	5 15	7 16	8 25		9 20	10 40	RR			8 47	
Bedminster ,,						1 10														
Pylle Hill ,,	7 40	8 40	9 30	11 40	11 40	2 15	2 15	3 10	4 5	4 55	5 19	7 20		9 25	10 55				8 50	
Bristol ... arr.																				

The Portishead Branch : The 1886 Timetable.

Sometime during the 1890s a returning excursion, from Portishead, unloads its passengers at Clifton Bridge. Note the former signal cabin on the Up platform.

Bristol City Museum

The year 1888 found the signal cabin at Portbury in control of six signals, three points and one bolt lock. Two years later, in January 1890, the platform was extended, while the siding serving the second platform on the Up side was removed sometime during the same year.

During the mid and late 1890s additional siding accommodation was installed by the GWR at Portishead. In 1885, for example, £193 12s 6d was spent on this work. More tracklaying took place into and through 1886 and 1887. By March 1889, the total account for all these extra sidings stood at nearly £1,800. From 1891 through into 1892 more work was carried out until, by July 1891, £2,330 18s 11d had been spent. Expansion was still the name of the game at Portishead even though the dock's financial results had not been all that encouraging, for example, the dock sustaining a loss of over £2,600 in 1886.

At the same time as the sidings were being laid in at Portishead, further quarrying developments were under way in the Avon Gorge. Under an agreement dated 1st October 1891, the GWR and the United Alkali Company (of Netham, Bristol) agreed to the building of a subway under the Portishead branch between No. 2 and No. 3 Tunnels. This would allow United Alkali, the quarry owners, access from its Greenland Quarry to a jetty then in existence in the River Avon. The bridge was brought into use in the spring of 1892.

Again in the Gorge, destructive events took place in 1899. Severe flooding, which affected various parts of Bristol, including St. Phillip's Marsh, some areas of Bedminster and Ashton Gate, also engulfed the station at Clifton Bridge to a depth of several feet. Incidentally, by this time, the station at Clifton Bridge had been renamed Rownham. In March 1891, in order to clear up any confusion that may have existed in passengers' minds concerning Clifton Station on the Port & Pier line, (this was renamed Hotwells), Clifton Down Station on the Clifton Extension Railway remained unchanged in name, whilst Clifton Bridge, on the Portishead branch, became Rownham. By 1910 the latter station had reverted to its original title of Clifton Bridge.

Quietly, unspectacularly, and with an uncertain future, the line slipped into the twentieth century. It was reckoned that between 1886 and 1902 the deficit at Portishead Dock had been nearly £160,000. With new developments taking place on the Avonmouth side of the river, Portishead and its railway looked as if they were in for very dark days. Let us turn the page into the twentieth century and see what actually happened.

Portishead, The Railway Station

Kelly's Directory for 1894 gives the following names of railway personnel working at Pill, Portbury and Portishead:

PILL: Stationmaster — John Hitchcock.

PORTBURY: Stationmaster — Oliver Heywood. There was also a telegraph office at the railway station for those wishing to use this service.

PORTISHEAD: Stationmaster — George Active. For those people wishing to travel on to Clevedon, there were omnibuses daily at 10.35 a.m. and 6.00 p.m. from the railway station. At the Custom House, James Alfred Goodall was the examining officer, while in the Dock Authority itself, the general manager was Francis Brooke Girdlestone. Tom Butler was traffic manager, while the dock and harbour master was E. W. Harvey. The GWR was represented by L. Wilkinson, goods superintendent (docks). The MR had a branch office with William Rich as its agent. The gas company had A. V. Daniel as its manager

Chapter Four

We have already seen how closely intertwined the destinies of the dock and the railway were at Portishead, and so we must continue to follow the myriad schemes put forward, in the latter years of the nineteenth century, to improve and develop the three docks now under corporation control. Support for new plans during the 1890s was split between three main groups of schemes; namely, those who favoured a second dock at Avonmouth; those who supported the idea of an extended dock at Portishead and those who were still keen on the idea of a dockised River Avon, with large locks at the mouth of the river.

In January 1896, the engineer, Mr Wolfe Barry, had produced an impressive report for the Docks Committee, and this did, indeed, look at these three alternatives,; dockisation, an extension of Portishead Dock into the Portbury Marshes and a new dock at Avonmouth based upon a scheme submitted in 1892. In 1900, a plan was put forward for a new dock at Avonmouth. This was accepted by the council and a Bill, providing for the new dock's construction, was made law on 17th August 1901. Dockisation was finally dead and the future was far from bright for the Portishead Dock. The Avonmouth Dock supporters had finally won with the new Royal Edward Dock which was opened on 9th July 1908.

The GWR had been inclined to oppose the Bill for the new dock at Avonmouth. They argued that the new dock would divert trade away from Portishead, where it had a monopoly of rail traffic over the branch to Bristol and beyond. Avonmouth, on the other hand, was served by both the GWR and the Midland and there was very little love lost between these two companies in the Bristol area. However, all was not lost and in order to show good faith towards the Portishead Dock, the Docks Commitee agreed to spend money on the then undeveloped land on the Portbury side of the dock. In 1903 the Committee agreed to build a 600 ft. long timber wharf and a 200 ft. jetty in this area. Behind the wharf was a stacking ground of ten acres and this would give storage room for between 20,000 to 30,000 standards of timber, each standard equalling about three and a third tons of wood.

Up until this time, there had been very little timber brought into Portishead, but once the traffic began, the railway naturally reaped the benefit. One interesting sideline here is, that in a 1913 report to the Docks Committee, it was revealed that timber for use in and around Bristol could not be brought from Portishead and so other local ports, Sharpness, for example, did the job instead.

'But what was wrong with the rail route, the exclusively GWR route from Portishead? . . . One can only wonder if the competitive railway rates for timber via the Midland Railway via Sharpness were appreciably lower than the monopolistic rates of the GWR from Portishead to Bristol. Possibly the single line was already at or near capacity, so as to lower the railway rates on timber could not attract additional traffic to make good the money lost by rate reduction . . . '

Text: G. W. Neale

The growth of the timber trade at Portishead undoubtedly helped the railway's trade in the difficult years before World War I. Not long after these developments had taken place, in June 1908 to be exact, British Petroleum, acting on behalf of the Anglo-Saxon Petroleum Company, reached an agreement with the Port of Bristol for a lease covering approximately three acres of land situated on the Portbury side of the lock at Portishead. On this, the company built tanks for storing petrol which was brought in by tank steamers. These installations were quickly brought into use and traffic flourished.

The three acres of 1908 grew to six acres by 1911, while, by 1913, the total area devoted to the storage of petrol had grown to nearly seven acres. There was even a small refinery here to treat the crude oil. The oil tanks and refinery were rail connected by a line, within the dock property, that ran parallel to Portbury Stream. It then ran through a sharp curve towards Portbury, joining the main Portishead branch at Timber Wharf ground frame. Presumably the railway benefitted in no uncertain way from the infusion of this new traffic. It would benefit even more during the Great War.

Although a detailed history of the Weston, Clevedon & Portishead Light Railway is beyond the scope of this book, various events took place on that railway in the seven or eight years before World War I that relate very closely to the story of the GWR line. For example, in a newspaper report, published in February 1907, it was reported that the new connecting spur, between the WC&PLR and the GWR at Portishead was complete, but was, at that point in time, blocked by an earth embankment which had been piled across the rails.

On Wednesday, 7th August 1907, the extension of the WC&PLR from Clevedon to Portishead was quietly opened. The honour of hauling the first train from Clevedon to Portishead was given to a Manning Wardle saddle tank *Portishead* which left with the 8.10 a.m. workmen's train. As for the GWR/WC&PLR connection itself, the first train negotiated that on 2nd November 1908. This link was reported to have involved over 1,000 yards of sidings and crossovers, in addition to a considerable amount of work undertaken on new sea defences.

which this photograph was taken, circa 1900. The engines were built from 1869 to 1899 and, as this picture shows, were apparently kept in beautiful external condition.

M. J. Tozer Collection

The *SS Vita Nova* unloads grain at Portishead Dock during the early years of the twentieth century. On the left can be seen Port of Bristol Authority internal user wagons, Nos. 47 and 57. At its height, the dock had a fleet of eighty of these wagons which were known as BDs. Hand unloading is the order of the day and the photograph gives a fine glimpse of the one time close co-operation that once existed between rail and water at Portishead.

Port of Bristol Authority

The *SS Nordberg* and the *SS Uddeholm* unload timber at South Wharf, Portishead, in 1954. In the foreground is the, then, newly delivered 0-4-0 diesel locomotive *Gordano*.

Port of Bristol Authority

These sea defences were evidently of little use against a very violent storm that thrashed Portishead in December 1910. This caused a great deal of damage and destruction with the whole of the low lying land inwards from the dock being completely under water. At the same time as the storm raged, incoming tides forced the water to move inland at great speed and with great force. The Light Railway Station and the approach to it were totally impassable, as was the approach to the gasworks. So much water was around, in fact, that the flooding of the gasworks cut off the gas supply to the town.

Staying with the theme of the WC&PLR, in November 1912 there was a sizeable amount of local interest in the news that the GWR directors were considering the building of a new station at Portishead. This would have been built at the bottom of Nore Road and would have catered for traffic on the Light Railway. The local newspaper, reporting this suggestion, welcomed the idea, adding that the old station should be retained for the use of the dockers. Unfortunately, nothing came of the project and Portishead had to wait until 1954 when a new station was built in the position recommended in the 1912 proposals.

Back on the GWR branch a new signal box had been opened at Clifton Bridge on 25th August 1907, while at Portishead a new box was brought into use on 16th June 1908. In the Ashton area, the new connections from the newly completed lines to Wapping and Canon's Marsh, (for more on this subject see Chapters 9 & 10) were brought into operation on 4th October 1906. The box at Ashton Junction, controlling these connections, was opened on 20th May 1906.

At 121 miles 30 chains a new halt was opened on 1st October 1906. Close to Bristol City's Football Ground, it was named Ashton Gate Platform and was a simple, wooden structure. It had, in fact, opened for football traffic only on 15th September 1906, was later closed because of World War I austerity, reopening to traffic again on 23rd May 1926.

It is at this point that I would like to introduce the oldest contributor to my book, Mr Hy Goodhind (93 in 1980). From 1905/6 he was signal porter, and later signalman, at Clifton Bridge Station. He returned here in 1907 and stayed until 1909. He was then appointed one of the first two signalmen to operate Ashton Swing Bridge South signal box when it opened on 4th November 1906. In 1909 he moved to Montpelier Station on the GW & Midland Joint line, as it then was, from Ashley Hill Junction to Avonmouth. He finally left the Bristol area in 1911.

Bristol, Clifton Down and Avonmouth.

All Trains shewn below convey Third Class Passengers.

DOWN TRAINS. WEEK DAYS ONLY.	A.M.	1,2.P. A.M.	A.M.	A.M.	A.M.	A.M.	A.M.	A.M.	A.M.	A.M.	A.M.	P.M.	P.M.	P.M.	P.M.	P.M.	P.M.	P.M.	P.M.	P.M.	P.M.	P.M.	P.M.	P.M.	P.M.	P.M.	P.M.	P.M.	P.M.	P.M.	1,2.P. P.M.
BRISTOL (T. Meds) dep.	6 50	7 15	7 30	7 55	8 30	9 0	9 42	10 15	10 40	11 5	11 50	12 45	1 20	2 10	2 35	3 10	3 30	4 10	4 45	5 10	5 45	6 15	6 40	7 5	7 40	8 30	9 10	9 45	10 25	10 45
Lawrence Hill — "	6 54	7 19	7 34	7 59	8 34	9 4	9 46	10 19	10 44	11 9	11 54	12 49	1 24	2 14	2 39	3 14	3 34	4 14	4 49	5 15	5 50	6 19	6 44	7 9	7 44	8 34	9 14	9 49	10 29	10 49
Stapleton Road...... "	6 57	7 22	7 37	8 2	8 37	9 7	9 49	10 22	10 47	11 12	11 57	12 54	1 27	2 17	2 42	3 17	3 37	4 17	4 52	5 20	5 55	6 22	6 47	7 12	7 47	8 37	9 17	9 52	10 32	10 52
Montpelier — "	7 2	7 27	7 42	8 7	8 42	9 12	9 54	10 27	10 52	11 17	12 2	12 59	1 32	2 22	2 47	3 22	3 43	4 23	4 57	5 25	6 0	6 27	6 52	7 17	7 52	8 42	9 22	9 57	10 37	10 57
CLIFTON DOWN...arr. "	7 5	7 30	7 45	8 10	8 45	9 15	9 58	10 30	10 55	11 20	12 5	1 2	1 35	2 25	2 50	3 25	3 45	4 25	5 0	5 28	6 3	6 30	6 55	7 20	7 55	8 45	9 25	10 0	10 40	11 —
CLIFTON DOWN ...dep.	—	7 33	—	—	—	—	10 0	—	—	—	—	1 4	—	2 27	—	—	—	—	—	5 32	—	—	7 25	—	—	—	—	—	—	—
Sea Mills — arr.	—	7 41	—	—	—	—	10 8	—	—	—	—	1 12	—	2 35	—	—	—	—	—	5 40	—	—	7 33	—	—	—	—	—	—	—
Shirehampton "	—	7 46	—	—	—	—	10 13	—	—	—	—	1 17	—	2 40	—	—	—	—	—	5 45	—	—	7 38	—	—	—	—	—	—	—
Avonmouth Dock— "	—	7 51	—	—	—	—	10 18	—	—	—	—	1 22	—	2 45	—	—	—	—	—	5 50	—	—	7 43	—	—	—	—	—	—	—
AVONMOUTH... "	—	7 53	—	—	—	—	10 20	—	—	—	—	1 24	—	2 47	—	—	—	—	—	5 52	—	—	7 45	—	—	—	—	—	—	—

UP TRAINS. WEEK DAYS ONLY.	A.M.	1,2.P. A.M.	A.M.	A.M.	A.M.	A.M.	A.M.	A.M.	A.M.	A.M.	A.M.	P.M.	P.M.	P.M.	P.M.	P.M.	P.M.	P.M.	P.M.	P.M.	P.M.	P.M.	P.M.	P.M.	P.M.	P.M.	P.M.	P.M.	P.M.	P.M.	1,2.P. P.M.
AVONMOUTH — dep.	—	—	—	—	—	—	11 30	—	—	—	—	1 35	—	—	3 20	—	—	—	—	6 10	—	—	8 5	—	—	—	—	—	—	—
Avonmouth Dock "	—	8 0	—	—	—	—	11 34	—	—	—	—	1 39	—	—	3 24	—	—	—	—	6 14	—	—	8 9	—	—	—	—	—	—	—
Shirehampton ...... "	—	8 13	—	—	—	—	11 41	—	—	—	—	1 46	—	—	3 31	—	—	—	—	6 20	—	—	8 16	—	—	—	—	—	—	—
Sea Mills — "	—	8 19	—	—	—	—	11 47	—	—	—	—	1 52	—	—	3 37	—	—	—	—	6 25	—	—	8 22	—	—	—	—	—	—	—
CLIFTON DOWN arr.	—	8 25	—	—	—	—	11 53	—	—	—	—	1 58	—	—	3 43	—	—	—	—	6 33	—	—	8 28	—	—	—	—	—	—	—
CLIFTON DOWN dep.	7 25	7 55	8 30	9 0	9 35	10 10	10 45	11 20	11 55	12 35	—	1 20	2 0	2 30	3 0	3 45	4 5	4 35	5 5	5 35	6 15	6 35	7 5	7 25	8 5	8 30	9 5	9 40	10 15	—
Montpelier — "	7 28	7 58	8 33	9 3	9 39	10 13	10 48	11 23	11 58	12 39	—	1 23	2 3	2 33	3 3	3 48	4 8	4 38	5 8	5 38	6 18	6 38	7 8	7 28	8 8	8 33	9 8	9 43	10 18	—
Stapleton Road... "	7 32	8 3	8 37	9 7	9 44	10 17	10 52	11 27	12 2	12 44	—	1 28	2 11	2 39	3 7	3 52	4 12	4 42	5 13	5 42	6 22	6 42	7 12	7 32	8 12	8 37	9 12	9 47	10 22	—
Lawrence Hill — "	7 36	8 8	8 41	9 11	9 49	10 21	10 56	11 31	12 6	12 49	—	1 33	2 15	2 34	3 11	3 56	4 16	4 46	5 16	5 46	6 26	6 46	7 16	7 36	8 16	8 41	9 16	9 51	10 26	—
BRISTOL (T Mds) arr.	7 40	8 12	8 45	9 15	9 55	10 25	11 0	11 35	12 10	12 53	—	1 37	2 20	2 38	3 15	4 0	4 20	4 50	5 20	5 50	6 30	6 50	7 20	7 40	8 20	8 45	9 20	9 55	10 30	—

Note.—Passengers are not conveyed locally between Sea Mills and Avonmouth, and intermediate stations by these Trains.

Bristol and Portishead.

DOWN TRAINS.	WEEK DAYS.								1,2.P.	Thrs only	Sundays 1,2.P.		UP TRAINS	WEEK DAYS.								1,2.P.	
	A.M.	A.M.	A.M.	P.M.	P.M.	P.M.	P.M.	P.M.	P.M.	P.M.	P.M.			A.M.	A.M.	A.M.	A.M.	P.M.	P.M.	P.M.	P.M.	P.M.	P.M.
BRISTOL (T. Meads) dep.	7 5	7 50	10 10	12 40	2 55	4 10	5 2	7 0	—	8 35	11 20	3 45	PORTISHEAD....dep	6 50	8 0	8 55	10 55	1 30	3 48	5 5	6 45	—	9 15
Bedminster — "	7 9	7 54	10 14	—	—	4 14	5 25	7 4	—	8 39	—	—	Portbury "	6 55	8 5	9 0	11 0	1 35	3 50	5 10	6 50	—	9 20
Clifton Bridge .... "	7 18	8 1	10 21	12 51	3 5	4 21	5 36	7 11	—	8 46	11 30	3 55	Pill "	7 2	8 12	9 7	11 7	1 42	3 57	5 17	6 57	—	9 27
Pill — "	7 29	8 12	10 32	1 2	3 17	4 32	5 47	7 22	—	8 57	11 42	4 7	Clifton Bridge — "	7 12	8 22	9 17	11 17	1 52	4 7	5 27	7 7	—	9 37
Portbury — "	7 37	8 20	10 40	1 10	3 24	4 40	5 55	7 30	—	9 5	11 50	4 15	Bedminster — "	7 20	8 30	9 25	11 25	2 0	4 15	5 35	7 15	—	9 45
PORTISHEAD — arr.	7 42	8 25	10 45	1 15	3 30	4 45	6 0	7 35	—	9 10	11 55	4 20	BRISTOL (T. Meds) arr	7 25	8 35	9 30	11 30	2 5	4 20	5 40	7 20	—	9 50

The Portishead Branch : The 1910 Timetable.

WC&PLR Portishead Station in the mid-1930s, showing the wooden station buildings, the run-round loop and the water tower. The view is taken looking south towards the next station on the line, Portishead South.

C. R. L. Coles

Unlike the situation on the Portishead line which handled both freight and passengers, the Canon's Marsh and Wapping lines were freight only. The City Docks' lines were both double track at Ashton Swing Bridge North signal box, but the Wapping line reverted to single track 9 chains further on towards Wapping alongside the New Cut at Cumberland Siding ground frame. Hy remembers the use of saddle and side tank engines here, but he could not recall an engine with tender being used in those days. The push-pull passenger trains on the Portishead branch had side tank engines.

The lines in the City Docks area were seen by the railways as 'training grounds' for new signalmen and as such gave men opportunities to acquire confidence about their skills as the days went by. Both the Wapping and Canon's Marsh lines were comparatively little-used at this time but, nevertheless, things would happen from time to time which would make individuals apply the rules that were relevant to the particular incident.

Hy also brought to mind the rapid construction, by the GWR, of the platform at Ashton Gate. Opened in October 1906, when Bristol City Football Club had got into the First Division, football specials were soon running to it. Having arrived and discharged their loads, the special trains would run empty to Clifton Bridge Station, only 33 chains away. Here the engine would run round the empty coaching stock and would then pull it back towards Bristol when required. Hy well remembers empty trains being stabled in Ashton Meadows sidings on the Canon's Marsh line until the matches were over. They would then take the crowds home again to local stations such as Clifton Down on the Clifton Extension Railway.

Down the line at Pill, the loop was extended at both ends on 7th March 1912 and, at the same time, a goods yard was added at the Portishead end. The platforms, extended in January 1880, were again lengthened at the same time as the above alterations took place. It was not until the end of World War I that a new signal box was built. The frame for this was ordered on 2nd August 1918, it was probably built, therefore, in 1919. Having mentioned the war, the next chapter investigates the role of the railway and the dock in that great struggle.

Portishead in the early years of the century. This photograph, taken to show the new footbridge spanning the station throat, shows a member of the Armstrong standard goods class of 0-6-0. It is possibly engine No. 688, although the photograph is

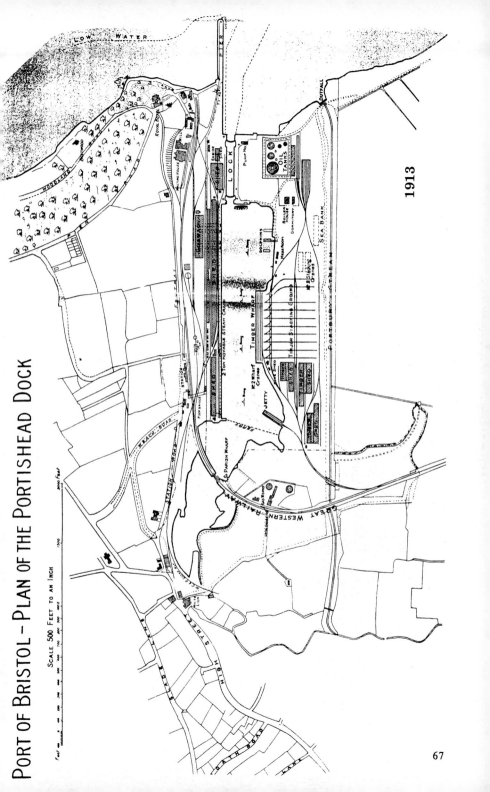

PORT OF BRISTOL – PLAN OF THE PORTISHEAD DOCK

SCALE 500 FEET TO AN INCH

1913

67

The Up railmotor, No. 58, seen at Pill, circa 1910. In a couple of years, the passing loop will have been lengthened and a goods yard installed and opened at the Portishead end (behind the railmotor).

M. J. Tozer Collection

Chapter Five

One of the more senior 'senior citizens' that I talked to, about the Portishead Railway, was Mr Henry Arberry. In March 1913, Henry's father, Mr George Arberry, moved to Portishead where he took up the post of Lock Gateman. In the same month, Henry started at Luckwell School in Bristol and, until Easter 1915, he travelled daily from Portishead to Clifton Bridge. In June 1915, he began work at Temple Meads where he remained until June 1916. In the meantime, however, in March 1914, Henry's father had applied to the GWR to become Pier Master at Portishead, for the pier was, in those days, still owned by the GWR's Marine Department. His father was successful; he became Pier Master, a job which he held until his retirement on VE day in 1945. The job, incidentally, disappeared from the payroll on his retirement.

Henry assures me that the trains on the line were always clean and comfortable and that, generally speaking, they kept good time. Indeed, throughout the line's later history, it appears to have had a good record for punctuality. However, if trains were running late, there was always the consolation of clean waiting rooms, with warm, cheerful, open coal fires. The staff were well trained and invariably courteous to passengers. They were still well respected members of the community in those early years of World War I, a war that brought about great changes, not only on the railways, but in many other aspects of English life as well.

On the freight side, one working that Henry particularly remembers concerns the working to the Timber Jetty at mile post 129½. This connection, and the ground frame that worked it, was installed on 22nd April 1903 to cater for the increase in the timber traffic then developing. When an engine and crew wanted to shunt the Timber Jetty and the docks, the single line staff would be taken, from the signal box, by the porter, who travelled out on the engine, and who would return, on foot, to the Portishead signal box, with staff in hand. When the engine wanted to return, it would 'blow-up'. The signalman would again draw the staff and the porter would again walk out with it, probably cursing and swearing, particularly if he was busy or the weather was bad! Often, this movement occurred several times a day and so, whatever else happened, the porter would remain fit! Of course, once the staff had been handed over to the engine crew, and the point out on to the main line had been changed, the engine would return to the station plus one porter on the footplate.

At that time, in the early years of the war, the majority of the workings were handled by saddle tanks, although occasionally a tender engine would be seen. During the 1913—1916 period, two or three services a day would be made up of 'motor trains'. In those days the first train of the day, the 6.50 a.m. from Portishead, called at Portbury around 7.00 a.m. and here it would pick up three or four churns of milk, a regular product from the local pastures. Also, before this particular train left Portishead, the station's porter would ring a handbell in order to hurry passengers along.

Other traffic on the line, during the war, included the movement of troops, and their horses, to and from Bristol. On one occasion Henry remembers mules being carried by train to Bristol, en route to military camps located at Shirehampton and Salisbury Plain. Indeed, a special wartime depot for mules had been established at Clifton Bridge Station and this handled mule traffic from all the local docks. At Portishead Dock itself, apart from the timber traffic already mentioned, any overflow of ships from Avonmouth would be handled, as and when necessary. For example, Henry recalls several occasions when Portishead handled some of Avonmouth's regular banana traffic, and this, presumably, would have meant that special trains would have run along the branch to handle this out of course traffic. In addition, more uneventful, and regular, loads of stone were transferred from the WC&PLR.

One clear reflection that still remains in Henry's mind relates to the River Avon and its boats. Some became stuck on the river mud, and he remembers seeing them from the carriage windows of Portishead branch trains. He remembers a fairly long list of boats that used the City Docks. These included the John Hill's City Line of boats from Bristol to New York and Montreal; Bristol to Dublin and Glasgow boats; the Bristol—Holland and Bristol—Hamburg boats, and, finally, the cattle boats from Ireland to the Cumberland Basin.

The war led to a tremendous increase in the amount of traffic handled by the railways and the companies stopped running excursion trains so as to increase their capacity. The cessation of these trains led to the death of an international exhibition then being held near Clifton Bridge Station at Ashton Meadows. The exhibition, with its ornate, temporary, buildings, dubbed 'The White City', was taken over by the War Office after the exhibition closed in August 1914.

In September 1914 the Port of Bristol Authority had two engines at Portishead. Two more were then purchased by the authorities. Both locomotives were outside cylindered 0-6-0 saddle tanks, one built by the firm of Peckett, the other by the firm of Avonside. Both of these new engines, *Alfred* and *Edward*, went to Avonmouth and this, in turn, led to the transference of one of the twelve locomotives, then working at Avonmouth, to the dock at Portishead to help out with the latter's growing war work. In 1915

The Avon Gorge looking towards the sea. The railway on the left runs to Portishead.

Author's Collection

two more locomotives were purchased. One, *Hudson*, was built by Avonside. This locomotive went to Avonmouth to work, while the other locomotive, *William*, again an Avonside product, went to Portishead. Coincidentally, both locomotives were eventually scrapped around 1964.

Not unnaturally, the war also affected the commercial trade of the dock. Although still busy in these trades, there was a marked fall in grain and timber at Portishead, although this was more than amply compensated for by the very large imports of petrol that took place for the use of the Government. Portishead was, for a long time, the main depot for the supply of petrol for road and air transport in France. Petrol was canned here and this led to the storage capacity of the refinery, mentioned in the last chapter, being greatly increased. During those dark, war-torn, days the dock was a hive of activity, both day and night. Imports amounted to 116 million gallons, while exports ran to 72 million. Very large consignments of petrol were, almost certainly, put on to rail here and then despatched to centres further inland where it was used for military purposes. The original directors and shareholders of the line and dock would have been in awe at the traffic that their successors were handling.

Another dangerous cargo handled at the dock, and by the railway, was that of toluol. This was the basic ingredient of TNT which was widely used in the manufacture of shells, bombs and mines. When war broke out, Britain relied upon coal as the source of materials for high explosives. However, it was known that crude petroleum offered an alternative supply and, so, when the Shell Company offered to supply the Government with large quantities of toluol from a source in far off Borneo, the offer was eagerly accepted.

However, as always, there were problems. Although the source was now guaranteed, there was no distillery available in this country to separate the toluol from the raw mineral oil. However, Shell did have a distillery at Rotterdam and they moved this, piece by piece, to Portishead. Speed was of the essence. The site at Portishead was prepared and in six weeks the new factory, sited within the Port of Bristol's boundary, was in full production. Since the conversion of toluol into TNT took place elsewhere, one can assume that much of this product was taken out of Portishead by rail. With petrol also being carried in large quantities, the railway was fast becoming a less than safe place to be.

From January 1917, Clifton Bridge, Pill, Portbury and Portishead Stations were all closed on Sundays and this, allied with a 50 per cent fare increase on the railways in the same month, made it apparent that much was being done to curb the passenger traffic in order to hurry the wartime freights through. However, plans were afoot for the line that would mean increases in both freight and passenger traffic.

One of these increases was due to wartime developments on the north side of the River Avon. These led, in turn, to changes taking place on the south side of the river at Clifton Bridge Station. In May 1917 work came to a halt at the new munitions factory, then being built, at Henbury, on the Avonmouth—Filton line. This was due to the entry into the war of the United States. As part of the expansion of the GWR's facilities to handle passenger traffic to this factory, permission had been given to convert the headshunt on the Down side at Clifton Bridge into a running loop. The estimated cost had been £641 and when work stopped on the Henbury project a decision had to be made, as to whether the Clifton Bridge facility would now be required. The GWR decided that it should go ahead, the Government paying for the work. The permanent way conversion was brought into use in January 1918. It was at some later, unknown, date removed.

In July 1917, Parliament approved the setting up of a National Shipyard Company. This company had to ensure the rapid replacement of ships lost by enemy action. Three shipyards were to be built, all in the Bristol Channel area. These were to be located at Chepstow, Beachley and Portbury. Fitting out facilities, for the use of all three, were to be provided at Avonmouth, and, because of its proximity to this dock, Portbury was chosen as the location for the central management offices. The new shipyard meant traffic and change for the Portishead branch.

Although the shipyard has always been known as Portbury Shipyard it was, in fact, sited at Sheephouse Farm, Easton-in-Gordano. A thousand men took part in the dock's construction, all were troops in the Royal Engineers. At first they were billeted in homes in Pill but as work progressed a vast camp was built at Sheephouse. A railway branch, from Portbury sidings on the GWR line, led down to extensive sidings at the shipyard site. Roads were constructed and water was piped in from Failand. The foundations for the slips were laid down but the Portbury project was never finished and, with the end of the war, the project was abandoned. As with the navvies who built the original B&PP&R Company's line, many of the soldiers stationed in the camp remained in the Pill area once they were demobbed. By 1918, the sum of £238,000 had been spent on the Portbury Yard and, as can be imagined, its effect on life in Pill and Easton-in-Gordano had been tremendous. Many troops brought their wives and families, with them, into the villages. There was a great increase in trade and movement generally. Towards the end of 1918, the 'Camp', as the locals called it, was a centre for the Admiralty, employing many civilian clerks and typists and justifying a station of its own at Duck Lane. The return fare from Pill was 1½d, Clifton Bridge to Portbury was 3d, while Bedminster to Portbury Shipyard was 6d return.

A few more railway details might not go amiss at this point. In October 1917, the GWR authorized the spending of £10,775 on the provision of siding accommodation at Portbury. The traffic running into the site soon started to grow and problems were experienced in handling the construction traffic. A plan showing proposed changes at the junction of the GWR and the line running down to the slips reveals the following items. On the GWR line itself, a new loop and sidings were to be put in between mile post 127 and mile post 127¾. The additional carriage and other two sidings were to be built to hold 44 trucks each. To control the new signals and connections, the GWR proposed building a 57 lever frame signal box. Finally, provision was made for a proposed office, 20 ft. x 8 ft. This building was divided into two parts: one office, 8 ft. x 8 ft., was for the use of checkers, while another slightly larger one, 12 ft. x 8 ft., was to be for clerical use. The signal box and sidings were constructed and were brought into use on 29th January 1918. The previously mentioned station first opened for passenger traffic on 16th September 1918. It was finally closed on 26th March 1923. The crossing loop, found here, was brought into action on 10th April 1928. The box, loop and sidings were finally taken out of use less than 40 years later, just before the line's closure, on 14th April 1964.

By the end of hostilities the total expenditure on strictly railway projects, in connection with the shipyard, had reached nearly £19,000. This figure was broken down in the following way. Over £11,600 had been spent at Portbury itself, while the other £7,300, approximately, was split between the provision of sidings at Clifton Bridge Station and West Depot. The former were not required once hostilities ceased, anyway, while the latter would have been retained had the shipyard been developed. It did not, of course, and it would seem that the actual provision of these sidings at West Depot was overtaken by events.

Before leaving the subject of the shipyard, it is worth having a look at the rather complex matter of locomotives used on the shipyard site. This is rather a difficult matter in that Portbury worked in conjunction with Beachley and Portishead and so there is some doubt as to the exact allocation between them. Two locomotives definitely recorded as being at Portbury were *Greenheys*, an outside cylindered 0-4-0 saddle tank built by Hunslet (288/1882) and IWD No. 34 *Portbury*, an outside cylindered 0-6-0 saddle tank built by Avonside (1764/1917). However, to complicate matters even further, it is known that at a sale that took place on site on 30th March 1920, the locomotives available included three 0-6-0 standard gauge, two 0-4-0s, again standard gauge and one 2 ft. gauge 0-4-0.

At these sales, however, locomotives were often brought in from other depots for the occasion, and one cannot assume that Portbury had six locomotives operating there. To complicate matters still further, there were three later sales of plant from all three sites at Beachley, Portishead and Portbury, and from the advertisements there is no way of telling what locomotives were located at any one place. These sales included the following items:

28th May 1920   3 — 0-6-0 saddle tanks (12 x 18)
                       1 — 0-6-0 saddle tank (13 x 18)
                       1 — 0-4-0 saddle tank (12 x 18)

19th September 1920	1 — 0-4-0 saddle tank (12 x 18) by Hudswell Clarke and Rodgers (standard gauge)
	1 — 0-4-0 Kerr Stuart 2 ft. gauge
	1 — 0-6-0 Kerr Stuart 2 ft. gauge
	1 — 0-6-0 Robert Hudson
22nd March 1921	5 — standard gauge 0-4-0 and 0-6-0 locomotives

GREAT WESTERN RAILWAY.

Weston-s.-Mare.

THE GRAND PIER AND PAVILION.

HERR KANDT'S BAND.   VARIETY ENTERTAINMENTS.

AMUSEMENTS AT BIRNBECK PIER.
KNIGHTSTONE PAVILION. — GROVE PARK.

Attractive Steamer Trips to Bristol Channel Ports.
Lovely Drives through Kewstoke Woods, Mendip Hills, Cheddar, &c.

HIGH-CLASS, BEAUTIFULLY ILLUSTRATED

TRAVEL BOOKS

Price 3d.

"DEVON
The Shire of the Sea Kings."

"The CORNISH RIVIERA,
Our National Health & Pleasure Resort."

"SOUTH WALES,
The Country of Castles."

"NORTH WALES,
The British Tyrol."

"Southern IRELAND,
Its Lakes and Landscapes."

"HISTORIC
Sites and Scenes of England."

Price 1d.

"RURAL LONDON."

"HOLIDAY HAUNTS."

And List of Seaside and Country Apartments, &c.

Can be obtained at Offices and principal Stations of the Company.

On Wednesday, July 31st, 1907,

A DAY-TRIP EXCURSION WILL RUN TO

PORTISHEAD, CLEVEDON,

AND

WESTON-S.-MARE

AS UNDER:

LEAVING	AT	RETURN FARES, THIRD CLASS.		
		To Portishead.	To Clevedon.	To Weston-s/M.
	A.M.			
Swindon	7 50			
Wootton Bassett ...	8 2	3/3	3/3	3/3
Dauntsey	8 10			
Chippenham	8 24	— 2/9	2/9	2/9
Corsham	8 35	2/6	2/9	2/9
Box	8 45			
Bathampton ...	8 52	— 2/3	2/9	2 9
Bath	9 4	— 2/3	2/3	2/9
Saltford	9 18	— 1/9	2/3	2/3
Keynsham	9 24	— 1/9	2/-	2/-

The Return Train will leave

WESTON-SUPER-MARE (Excursion Platform, Locking Road.) at 8.4 p.m.
CLEVEDON at 7.40 p.m., and PORTISHEAD at 7.35 p.m. the same day.

Passengers for Portishead change at Bedminster in both directions, and those for Clevedon at Yatton.

Weston-super-Mare.—Electric tramcars run every few minutes from and to the Excursion Platform (Locking Road) and the Sanatorium, Grand Pier, Knightstone Pavilion, Birnbeck Pier, &c.

BATH.—Excursion and cheap tickets can be obtained in advance at the G.W.R. Office, 20 Bond Street.

Children under Twelve Years of age, Half-price.   No Luggage allowed.

The Tickets are not transferable. Should an Excursion or Cheap Ticket be used for any other Station than those named upon it, or by any other Train than those specified, it will be rendered void, and therefore the fare paid will be liable to forfeiture, and the full Ordinary Fare will become chargeable.

For information respecting Pleasure Party arrangements, and Excursion and Special Trips on the Great Western Railway, application should be made to Mr. C. Kislingbury, Divisional Superintendent, Temple Meads Station, Bristol ; or at any of the Stations.

Paddington, July, 1907.   JAMES C. INGLIS. General Manager.

(Bristol—3,500 R. 8vo, 2 sides)   Arrowsmith, Printer, Quay Street, Bristol.   (B 559)

Handbill: *Michael Wyatt and Photography Steve Smith*   75

By 1926, the former shipyard at Portbury had become Central Stores Depot No. 367 and, at a sale of plant there on 31st October 1926, engine IWD No. 7, an 0-6-0 saddle tank 12 x 18, believed to be Manning Wardle 1529, was one of the items included.

Further back in time and along the line in the Ashton area, other developments were taking place. On 27th July 1918 an agreement was signed, between the Imperial Tobacco Company and the GWR, to provide a set of private sidings serving the firm's premises alongside of what is, today, Ashton Containers' main works. Under this agreement with Imperial, two loop sidings, capable of holding twenty trucks, and a headshunt were provided. These sidings were brought into use on 7th December 1918.

In January 1920 Ashton Saw Mills took over Imperial's interest and in turn Ashton Saw Mills became Ashton Containers. This latter change took place in July 1937. Under a further agreement between the GWR and Ashton Containers, signed on 31st October 1947, the private sidings were extended around the side of the firm's factory, virtually reaching as far as Winterstoke Road.

In the 1920s the line's traditional holiday traffic started to return. In addition, the Campbell Steamers still called at the pier and there were numerous occasions when they picked up people who had arrived at Portishead by connecting train. As an example, on Sunday, 15th August 1926, one hundred and thirty three people went down to the resort by train to pick up the *Britannia* which called at the pier on its way to Ilfracombe. Tradition was re-asserting itself and the old patterns were becoming re-established. Indeed, new stations were being opened, and, in one case, re-opened, on the branch to develop the passenger traffic. On 23rd May 1926 Ashton Gate Platform was re-opened while, in the winter of the same year, Ham Green Halt was opened near Pill to serve the neighbouring hospital at Ham Green itself. The final new addition, to the complement of stations and halts on the branch, was the new platform opened, in July 1928, for the summer season only, at Nightingale Valley. This halt, situated almost directly under the Suspension Bridge, was closed in September 1932, having remained open for the summer seasons of the intervening years, its provision having been an almost total failure.

There were also changes occurring at Portbury when, in April 1927, the GWR purchased, from the War Department, the land on which Portbury Shipyard loop and sidings were laid. The limit of the GWR's land appears to have run down the middle of the passing line, on the shipyard side, and so, virtually with an intensification of the passenger service in the offing, it would seem that the GWR felt that the time was ripe to purchase the land. The map accompanying the conveyance shows the station at Portbury

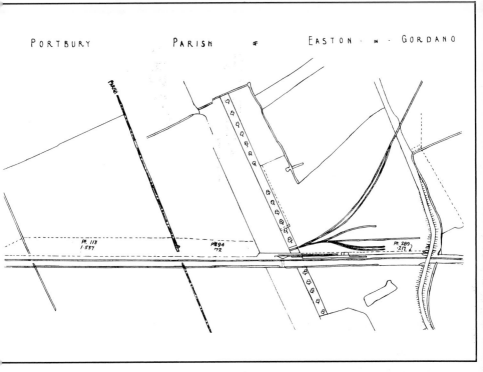

A 1927 plan showing Portbury Shipyard Station and its associated branch.

Portbury Station, looking towards Portishead.

M. E. J. Deane

Shipyard and the connections and sidings, leading away from the GWR line, still in place in 1927. Also, in the same year, the GWR initiated its own bus service between Portishead Station and Redcliffe Bay. This service began on 28th June 1927 and ran until 19th July 1931 when it succumbed to competition with the Bristol Omnibus Company.

Even greater things were happening in Portishead in the mid-1920s for the then Electrical Commissioners, under the terms of the 1926 Electricity Supply Act, chose a site at Portishead for the construction of one of their large West Country power stations. This was to be known as Portishead 'A' Power Station and was situated on the hill behind the railway station. The firm chosen to build this power station was that of William Cowlin of Bristol and so an agreement was signed, between the firm and the GWR, to lay in sidings and connections between the firm's depot at Portishead and the GWR running lines on the Down side of the GWR station and the pier. It was through these connections and sidings that material for the power station's construction was to come.

For the latter's construction one of the contractors, Charles Brand, employed two 2 ft. gauge outside cylindered saddle tanks. Both were 0-4-0s, one being built by Andrew Barclay in 1921 (1730) while the other had been built in 1916 (2471) by Kerr Stuart. The power station opened in 1929 and on 1st February of the same year the sidings serving the Generating Station were brought into use.

Under another agreement dated 14th December 1927 between Severn Kraft Company and the GWR, a private siding was built leaving the main line just outside Portishead at 129 miles 33 chains. A new ground frame was also provided in association with this work, while the siding itself was brought into use on 13th February 1928. It remained in service until the firm ceased trading in the 1930s.

At Oakwood, between Nightingale Valley and Ham Green Halt, a loop and controlling signal box were brought into use on 14th May 1929 in readiness for the intensive passenger service introduced to the line by the GWR in July 1929. This service was hourly but at certain times of the day the frequency was increased to half-hourly. For the service most trains crossed at Pill or Portbury Shipyard, although the new loop at Oakwood ensured flexibility for the occasions when trains were running out of course. The intensive service continued, with minor changes, until the outbreak of World War II and beyond. The box and loop at Oakwood were taken out of use in September 1960.

At the same time as the expansion work was being undertaken, related changes were also taking place at Portishead Station in order to ease problems caused by the new passenger service. At the station a carriage loop was converted into a passenger run round road, while a new platform was built against this new loop. The Portishead facilities were brought into use on 9th March 1930 in readiness for the year's summer service.

In the early 1930s an ambitious series of improvements was undertaken by the GWR in the Bristol area. The scheme provided for the enlargement of Temple Meads Station and for the provision of two additional running lines between Filton Junction and Stapleton Road; Dr Day's Bridge Junction and Temple Meads and also between Temple Meads and Portishead Junction. This gave at least four running lines between Filton Junction and Portishead Junction, a distance of nearly seven miles. This work meant the rebuilding of Horfield and Ashley Hill Stations to the north-east of Temple Meads, and Bedminster and Parson Street Stations on the Weston-super-Mare main line to the south-west of Temple Meads. A number of bridges in the station area around Temple Meads itself also had to be rebuilt and widened.

These works involved the engineering of extensive earthworks and numerous bridges, as well as the rebuilding of Horfield, Ashley Hill, Bedminster and Parson Street Stations, while many miles of track had to be rebuilt and realigned. Between Bath Road Bridge and Portishead Junction, for example, the track widening work was very heavy in that it entailed many new earthworks and high retaining walls. In the case of the retaining wall on the Down side near St. Luke's Road, in Totterdown, the contractors resorted to a new approach in that they had reinforced concrete uprights and struts bedded into the concrete foundations instead of the usual timbers to support the ground. The point about this was that these concrete uprights and struts did not need to be withdrawn. They were embedded in the wall to form part of the permanent structure, so avoiding the chance of any ground movement when the 'timbers' were withdrawn.

One other structure of note on the Temple Meads—Portishead Junction section was the large skew arch of 56 ft. square span that still carries the Bedminster Down Road over the railway. The angle of skew on this particular bridge is very marked and so, when it was being built, the two skew faces were formed in concrete, strengthened with steel bar reinforcements, while the middle section was constructed in brickwork. This bridge was one of two replacement bridges built on the south-western section of the main line from Temple Meads to Portishead Junction, the other being at

RAILWAY STATION, PORTISHEAD

Photographs of stations have always been of interest both to the railway enthusiast and the general public. In the early 1900s, in particular, there were thousands of postcards sold of 'The Railway Station'. It was a part of the locality, like the church, the ancient pub and the market place. It was so often the scene of joyful meetings and sorrowful departures. Everybody knew the station and respected the stationmaster who was an important person and opened carriage doors for the first class passengers. He was equally up to the occasion if young Fred was troublesome and had to be fiercely told to 'op it quick'.

Photograph Lens of Sutton and text Jeoffrey Spence

Pill Station in later years.   *C. J. Maggs*

◁ GWR '4500 class 2-6-2T, No. 4551, crosses at Oakwood in the mid-1930s.
C. R. L. Coles   81

Parson Street itself. The two former bridges were demolished on Sunday, 26th April and Sunday, 15th November 1931. On both occasions passenger trains to the West Country were diverted to the harbour line running via Wapping, Ashton Swing Bridge and West Loop North and West Depot signal boxes.

One of these bridges was that of Bartlett's Bridge at Bedminster, which was reduced to rubble on Sunday, 26th April 1931. The original bridge here was constructed of rough stone when the Bristol to Exeter line was laid in 1844. A facing of brickwork was later added. Preparatory work, in connection with the demolition, was begun early in the morning. Rain made things difficult but by 7.30 a.m. the permanent way beneath the bridge had been protected by masses of timber and 10 lb of gelignite had been placed in three rows at either end and in the centre of the bridge.

Owing to a short circuit only the first charge fired at both ends of the bridge, which rocked but stayed in position. The second charge cut it in half. The third, at 8.00 p.m., hurled the remainder, nearly 200 tons of it, to the ground. The lines were clear for traffic by noon.

The station at Parson Street, opened 29th August 1927, was thoroughly rebuilt only a few years later as part of the quadrupling, the latter being brought into use, in stages, throughout 1933. The signal box at Portishead Junction was replaced by Parson Street signal box which was sited fifty yards west of the old box, at 120 mile 33 chain. The new box was brought into use on 13th November 1932. Later in the decade the signal box at West Loop North Junction was abolished on 10th May 1936. With all these changes taking place on the line, let us now see what it was actually like to work at some of the stations during the 1920s and 1930s.

One regular traveller on the line, in the 1930s, was Mr L. F. Tucker, currently living in Bath. He used the Portishead branch on many occasions during the period 1929 to 1937, mainly during the summer months. Setting off from Parson Street, his destination would usually be Portishead, although Clifton Bridge was also a popular stop as well. He always used the line for pleasure sometimes going to Portishead to change on to the W C & P L R.

He comments that travelling on the W C & P L R was a little rough and, in places, the track left a lot to be desired! The rails were spiked to the sleepers, there being no chairs. The W C & P L R Station at Portishead was a rustic timber structure with a shelter and a ticket hut.

In those days, Portishead, like its neighbour Clevedon, was quiet, attracting mainly weekend and day trippers from Bristol. Of course, Mr Tucker made use of the combined rail/boat tickets for use with the excursions offered by P. & A. Campbell of Bristol. Of all the stations on the branch itself, Mr Tucker liked Clifton Bridge best. This was due to its really pleasant setting in the Avon Gorge with the Suspension Bridge in the background. He suggested it was the most useful station in that when the Rownham Ferry was in operation (it ceased working in 1932), it served the dock and power station workers who travelled to Portishead from the Hotwells district, in addition to those members of the public who lived on that side of the river. It was also handy for access to the river bank on the (then) Somerset side, where the path alongside the Avon was very popular at weekends and during the holiday season.

One rather special occasion recalled, occurred when Mr Tucker travelled from Bristol (Temple Meads) to Plymouth via the City Docks' lines via Wapping (the 'back-door' route as he called it). This diversion was brought about by the dismantling of the 'forming structure' under the then newly constructed A38 road bridge by Parson Street Station. On this particular Sunday, all Down main traffic was put through the City Docks' lines at Wapping, via the Bristol Harbour line, and then on along the New Cut to Ashton Swing Bridge North Junction. He recounts how strange it seemed to be travelling through the city centre by passenger train.

By the 1930s, the Smith family were a well established railway family in the Pill and Portishead areas. Between 1929 and 1934 Mr Philip Smith was employed by the GWR at Temple Meads, but until the age of 18 he lived with his parents in the Cheddar Valley. His parents then moved to Pill where his father, Mr Walter Smith, was, between roughly 1932 and 1939, stationmaster. Portishead was Philip's father's home, while his grandfather, Mr James Smith, was, for many years, the GWR Inspector in charge of the Portishead Dock. The Smiths lived at Pier Cottage, Portishead for something like thirty years.

In the short time Philip was living at home, he commuted daily to Temple Meads, where he worked in the stationmaster's office. The stationmaster in those days, was termed Station Superintendent, and the occupant of that office was one Amos Follows. The arrangement there was that the GWR and the LMSR used to appoint the Station Superintendents in turn, and Mr Follows was an LMS man, previously stationmaster at Nottingham. Follows' father was a Vice President of the LMSR.

Temple Meads Station was somewhat unusual inasmuch as its staffing was organized by the GWR (apart from the post of Station Superintendent) but it sheltered under the title of Bristol Joint Station, with the buttons on the uniform marked 'BJS'.

Returning to the workings on the branch, the Portishead line was, it seems, regarded as being quite important in the 1930s. It had a regular hourly service in each direction, having the, more or less, exclusive use of the bay in No. 1 platform at Temple Meads. Awkward questions quickly followed any delay to trains on the branch because it carried a great number of commuters into and out of Bristol. As a youngster, Philip had the decided impression that the importance accorded to the branch was also related to the number of railway officials who resided along its route!

Philip's brother, Gordon, who spent the greater part of his life based in the Pill and Portishead areas, also reflected upon life at Pill Station and on the Portishead line during the mid and late 1930s. As a schoolboy he travelled backwards and forwards between Pill and Temple Meads five days a week during the school terms. Later, after leaving school and aspiring to the heights of laboratory boy, at Bristol University, while waiting to go to sea, his journey was between Pill and Clifton Bridge Station. From here he would walk along the rather pleasant path that led to the Swing Bridge spanning the New Cut, over it and along towards Hotwells, taking various short cuts along the dockside railway track. In all, he travelled the line regularly for about eight years.

Gordon told me that he vividly remembers the dusty seats and the fact that when you whacked the upholstery with your hand, visibility in the compartment was virtually reduced to nothing. He also recalls the hot steam pipes running beneath the seats and steam rising up from beneath the running board of a stationary train in winter time. One vital fact for a young schoolboy was that a 'Woodbine' cigarette lasted from the former No. 1 platform at Temple Meads to just beyond Ashton Gate Station, and that it took from there to the Bristol side of Ham Green Tunnel, with one's head out of the window, to destroy the evidence before getting home!

Vandalism was not a very serious problem. It amounted to throwing light bulbs out of the window, whilst travelling through Ham Green Tunnel, just to hear them 'pop'! On a couple of occasions someone pulled the communication cord; then you had

◁ GWR '4575' class 2-6-2T, No. 5508, at Portishead in the mid-1930s. The engine, built in October 1927, was withdrawn from service in December 1964. This class of locomotive gave sterling service on the Portishead branch.

C. R. L. Coles

Portishead South Station (WC&PLR), circa 1934/5. Note the stone wagons in the siding. Clean, crushed stone left the WC&PLR via the connection at Portishead in common user wagons, although some traffic was taken out in the quarries' own private owner wagons. When the stone traffic was at its peak, some forty loaded wagons a day would be put over on to the GWR. Inwards traffic would consist of empties for the quarries, while tar and bitumen would come in by rail tankers. Coal was also a common incoming traffic. Mustads' nail factory at Portishead also imported its iron by rail.

Photograph C. R. L. Coles and information for text C. Redwood

Ham Green Halt looking towards Bristol. The halt was opened on 23rd November 1926 to serve the neighbouring hospital and village of the same name. It was closed, along with all the other stations on the branch, on 7th September 1964.

C. J. Maggs

to be watchful in case the offenders, who might well be in the next compartment to your own, did not poke the chain through the communication pipe so that the slackness appeared in your compartment. There were also old photographs, being mainly of holiday places covered by the GWR network, adorning the compartments. Quite often there was one of a middle-aged lady, with her skirt tucked into the lower part of a pair of voluminous knickers, paddling near the pier at Weston-super-Mare. But, without fail, on every train, there was the picture of a very large lady, struggling up the cobbled street at Clovelly, astride a mule about half her size. This seemed to be the GWR's favourite, because there was one in almost every compartment. The RSPCA would not stand for it today!

One well remembered incident, in Gordon Smith's life at Pill, arose as a result of his digging up about twenty detonators from a non-productive part of his father's garden. Whoever disposed of them in that way could not have been overblessed with intelligence because, had Gordon pierced one with his garden fork, the whole lot would have gone off in his face. They were about the size and shape of a large poached egg, and just one went off with a terrific bang. Gordon kept the discovery of this little arsenal to himself and waited for an opportune moment. Without thinking of the consequences, he clamped about a dozen of them to the rails, just below the booking office where his father was working, one late afternoon.

BRISTOL AND PORTISHEAD. Week Days.

Mls			a.m.	a.m.	a.m.	a.m.	a.m.	a.m.	a.m.	noon	noon	p.m.	p.m.	p.m.	p.m.	p.m.	p.m.	p.m.	p.m.	p.m	p.m	p.m
	Bristol (Temple Meads)	dep	7 0	8 17	9 0	9 30	10 24	11 30	noon	0 12 30	12 57	1 30		2 30		3K30	4 30		5 30 5 K 49	6 30		7 30
1	Bedminster	,,	7 4	8 21	9 4	9 34	10 33	11 34	12 4	12 34	1	1 34	2E 4	2 34		3K34	4 34	5K 5	5 34 5 K 53	6 34		7 34
1½	Parson Street	,,	7 6	8 23	9 6	9 36	10 35	11 36	12 6	12 36	1 5	1 36 2E 6		2 36		3K36	4 36	5K 5	5 36 5 K 56	6 36		7 36
3	Ashton Gate	,,	7 10	8 27	9 10	9 40	10 40	11 40	12 10	12 40	1 10	1 40 2E 10		2 40	3E 10	3K40	4 40	5K15	5 40	6 10	6 40	7 10	7 40
3½	Clifton Bridge	,,	7 13	8 30	9 13	9 43	10 43	11 43	12 13	12 43	1 13	1 43 2E 13		2 43	3E13	3K43	4 43	5K19	5 43	6 13	6 43	7 13	7 43
4	Nightingale Valley	,,									1 45 2E 15		2 45	3E15	3K45	4 45	5K21	5 45	6 15	6 45	7 15	7 45
7	Ham Green Halt	,,	7 21	8 38	9 21	9 51	10 51	11 51	12 26	12 51	1 51	1 51 2E 21		2 51	3E21	3K51	4 51	5K27	5 51	6 21	6 51	7 21	7 51
7½	Pill	,,	7 24	8 43	9 24	9 54	10 54	11 54	12 29	12 54	1 54	1 54 2E 24		2 54	3E24	3K57	4 54	5K30	5 54	6 24	6 54	7 24	7 54
9½	Portbury	arr	7 32	8 47	9 29	9 59	10 59	11 59	12 34	12 59	1 59	1 59 2E 29		2 59	3E29	4K 2	4 59	5K35	5 59	6 29	6 59	7 29	7 59
11	**Portishead**	,,	7 39	8 53	9 35	10 5	11 5	11 12	12 40	1 5	2 5	2 5 2E 35		3 5	3E35	4K 8	5 5	5K41	6 5	6 35	7 5	7 35	8 5

Week Days—contd.

		p.m.	p.m.	p.m.	p.m.	p.m.
Bristol (Temple Meads)	dep	8 30		9 30	11 0
Bedminster	,,	8 34		9 34	11 3
Parson Street	,,	8 36		9 36	11 6
Ashton Gate	,,	8 40	8K10	9 40	11 10
Clifton Bridge	,,	8 13	8 43	9 43	11 13
Nightingale Valley	,,	8 15	8 45		
Ham Green Halt	,,	8 21	8 51	9K21	9 51	11 21
Pill	,,	8 24	8 54	9K24	9 54	11 24
Portbury	arr	8 29	8 59	9K29	9 59	11 29
Portishead	,,	8 35	9 5	9K35	10 5	11 35

Sundays.

		a.m.	p.m.	p.m.	p.m.	p.m.	p.m.	p.m.	p.m.	p.m.	p.m.	p.m.	p.m.
		10K15	1 30	2K 0	2K30	3K 0		4 18	4E48	5 18	6 4		7 30	8 30
		10K19	1 34	2K 4	2K34	3K 4		5K30	6 30	7 0	7 30		8 34
		10K21	1 36	2K 6	2K36	3K 6		5K34	6 34	7 4	7 34		8 36
		10K25	1 40	2K10	2K40	3K10	3 40	5K36	6 36	7 6	7 36		8 36
		10K28	1 43	2K13	2K43	3K13	3 43	5K40	6 40	7 10	7 40	8 10	8 40	9 10
			1 45	2K15	2K45	3K15	3 45	5K45	6 45	7 15	7 45	8 15	8 45	
		10K36	1 51	2K21	2K51	3K21	3 51	5K51	6 51	7 21	7 51	8 21	8 51	9 21
		10K39	1 54	2K24	2K54	3K24	3 54	5K54	6 54	7 24	7 54	8 24	8 54	9 24
		10K44	1 59	2K29	2K59	3K29	3 59	5K59	6 59	7 29	7 59	8 29	8 59	9 29
		10K50	2 5	2K35	3K 5	3K35	4 5	6K 5	7 5	7 35	8 5	8 35	9 5	9 35

See page 41 for Explanatory Notes.

PORTISHEAD AND BRISTOL. Week Days.

		a.m.	a.m.	a.m.	a.m.	a.m.	a.m.	a.m.	p.m.	p.m.	p.m.	p.m.	p.m.	p.m.	p.m	p.m	p.m	p.m	p.m	p.m	p.m
Portishead	dep	6 47	7 57		9 30	9 53	10 53	11 53	12 48	1 48	2 48	2K38	3 48		4 18	4E48	5 18	6		6 18	6 48	7 18	7 48	8 18
Portbury	,,	6 52	8 2	8 35	9 23	9 53	10 53	11 53	12 53	1 53	2 53		4 23	4E53	5 23	5 53		6 23	6 53	7 23	7 53	8 23
Pill	,,	6 57	8 7	8 42	9 30	10 0	11 0	12 0	1 0	2 0	3 0		4 30	5E 0	5 30	6 0		6 30	7 0	7 30	8 0	8 30
Ham Green Halt	,,		8 9	8 44	9 33	10 3	11 3	12 3	1 3	2 3	3 3		4 33	5E 3	5 33	6 3		6 33	7 3	7 33	8 3	8 33
Clifton Bridge	,,	7 7	8 18	8 53	9 42	10 12	11 12	12 12	1 12	2 9	3 9		4 39	5E 9	5 39	6 9		6 39	7 9	7 39	8 9	8 39
Nightingale Valley	,,									2 9	3 9		4 39	5E 9	5 39	6 9						
Ashton Gate	,,	7 9	8 20	8 55	9 44	10 14	11 13	12 14	1 14	1 13	2 14	3 14	4 14		4 44	5E14	5 41	6 14		6 44	7 18	7 44	8 14	8 44
Parson Street	,,	7 13	8 24		9 49	10 18	11 17	12 18			2 18		3 18		4 48	6E18		6			7 22		8 20
Bedminster	,,	7 16	8 28	9 2	9 53	10 22	11 20	12 22	1 19	2 22	3 22	4 22		4 52	5E22		6 22			7 26		8 24
Bristol (T. Meads)	arr	7 19	8 31	9 6	9 56	10 25	11 23	12 26	1 22	2 25	3 26	4 26		4 55	5E25		6 25			7 29		8 27

Week Days—cont

		p.m.	p.m.	p.m.	p.m.	p.m.	p.m.	p.m.	p.m.	p.m.	p.m.	p.m.
Portishead	dep	8 48	9 18	9K48	10 18	11 6	2 18	2 48	3 18	3 48	6K18	7 18	7K48	8 18	8K48	9 18	9 48
Portbury	,,	8 53	9 23	9K53	10 23	11 10	2 23	2 53	3 23	3 53	5 23	6K23	7 23	7K53	8 23	8K53	9 23	9 53
Pill	,,	9 0	9 30	10K 0	10 30	11 17	2 30	3 0	3 30	4 0	5 30	6K30	7 30	8K 0	8 30	9K 0	9 30	10 0
Ham Green Halt	,,	9 3	9 33	10K 3	10 33	11 20	2 33	3 3	3 33	4 3	5 33	6K33	7 33	8K 3	8 33	9K 3	9 33	10 3
Nightingale Valley	,,	9 9					2 39	3 9	3 39	4 9	5 39	6K39	7 39	8K 9	8 39	9K 9		
Clifton Bridge	,,	9 12	9 42	10K12	10 42	11 29	2 42	3 12	3 42	4 12	5 42	6K42	7 42	8K12	8 42	9K12	9 42	10 12
Ashton Gate	,,	9 14	9 44	10K14	10 44	11 31	2 44	3 14	3 44	4 14	5 44	6K44	7 44	8K14	8 44	9K14	9 44	10 14
Parson Street	,,	9 18	9 48	10K18	10 48		2 48	3 18	3 48	4 18		6K48		8K18		9K18	9 48	10 18
Bedminster	,,	9 22	9 52	10K22	10 52	11 39	2 52		3 52	4 22	5 52	6K52		8K22		9K22	9 52	10 22
Bristol (T. Meads)	arr	9 25	9 55		11 10	11 42	2 55		3 56	4 25	5 56	6K55		8K25		9K25	9 55	10 25

E—Weds. and Sats. only.

G—Saturdays excepted.

K—Through train to or from Lawrence Hill and Stapleton Road.

S—Saturdays only.

The Portishead Branch : The 1932 Timetable.

◁ 'Dean Goods' No. 25 26 simmers gently at Portishead, the granary dominating the background landscape. The locomotive, built in 1897, saw service until World War II when it was withdrawn in October 1940.

C. R. L. Coles

With the platform full of Avonmouth dockers returning to their homes in and around Portishead, in came the train bursting at the seams with tired businessmen quietly dropping off to sleep. Then a dozen detonators went off like an exploding ammunition dump! One or two of the old salts, who were walking up and down the station bridge, took off like sixteen year olds. The dockers dived for cover round the back of the signal box. Gordon's father came rushing out of the booking office like a tom-cat two jumps ahead of the vet! Resulting from this burst of high spirits, Gordon suffered a row of early nights lasting some three months. There was also a substantial adjustment to his pocket money and this, to a nine year old boy, was sheer tragedy.

Gordon's father, as stationmaster at Pill, was also in charge of the halt, and the chocolate machine on the halt, at Ham Green. This particular platform was made of wooden timbers and, quite often, while attempting to put money in the machine, passengers would fumble and drop the coins down between the timbers. However, because, more likely than not, their train was approaching, they never had the chance to retrieve any of their coins. Knowing when the halt was quiet, Gordon would often go under the platform and search out this useful source of additional pocket money.

At Pill itself, the railway track came in rather lower than the surrounding roadway system and was, therefore, spanned, at the Bristol end of the platforms, by two bridges, close by the ticket office. This was a focal point for many of the old retired ships' pilots who walked back and forth, as they had done during their working lives. Gordon learned to walk back and forth with them listening to tales of long ago, of oceans far away. It must have done the trick because eventually Gordon himself became a pilot as well.

One night, further along the line at Portishead, two of the Bristol Channel pilots came ashore at the town's pier after having taken some ships down-river. They wanted to catch the last train back to Bristol so they gasped their way along the seemingly endless path from the pier to the station. Since they were in a hurry they decided not to go to the ticket office since that would take up too much time. They would get their tickets from the guard on the train. They staggered along the platform and threw themselves into the last coach of the train which, fortunately for them, was still in the station. After all that rush, they were pretty pleased to have caught the train, it was a long walk back to Bristol. Anyway they chatted, and waited, and chatted and waited , . . . and waited, and waited. Twenty minutes, thirty minutes and so, wondering what the delay was, they looked out of the window to see that theirs was the only coach left in the platform! The rest of the train had left long ago . . . !

A view showing Bailey's Mill at Portishead Dock. This photograph was taken in May 1935 and shows a rather nice collection of rolling stock.

Port of Bristol Authority

As with a lot of branch lines, just prior to World War II, there were rumblings about closure of some stations, or perhaps the suggestion that one stationmaster could look after two stations. So, at that time, it was only reasonable that each stationmaster looked with more care, and some apprenhension, on freight and ticket receipts. This might well have been the case with the Portishead branch in that, by 1938, trade had fallen to such a low level at the dock itself, that the Port of Bristol Authority had seriously considered closing the whole thing down.

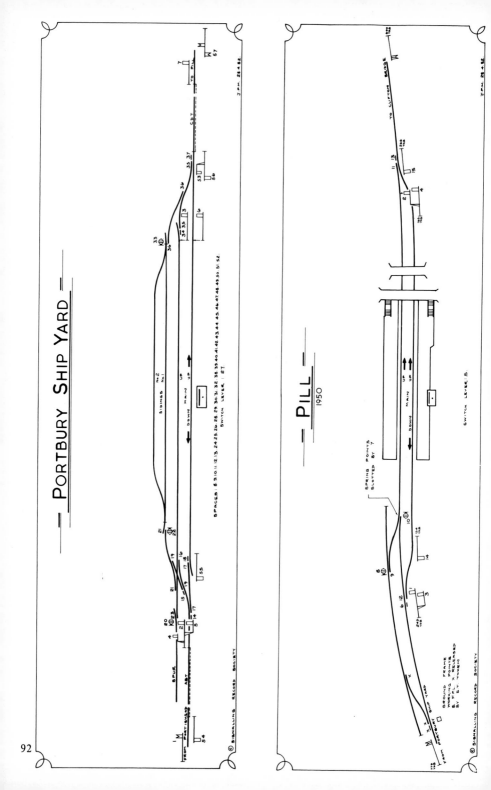

PORTBURY SHIP YARD

PILL

1950

92

At Pill Station, there was a road running adjacent to the track, although the former was a good deal above the latter, and was separated from the platform by a high bank. About the time of the threatened closures Mr Walter Smith noticed a couple of schoolgirls come regularly bounding out of their house, tear down the bank and get on to the train, at the last second, without buying a ticket from the booking office. Obviously they got one at the other end, Clifton Bridge in this case, where they had a bit more time to spare. Possibly Mr Smith considered that the loss of two return tickets several times a week to Clifton Bridge was not a good thing. Consequently, he used to take up 'battle stations' on the platform and would chase the poor girls back up the bank into the road and round through the booking office, whilst train, driver and guard waited patiently below.

At Portbury Station, the stationmaster had a lovely garden alongside the track, right opposite the booking office, and, like Mr Walter Smith during his Cheddar Valley days, also went in for hanging baskets. The stations, like the gardens, were very well looked after. The wooden floors of the waiting rooms were scrubbed clean, there was no sign of litter and an almost clinical attention to the lavatories existed, whether these were at stations or on trains.

Although having little to do with the actual Portishead line itself, one of the touches that Gordon Smith well remembers about coming home to the Bristol area by train after a long voyage away at sea, was returning, perhaps via Hull or Glasgow, and listening to the local accent of the various station announcers. Gradually the accent would get a little closer to the one you wanted, and then it would happen, that wonderful warm West Country . . . 'the train now arrivin' at platform vive . . .' The Dock may have had its financial problems in the late 1930s but the railway still welcomed people back.

GWR — PILL

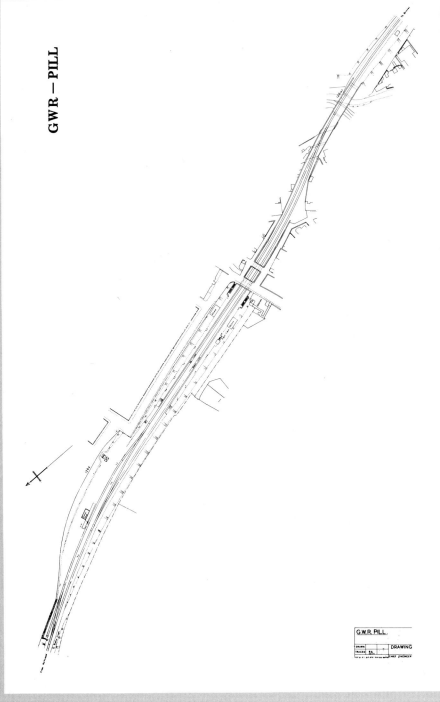

G.W.R. PILL.

| DRAWN | | DRAWING |
| TRACED | B.S. | |

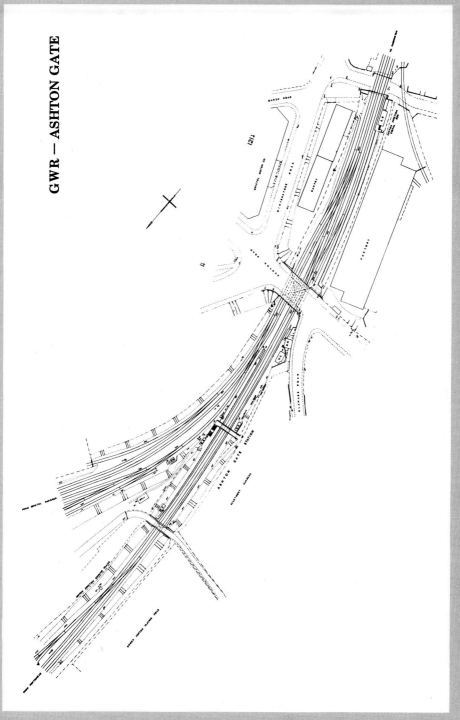

GWR — ASHTON GATE

An excellent aerial shot of Portishead taken just after World War II, in 1947. Items to note include, (from left to right), the timber wharf, in the far middle distance, the goods yard with the old GWR station in the middle distance, the 'A' power station, suitably camouflaged for wartime activities and, in the centre foreground, we can see the PBA granary, Bailey's Mill and the old Pier Station. One very interesting point to note is that there seems to be next to no railway wagons, coaches.

Chapter Six

Towards the end of World War I at Ashton, the factory at Ashton Containers was opened, and, in the past, this particular factory provided a good deal of traffic for the railway. Before World War II, rail traffic was essentially in the outward direction and consisted of wooden cases and heavy fibre board. The wooden cases were collapsible and, once returned, could be re-used and sent out again. During World War II there was a fair amount of this traffic, which continued after the war, when it was added to by fibre case traffic as well.

Some chemicals and adhesives were also brought into the factory. Wood was another rail-borne traffic and this was stored in a timber yard on the site now occupied by Ashton Containers' modern offices. This yard often contained large amounts of timber and paper in storage and was, in the days of steam haulage, a real fire risk. In 1938 the firm acquired a new 0-4-0 diesel-mechanical locomotive (22288), from the firm of John Fowler, for shunting wagons from the firm's private sidings alongside the Portishead branch into the factory premises themselves. It is believed, however, that pre-1938 the firm employed a steam locomotive to do its work, although, as yet, no details have come to light. In the later days of the firm's dealings with the railways, during the 1950s and early 1960s in particular, the diesel locomotive was kept in the paper store. Occasionally, when it broke down, the firm would hire a shunter from British Railways. The diesel was kept in spotless condition, there being two drivers on the firm's staff, one acting as shunter in addition to his normal driving duties.

Also in the Ashton area, railway interest would centre around the tobacco bond warehouses, near Ashton Containers' site, on the Winterstoke Road. These were built just before World War II and were rail served. This facility proved most useful during the war when the bonds were used for aero-engine work. The railway sidings behind the bonds were also well used by trains bringing food into the area for American soldiers. These men were stationed locally to guard the POWs being held in a camp situated close to the level crossing at Ashton Junction. It is interesting to note that, in post-war years, the bonds often proved a boon to the workers at Ashton Containers in that 'empty' vans, which came to the latter firm for loading, sometimes still had some cigarettes and tobacco in them.

Unfortunately, times have changed and, with the growth of road transport, Ashton Containers decided, in the early 1960s, to move its products by road. Rail traffic ceased from 13th May 1965 and,

An 0-4-0 diesel-mechanical locomotive, Works No. 22288, busies itself shunting Ashton Containers' traffic. The photograph was taken beside the Up line of the Portishead Branch, the exact position being clearly denoted by the milepost in the foreground.

Arthur Day

around two months later, in July 1965, the 0-4-0 diesel went to Pugsley, the Bristol scrap merchant, for breaking up. Today, only disconnected and lifted track remain of this once busy area for rail traffic.

Still in the Ashton district, other wartime additions to the rail network were occurring. On 28th March 1940, an agreement, between the GWR and the Bristol Tramways Company, was

Even during the lean years of wartime, the routine jobs have to be done. Mrs Durbin and Miss Lancastle clean the oil lamps at Clifton Bridge.

Terry Dart

signed to make use of a point already installed in the Up main line near Ashton Junction. The connection led into a siding that had a capacity of three wagons. The siding itself was paid for by the Tramways Company, but it was built by the GWR. One question that remains in my own mind is, what was this remarkably short siding used for?

In 1942, another agreement, between the GWR and F. W. Toogood, was signed to enable the latter company to use the siding in addition to the Tramways Company. A lot of activity evidently went on in this short three truck capacity siding! It was eventually removed in March 1965.

On the branch during the war, Terry Dart worked at Clifton Bridge Station from 8th June 1942 until 19th March 1944. He recalls that on the passenger side the service was still very intensive. Down trains usually left Bristol on the half-hour and they generally crossed at Clifton Bridge or Pill. At night the engine of the last passenger train Down (the 11.00 p.m. ex-Temple Meads) used to bring back a goods train from Portishead. The signal boxes at Portishead and Clifton Bridge remained open until this last Up train had been cleared. In the same manner, the engine of the first goods train of the day (the 5.00 a.m. Down) formed the first passenger train Up, the goods stock being put away at Portishead.

During the war many Bristol people were evacuated to the Pill and Portbury areas, and a goodly number of these evacuees came up on the first train of the day to Clifton Bridge Station. From here they would walk to their work at Ashton Containers, or W. D. & H. O. Wills, etc. War or no war, schoolchildren were, as ever, a prominent feature. During the air raids on Bristol, people would often sleep in the 59 yard length of Clifton Bridge No. 1 Tunnel. Built to fairly generous standards, the tunnel was home to those who would walk along the towpath from Clifton Bridge Station to gain shelter in it from the Bristol 'blitz'.

At the Ashton end of the station, coaches were stabled. At night two sets were stored here, one in the station's Down loop, the other in the Down spur. People sometimes slept in these coaches, again, in order to get away from the air raids. Sometimes the coaches were 'unofficially' used by courting couples! The two sets of coaches were picked up in the morning and both formed Avonmouth line trains. In 1943 three new Up sidings were constructed in this locality and these were brought into use, along with Ashton Junction ground frame, on 2nd April 1944.

Although wartime freight traffic to Portishead was heavy, it was not as great as that handled by the yards and sidings at Canon's Marsh and Wapping, since these took in more of the convoy work. However, Portishead still handled a good deal of inwards timber and also dealt with a fair amount of van traffic. Because of the general level of traffic on the branch, long stints were worked by the railwaymen in order to keep traffic moving, signalmen, for example, worked overtime to release staff to, in turn, make up gangs to rope and sheet wagons at Portishead on an 'as required' basis.

As for particular freight workings, the 5.00 a.m. Down goods was 'through' at Clifton Bridge. Later in the morning, the local 'pick up' goods would come down after the 9.30 a.m. ex-Bristol passenger train. This local would put off freight at all stations and would later form the mid-afternoon 3.07 goods from Portishead back to Bristol. The line was often used to capacity by the heavy wartime passenger and freight traffic, with stock often being stabled at such places as the mileage sidings at Portbury Shipyard signal box.

When Terry was at Clifton Bridge, he worked under James Henry Almond, the stationmaster at that time. Almond, a good singer and member of the Leigh Woods Choir, was reckoned to be a very good stationmaster. He would give Christmas presents to his staff, while, when Almond's wife used to bring around her husband's 'elevenses' she would include some for the other members of staff as well. Incidentally, other wartime staff at Clifton Bridge included two women, namely Mrs Durbin and Miss Lancastle, working full time as porters.

A description of the buildings at Clifton Bridge would tell of a long building, in which the one room, which ran the full length of the downstairs area, had been partitioned off into a waiting-room, a booking office and a stationmaster's office. In addition, there was also a room downstairs with a coal boiler providing hot water for the washing facilities. Coming in from the rather pleasant station forecourt, you would turn right into the booking office. The entrance to the waiting-room was directly from the platform. Upstairs, there was complete living accommodation of a generous size. This area was served by its own private stairway.

At Clifton Bridge, there was a short spur on the Down side that would hold two or three wagons. This spur, with its tight clearances, was greatly used during the war. Here women members of the Land Army would load timber cut from the nearby woods, while they would off-load commodities required in the local community. One incident of railway interest occurred when an old wagon was being shunted into this spur. The wagon, a particularly poor runner, was pushed up hard by the shunting engine. The engine hit the truck rather hard, which in turn hit the buffer stops rather violently. It then came to a halt. Unfortunately, although the chassis had come to a full stop, the body of the truck moved rather badly off the chassis!

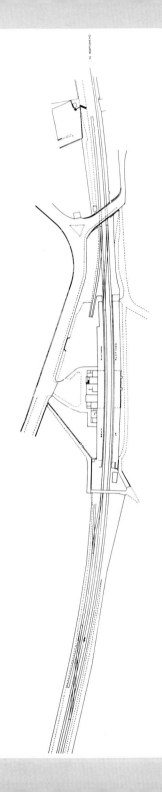

TO PORTISHEAD

G.W.R.   CLIFTON
BRIDGE.

DRAWN   DRAWING Nº
TRACED   D.41.
SCALE 1 FT TO THE MILE   CHIEF ENGINEERS OFFICE
                         PADDINGTON.

Alongside this Down spur there was a beautiful garden and, although there was a war on, it was such a fine place to be on a warm, sunny day, it was sometimes possible to forget there was a war being fought. Terry recalled other beautiful settings on the line, such as the erstwhile halt at Nightingale Valley with its sleeper built platform and its name echoing the tranquility to be found in the adjacent woods. The pace on the branch could be leisurely, but the job was still not an easy one. Two cases that sprang to Terry's mind were those of Ernie White and his mate, Arthur Parker, both of whom worked at Clifton Bridge during the war. Arthur, a shunter, lost his leg working for the railway, while Ernie, who lived at Pensford, near Bristol, cycled into work at Clifton Bridge for 5.00 a.m., cycling home again after 1.00 p.m. Incidentally, it is also worth remembering that in the early days, many of the signal boxes on the Canon's Marsh line were manned by disabled men. Is it because of this that the Harbour line was nicknamed the 'Holiday Line'?

At Clifton Bridge the following working arrangements applied for the signalmen:-

First Signalman	on at	5.00 a.m.	off at	1.00 p.m.
Signal Porter	on at	1.00 p.m.	off at	4.45 p.m.
Second Signalman	on at	4.45 p.m.	off at	12.45 p.m.

As signal porter, Terry would work from 6.35 a.m. until 4.45 p.m. His first duty was as front guard on a train to Avonmouth, the empty coaching stock of which had been stabled at Clifton Bridge overnight. He would then come back to Clifton Bridge on the 9.30 a.m. Bristol—Portishead passenger train, working on station duties until 1.00 p.m., where, until 4.45 p.m. he would work his 3¾ hours stint in the signal box. Coincidentally, four hours was the minimum time a man could work to qualify for the full signalman's rate.

The box at Clifton Bridge involved some interesting working, in that it had staff instruments linking the box directly to Portishead (for Sunday working, etc.) or it could be linked to the neighbouring box, at Oakwood, down the line. The intervening sections, between Clifton Bridge and Portishead, were Clifton Bridge—Oakwood, Oakwood—Pill, Pill—Portbury Shipyard and Portbury Shipyard—Portishead. The boxes at Portishead and Clifton Bridge were normally switched in at 5.00 a.m. while the intervening ones at Oakwood, Pill and Portbury Shipyard came on-line at 7.00 a.m. Naturally, before switching in could take place the section between Clifton Bridge and Portishead had to be clear and then, if this was the case, after telephone confirmation, each box was switched in separately, firstly the one at Pill and then those at Oakwood and Portbury Shipyard. The boxes were, of course, released both mechanically and electrically. At Clifton Bridge tokens were exchanged by hand at the box, but the token could also be taken from an intermediate token release instrument at the end of the Down platform.

In those days, there was an independent family firm using the station that had a large trade in herbal medicines and the suchlike. The family concerned lived at Leigh Woods and their traffic, loaded in station trucks, would go from Clifton Bridge mainly to the South Wales area. Clifton Bridge was also credited with the traffic from Ashton Containers. This firm handled a good deal of wood and cardboard type traffic as we have seen earlier in the chapter, and all the labelling for its traffic was actually done at Clifton Bridge, although all the accounting was handled by Bristol Temple Meads. A new post of male checker had been created for this traffic at Clifton Bridge. Sid Broome filled this post and he spent much of his day between Clifton Bridge, Ashton Gate Platform (then staffed by Mrs Harrison and Miss Dury) and the siding at Ashton Containers.

The section of line between Ashton Junction and Parson Street had a fair number of private sidings, as at Ashton Junction itself, where the timber firm of Toogoods had its sawmills and where its traffic was unloaded on the old colliery lines, the shunting being carried out by the Ashton Meadows pilot. Another timber firm, May & Hassell, had a Down ground frame connection between Parson Street Junction and West Loop North Junction. The ground frame controlled a single siding into a timber yard, the connection having been brought into use in January 1938. This much-used siding had wagons backed into it by the 9.30 Down goods from West Depot. On the Up line, just beyond Ashton Junction signal box, there was a catch point with a short siding (the Bristol Tramways Company siding), while right opposite Ashton Junction box, again on the Up side, in the Ashton Meadows' direction, was a spur across the Winterstoke Road leading to Lysaght's Works.

At Ashton Meadows, the shunters' cabin was staffed by three full time shunters, one on each turn, who were stationed here during the war. When convoys were in dock, trains were formed at Ashton Meadows through to destination. The traffic from the Canon's Marsh and Wapping areas was immense at that time, with pilots on duty 24 hours a day at both places. Ashton Meadows, although it did not have 24 hour pilot duty, was also kept tremendously busy.

One other wartime story was connected with the firm of Ashton Containers. In 1938, as we have read, it bought a new 0-4-0 diesel locomotive for internal shunting at the factory. However, in addition, a steam locomotive was borrowed from the GWR. This locomotive, one of the former WC&PLR 'Terrier' 0-6-0 tanks, was delivered, in steam, to the firm's premises with a label stating that it was 'to be signed for'. You had to go by the book on the Portishead branch! There were, in fact, two 'Terriers' taken into GWR stock. These were No. 2 *Portishead* and No. 4, which was never named. They were both allocated to St. Philip's Marsh. They were handed over after the WC&PLR closed in 1940. They were renumbered, No. 2 becoming No. 5 and retaining her name, while No. 4 became No. 6. This locomotive, No. 6 (GWR numbering) was used on shunting and harbour duties but was only used in this capacity for around 18 months. She was eventually condemned in January 1948. No. 2 *Portishead* was used, like No. 4, at Portishead Power Station and also on the construction of the US Army Depot at Wapley Common. She was eventually broken up in 1954.

George Woodland was senior porter at Pill Station during the 1939—45 period. In 1939, when he first went to Pill to work, he was living at Ashton. His first stationmaster at Pill, Walter Smith, was a strict disciplinarian. He made George move into digs in the village, and would not allow him to cycle to work, probably because the days, starting at 5.30 in the morning and finishing at 11.30 at night, were so long. Once Stationmaster Smith left, he was replaced by a chap called Mealings. George remembers him, perfectly dressed, always with a flower in his buttonhole. Mealings was also very strict, and, on a late shift, he would often stand in the garden of the stationmaster's house, stop-watch in hand, checking the time of trains crossing in the loop. Woe betide any laggards! It is important to remember that there was virtually an hourly service in those days and smart working was essential.

Of course, the stationmaster was then responsible for paying the staff under his control. Each station had to balance its own books. Mealings was a good accountant and it was from him that George learned his bookkeeping skills. Everything had to balance right down to the last halfpenny. Mention of money brings us on to the way it was transported to and from Pill. Wages would come down in a box chained to the guard's brake in the van of one of the passenger trains from Bristol Temple Meads. In the reverse direction the takings from the station would be put into a leather wallet, put inside the box and, again, this would be chained to the guard's brake on one of the Up trains.

As a porter the work was very hard. You had to be a 'jack of all trades' and, even more, you had to be 'master of them all'. For example, George would clean all the signal and Tilley lamps at Pill. He sometimes worked, 'unofficially', in the signal box and, when only 24, he was appointed relief stationmaster, for six weeks, at Clifton Bridge. In terms of staff, Pill then had one stationmaster, two porters and two signalwomen.

The station was busy in those distant war days. The first passenger train Down was the workmens' train which arrived at Pill around 5.20 a.m. This formed the early workmens' train back to Bristol from Portishead. During World War II the workmens' traffic was very heavy, with dock workers and with people working at the W. D. & H. O. Wills tobacco factory in Bristol. In addition, the power station and the nail factory at Portishead both provided passenger traffic, much of it coming in from the Avonmouth side of the river via the ferry at Pill. You could buy six day workmens' tickets, while there were, of course, regular season ticket holders to Bristol. Indeed, one of these season ticket holders later became George Woodland's wife!

During Bank holidays, train were packed, while local traffic was swollen by American GIs who were billeted in Pill and at the 'White City', Ashton and who used the local trains into Bristol. One of the signalwomen, Mrs Elsie Moore, recalls how, on one sunny Bank holiday, a two car 'B' set was provided to run the next service and, of course, the trains were packed out. On the next Bank holiday an eight car set was provided and it poured with rain all day! Perhaps things don't change that much after all! One of the benefits the line did offer passengers was provided by the station at Portishead. Here travellers could patronise the licensed refreshment rooms which were to be found on the station's main platform. These were run by landlord Sid Howe. It goes without saying that they were well patronised by both railwaymen and locals alike.

On the freight side, Pill was very busy during the last war. A good deal of shunting took place in the small yard and an interesting variety of goods was handled. Loads of straw and hay often passed through while a good variety of traffic was dealt with for the Ministries of Food & Supply. General goods, livestock, for example, pigs, sheep, ducks and chickens, were also fairly common. Boxes of supplies, gun barrels, for example, for the nearby Army installations at Easton-in-Gordano and Markham, all went through the yard at Pill. In addition, there was coal traffic through to Portishead although the bulk of this still came in by boat from South Wales. Ordinary parcel traffic was, of course, handled but sometimes a more interesting load was sent out; braces of pheasants and some rabbits — all added to the variety!

All lines have their unusual and humorous incidents, and thus it was at Pill. For example, on Sunday afternoons many people would come to Ham Green Halt to visit the nearby hospital. George remembers there being two particular Down trains which were always well loaded with intending visitors for this establishment. Ham Green Halt, like Portbury, was under Pill's jurisdiction and so George was sent there to collect tickets. The first train came down, he collected the tickets and there were no problems! However, it was such a beautiful, warm, Sunday afternoon that George went to sleep and missed the second train entirely! When he got back to Pill later that afternoon, he was not at all popular with the stationmaster who had been told, by the guard of the second train, that he had been inundated with tickets! George also remembers the occasion when the driver of a Down passenger train came into Pill Station without a token for the single line. George had to walk back to Oakwood box to get the token and, of course, by then, the train was badly delayed.

Animals sometimes strayed on to the line and George recalls an incident at the poorly used station at Portbury, where he was then porter on duty. He admits to leaving the station gate open and, because of this, a herd of cows escaped and walked up the line towards Pill. A late night light engine, on its way back to Bristol, careered into the animals and three or four of them were killed. In addition, more had to be put down. George was up 'on the carpet' about this, although he now admits that he was lucky enough to have escaped any real punishment. Incidentally, the regular porter at Portbury, a certain Mr Skelley, had a hook instead of a hand but, despite this handicap, was very adept at mending cars and radios and suchlike!

Another incident occurred at Portbury Shipyard signal box when an engine on a freight train came off the rails, ploughed through a fence, went across a ditch and ended up in a field. On another occasion, the Up local afternoon freight was stopped on the incline coming up to Pill from Portbury. By all accounts, when the train's load of trucks eased back on the couplings, the guard's tea urn, in the brake van, was completely upset. The guard, somewhat of a cider drinker, came up and complained to George about what had happened. Once George saw the guard's condition he refused to allow him to shunt the yard and promptly did the job himself.

In addition, there were a fair number of incidents due entirely to the conditions of war. For example, during the early years of the war when the German raids were at their height, Ham Green Tunnel was sometimes used as an air raid shelter, and in the middle of an air raid, freight trains sought shelter there. In order to prevent some of the attacks on the various docks in the locality, a profusion of barrage balloons protected the area around Pill, Portishead and Avonmouth. During an electrical storm one of these balloons exploded and its cable came down across the railway lines. A massive flash then travelled along the rails and George clearly remembers how terrifying a sight it was.

The line received no direct hits between Clifton Bridge and Portishead, although incendiary bombs were not infrequent visitors. Trains were often badly delayed and late connections ensued because of the Bristol blitz, and one of the most unreliable timekeepers was the 11.00 p.m. Down, ex-Temple Meads. This train, due Pill at 11.23 p.m., sometimes did not arrive until 1.00 a.m. and then it was often packed with soldiers who had no tickets because of the confusion in Bristol. To overcome this problem, George would put his cap out for the money and then go on to make out excess ticket slips for all those concerned.

Because of the war, women were widely used on the railways in such jobs as portering etc., but it was less usual to find women in the signal box. However, the Garland sisters worked the Pill signal box during the same period as George was working as senior porter. The two sisters, Mrs Elsie Moore and Mrs Barbara Voisey, were the only signalwomen working on the line during the war. Elsie worked on the branch from 1942 until October 1948 while Barbara, at first employed as a porter, 'graduated' to work, like Elsie, in the signal box at Pill. Both girls were given six weeks tuition, which then led to a severe test at Temple Meads where they were examined on such things as railway rules, bell-codes, etc. Both of them worked the signal box, the shifts in those days being: early, which was from 8.00 a.m. until 3.00 p.m. and late, which was from 2.00 p.m. until 10.00 p.m.

When she was a signalwoman, Barbara's duties included tending to the garden, and the Tilley lamps, in front of the signal box. However, at times the signal lamps would blow out and then porter Woodland used to relight them rather than get the women to do the job. As women, they often found the points hard to pull, especially on a frosty morning. They also found switching in the box rather difficult, the timing, of course, being absolutely crucial. One comment often made to the Garland sisters, by so many of the soldiers waiting for trains at Pill Station, was that the switch point leading from the yard gave the impression that it was wrongly set. Many times the women had to reassure them that it was correctly set and that things were all in order. Of course, in those pre 'Womens Lib' days, women did not get paid exactly the same money as that earned by men, and that was something of a sore point. However, they were classified as manual workers and this did entitle them to extra rations.

In terms of traffic, the sisters recall that coal traffic was as important as were general goods. In addition, because of the war, ammunition trains ran to Portishead. These trains ran at night and

Elsie Garland prepares to receive a Down train in the small, but neat, signal box at Pill. Her sister, Barbara, watches with interest.

Mrs Barbara Voisey

Barbara Garland exchanges tokens with the driver of a Down coal train at Pill Station. GWR '4500' class 2-6-2T, No. 4539, heads the train which was on its way to the power station at Portishead.

Mrs Elsie Moore

were non-stop through Pill. The girls had to make a difficult change-over of tokens, with token in one hand and lamp in the other. It was suggested that drivers would deliberately accelerate so that the handover would be made even more difficult!

In addition, there were other special trains carrying wire mesh, these were in addition to the usual relaying and permanent way trains. With a service of two passenger trains an hour, plus the freight traffic, the line was busy, particularly during the morning and evening peak periods. For example, the 6.53 a.m. train to Bristol was always well filled with passengers and was usually a long train. This, the first train Up was, seen from the outside, like all the trains running out of daylight hours, in complete darkness because the blinds were down due to the black-out regulations. Interestingly, in spite of all this traffic, or perhaps, because of it (?), punctuality was generally very good.

A fair number of stories related by the Garland sisters, centred around the stove in the signal box. The gangers wanted to cook their snails on a shovel in the fire in the signal box's stove, but the Garlands would not allow this! One advantage of the job was that if supplies for the stove were ever low, the girls could scrounge coal from the engine drivers. However, it didn't burn too well since it was steam coal! As a final point, Barbara remembers how she used to warm her feet on the stove. Chilblains have since followed!

During the bombing in 1942, the girls used to hide, when an attack was being experienced, under the signal box amongst the point and signal rodding. Elsie remembers the time when the line appeared clear and so she disappeared into the field behind the station in order to gather some mushrooms. Suddenly she heard the bell ringing in the box and had to rush back for one of the special mesh trains.

A couple more stories with a humorous touch, the first of which concerned the porter Ken Hurley. The girls remember him issuing tickets whilst wearing his pyjamas because he had overslept and, living close to the station, he had decided, at that time, that was the best thing to do! Lastly, while George Woodland and Elsie Moore were unloading a truck in the yard at Pill, they found the false arm of Mr Skelley, the porter at Portbury. He rang to ask if he could have it back, and, of course, they agreed, since they could 'see no 'arm in it' . . .!

Down towards Portishead, Don Harwood spent the middle years of World War II, from 1943 until 1945, working as a signalman at Portbury Shipyard signal box. Access to the box was usually achieved by taking one's push-bike along the line from Pill Station or, alternatively, putting the bike on the train to Portbury Station and cycling from there. When one looks at how easy access to the site is today, located as it is so close to the motorway and the access road to the Royal Portbury Dock, it is all too easy to forget that the box at Portbury, like the one at Oakwood, was once quite isolated.

The box at Portbury was fairly generous in its proportions, and it seems very clear that the railway authorities in World War I expected that the box would have to handle a goodly amount of traffic from the shipyard. When Don worked the box, it had nineteen levers operative in a fifty seven lever frame. There was token exchange apparatus installed for setting down and picking up on the Down line, while on the Up, only picking up facilities were provided. On the occasions when the signal box was out of circuit, the line was set for the Down main and the Stop signals for both Up and Down directions were put to clear. It was then possible to clear the distant signals which, when the box was in circuit, were locked in the caution position.

In normal conditions the box was usually lit by two Tilley lamps but, because of the wartime conditions, two brass lamps, with shades, were used instead. At Portbury the signlman prepared and changed the oil lamps of signals in the area around the box. The latter was not equipped with piped water and so, as was the practice at Oakwood, it was brought by train. The 8.12 a.m. railcar from Bristol to Portishead would pick up the empty cans on its way down the line. It would then work the 9.05 a.m. from Portishead and drop the full cans on its way back to Bristol. This was the same train that supplied Oakwood with its water rations.

Portbury was a fairly busy crossing place and it was not unknown to have three trains crossing at once; two passenger and one goods. Also, because of the provision of catch points at both ends of the loops, trains from opposite directions could enter the loops simultaneously. On one occasion, during the war, an LMS engine and brake van, going to Portishead to pick up a train, ran into the loop and became derailed at the catch point at the Down end. The signalman, who had got down from his box to pick up the token, watched amazed and helpless as the engine ran slowly past him and through the trap. Conversations with the driver, after the incident, revealed that the engine's brakes had failed!

Another incident occurred during 1943. The sidings at Portbury Shipyard were full of ammunition trucks, their contents ready for loading into ship at Portishead. One night, the authorities decided that they were ready to move them from Portbury Shipyard. Don was summoned from his bed by a telegram messenger boy. He cycled out to Portbury from his home in Knowle. The box was very isolated and it was a very dark night. As he drew near to the box, an armed guard leapt out of the darkness and challenged him with a hearty 'Who goes there'? Don, in his own words, frightened half to death by this individual, relates how well guarded wartime railways really were.

However, there were compensations for those involved in wartime work at Portbury Shipyard. Behind the box, where the access roundabout to Royal Portbury Dock is now to be found, a mass of blackberry bushes used to flourish and these often yielded a hand-

Portbury Shipyard loop was a busy place at times. It had four roads and timber trains were often held there. It was also there that an ammunition train came off the rails during World War II. During the latter years of World War I, a government shipyard was partially constructed nearby. The track for the connecting line from Portbury Shipyard loop on the GWR branch was laid on ashes and ran right down to a complex of tracks at the shipyard itself. On the GWR line there was a platform for troop trains and ordinary passenger trains, the latter for the use of those civilians who worked at the shipyard site. The platform and its shelter were managed by the stationmaster at Portbury Station. Inward goods traffic included stone and building materials, while coal was also handled. The connecting line started by Duck Lane Bridge, where there were steps up to the road, while the platform itself was roughly one and a half chains in the direction of the shipyard. The route of this line was, until fairly recently, easy to trace. However, of late, spoil removed from the site of the Royal Portbury Dock, during the latter's construction, has been dumped all across the area.

Photograph Don Harwood and text J. Clarke

some harvest. In the field opposite the box was a barrage balloon site, manned by women, and this must certainly have added to the interest. Mention of the dock access road leads one on to say that the box, closed in 1964 when the loop and sidings were taken out of use, was later knocked down to allow the Portbury Road Bridge to be built over the branch. Indeed, if the oft hoped for rail connection to the Royal Portbury Dock does go in, the actual junction point of that connection will be almost directly under this particular bridge. Incidentally, the bridge has been built large enough to take overhead electric wires, should these ever be required.

In terms of traffic flow, this was handled by GWR railcars and 55XX 2-6-2 tanks. One working that was the exception to this rule was the 5.58 p.m. Down passenger train from Bristol which was formed of an 'M' set (seven car non-corridor). This had started its journey from Avonmouth. On the freight side, coal traffic was heavy and, on arrival at Portishead, this would be shunted and sorted and later tripped, by the station pilot, into the power station sidings.

At Portbury the station received horse-boxes, cattle and open wagons, the latter being used to transport pit props away from the area. These props were usually loaded by female members of the Land Army. A prop of a different kind was a regular feature of the Up Distant signal at Portbury Station, since this was often used by Mrs Skelley to support her clothes line!

During Don's spell at Portbury, the line's generally heavy war-time traffic was made obvious at Pill, where the small yard handled a large amount of traffic. Freight for this yard was first taken to Portishead and then back to Pill so that it could be backed into the yard there. This level of activity contrasts severely with the now desolate and deserted site at Portbury Shipyard. Today, all that remains of this crossing place is the half ruined checkers' hut, some sleeper marks in the ballast, a white gate leading nowhere (in the past it led to the shipyard) and a stretch of continuous welded rail on the main line itself; quite a contrast to the bustling wartime days.

Wartime at Portishead was recalled by Mr Cyril Hayman, who was porter at the station at this time. Before moving here Mr Hayman worked at Wapping Wharf from January to April 1940, after a spell working at Temple Meads Goods Depot. In March 1940, after having failed his medical to join the Army, he applied for a transfer within the GWR and, from the following month, started work as a porter at Portishead under the then station-master, Mr Dinham. His move to 'Posset' meant the replacement of Mr Lesley Walters who had worked pre-1940 at Portishead Station.

Cyril Hayman's memory for names and faces of members of staff who worked at Portishead is excellent, and he clearly remembers Messrs Dinham, Paul and Richards, all of whom were station-masters during his long stay there. During and after the war the head shunter was 'Tot' Callard, so-called because he was from Totnes, ably assisted by Reg Dyke, the under shunter.

Among the women workers at Portishead were Mildred Roynon (booking office work), Molly May, Ingrid Berg (booking clerk), Mrs White (goods invoice office), Miss Atherton, Miss Phylis Ratcliffe (the stationmaster's stepdaughter, who worked as a booking clerk) and Mrs Chapman, all contributing to the railway's war work. Mr Frank Hassell (booking clerk) and Mr Dan Meacham (goods invoicing clerk at that time) were also working at the station in those war years. It was quite clear from this list alone that Portishead had, in those days, a large staff.

Signalmen at the old station included Bert Thorne, David Trudgian, a very conscientious railwayman, and John Elms who was a porter signalman. In addition, there was Charlie Coles, also a signalman at the old station, who died quite suddenly one Sunday in the signal box of the new station, opened in 1954.

During the war large numbers of American troops were billeted in the Pill and Portishead areas, although there were very few troop train movements on the line. Those that did occur, ran late at night when station staff were asked to stay on after their shift had finished, to help with these additional movements.

On the freight side, during the early years of the war, timber boats would unload on the far (Portbury) side of the dock, and they would then come across to the north side of the dock and load china clay. This had been brought in by special trains of sheeted wagons from Fowey, in Cornwall, and was bound for export to the United States. There was much picking up of the sheets used in connection with this traffic while the clay itself could be foul, and slippery stuff to handle when wet. Grain traffic was also handled in large quantities during the war.

In the build up of forces for the invasion of Europe, a load of anti-aircraft guns came into Portishead for shipping overseas. Un-fortunately, they proved too heavy for the dockside cranes to load and so it was decided to send them to another port for shipment. 'Tot' Callard, head shunter at the time, misjudged the length of the guns while they were being put away in the yard, and a nozzle of one of the guns ended up through the shunter's truck! No one was hurt, but the shunter's truck was derailed.

It was also during the early part of the war that a railway line was laid within the PBA's boundary fence at the Parish Wharf, known locally as the 'Viaduct', linking the lines on the north side of the dock with those serving the timber jetty on the Portbury side. The

115

line was laid on reclaimed ground, in an area that had formerly been part of Portishead Pill towards the head of the early dock. The area reclaimed used power station ash and the line's provision meant that the dock locomotives and wagons could use PBA tracks to move freight from one side of the dock to the other without using GWR tracks, as had been the case until that time.

Cyril's duties as a porter, at both the old and new stations, were very varied. On early shift the day would start at 5.45 a.m. in time to receive the first passenger train arrival from Bristol. Tickets would need collecting, parcels and newspapers had to be handled and rapidly dealt with, while, in order to get the train out for its return working to Bristol, the tail lamp would need changing from one end to the other. Once the early morning rush was out of the way, there were parcels delivery sheets to be made out, while parcels leaving Portishead had to be booked in. There were always windows, toilets and floors to be cleaned, posters and notices to be put up, while on Mondays and Tuesdays signal lamps had to be cleaned. Finally, the Up platform, ash covered as it was, needed weeding from time to time. Fortunately, the afternoon shift was a little more leisurely; all in all, a hard, but satisfying, life.

In the 1950s, one of the duties that Cyril performed, that used to bring in some overtime, was that of working, along with some of the other porters, at the pier, tending lights, reading gas and water meters, checking how much fresh water the railways sold to the pilot boats and so on. He followed a long line of railwaymen who had carried out this work, including Mr Arberry (the Pier Master), whose name crops up in another chapter of this book. After Mr Arberry retired, the job was taken over by Reg Dyke. On his retirement, Bert Brine took his place. (Note the somewhat apt surname!) When he, in turn, gave up the work owing to ill health, Cyril Hayman and Norman Jelley took charge of the work. In 1961, after 21 years of railway working, Cyril retired.

Portishead Old Station.

The grandiose approach to Clifton Bridge Station, in 1954.

Author's Collection

Chapter Seven

During the 1940—1942 period, work was still in hand on 'A' power station and the old station goods yard handled the steel structure for this. Additional materials, such as firebricks, also arrived by rail. A group of very large items, brought in for the power station, included some complete columns approximately 73 ft. in length and weighing 26 tons. These came in during 1941/2 and two trailers were used to get them from the station goods yard up to the site of the power station. At the same time, there was also a Dennis lorry which could carry a two ton load and was employed to carry loads of nails, from Messrs Mustad's nail factory, to the old goods yard to be loaded on to rail trucks for the journey out. This lorry was often used with a trailer which could carry up to six tons.

After the war, loads of Canadian wheat, and also cotton, was handled by the PBA at Avonmouth. This traffic was then brought, by rail, over to Portishead and was stored at the granary, which was demolished in 1951 to make way for yet another power station. In the early 1950s, goods traffic in the old goods yard, the sidings that had previously led to the connection with the WC&PLR, was handled by the fixed 6 ton crane found there. Goods taken onwards by road were dealt with by a Swiss-built road vehicle in use at that time. This had four wheel drive and four wheel steering and these were both useful qualities to have when considering the state of the building site for the new 1949 power station, of which more later, since the vehicle was frequently used to take equipment across from the yard to the new plant. In the main, coal was brought to the power station from the Somerset coalfield by rail. Some, however, came in from mines at Coalpit Heath. It was also brought in by road, two stroke Commer lorries bringing it in, again from the Somerset coalfield.

Immediately following the war, in 1946, a small housing estate was built on the river side of the Portway Road and the CER at Shirehampton on the north bank of the Avon. Both Nibley and Dursley roads were extended towards Sea Mills and, with the later phase II extension, the houses ran from the railway bridge at Hung Road to the Woodwell Road railway bridge. Most of the families housed on this estate were young families with one or more children.

Very few of these families had the now familiar motor car and the only way for them to get about with the children was by public transport. Thus, at weekends, families wishing to have a day out were generally faced with choosing between one of three alternatives; Bristol Zoo at Clifton Down, or the seaside at Severn Beach or Portishead. All three of these were served by the railway, the first two being reached by means of the GWR/LMS Joint from Shirehampton Station, the third by means of the GWR from Pill Station on the other side of the river. This latter alternative was, according to Stan Wiltshire, one of the young peple living in the area at that time, *the* day out. It could, of course, have been reached by taking the 'Great Way Round' via Shirehampton Station and Bristol Temple Meads, but the residents of Shire had an extra bonus that was a must for the children -- the Pill Ferry. Every Sunday in the summer, weather permitting, families could be seen walking down the hill, on the Shire side, to the Lamplighter's Hotel and then on down to queue at the riverside hut for the first highlight of the day, the ferry across the Avon. Once across, the families walked up the hill towards Pill Station, anxiously keeping an eye on the viaduct and hoping that the train wouldn't come too soon. Then, it was on by train to Portishead itself and the joys of the seaside.

Later in the day, it was the same journey in reverse, but, by that time, the excitement had turned to tiredness. These were days well remembered with the B&PP&R Company's line and the

'Port & Pier' virtually in sight of one another from Avonmouth to Clifton Down Tunnel and, quite often, with similar trains running on either side of the Avon, a Class 55XX with two, sometimes four coaches.

Post-war at Portishead, the old station was a typical GWR station with gas lights and coal fires and, in the 1950s, Mr George Richards was its stationmaster. This old station was, of course, a real social centre in that it had a very fine station bar run by Mr & Mrs Howe. At lunchtimes, and in the evenings, it would be well patronised by a wide cross-section of the local population including power station workers, bank managers, local travellers, etc. It was also a well-known place for the Railway Inspecting Officers who often spent their lunchtimes in the bar! Interestingly, no bar was allowed in the new (1954) station.

Passenger traffic was still fairly heavy, this being well catered for by an hourly service from Temple Meads. This ran from roughly 6.30 in the morning to around 10.30 at night. Bank holidays were still busy days, when 3,000—4,000 day trippers, many of them from Bristol, would demand the presence of two porters collecting tickets at the station's exit gates.

Local passenger services were usually well loaded, especially in the mornings and evenings with the rush hour traffic into and out of Bristol. Tom Pugsley, a former booking clerk at both the old and new stations at Portishead, told me that it was nothing unusual to take £80 to £100 in the first two hours of the day, many workmen's tickets being sold.

On the freight side, the station handled a wide variety of goods and, for a period when both the new 'B' power station and factory for Albright & Wilson were being constructed in the early 1950s, there was, in addition, a heavy volume of freight traffic; coal for 'A' power station, general goods and also parcels and pigeon traffic. The latter traffic went by ordinary train and, like many of the northern cities, there were a goodly number of pigeon fanciers in the area in those days. Inward rail traffic was also provided by the wire that was used in the manufacture of foundry and horse nails in the adjacent nail factory. This wire came in from Roath Docks, Cardiff, while the finished product, the nails, were sent to car plants at Longbridge and Dagenham. They also went for export, the latter in 28lb boxes. Incidentally, nails for export were bundled in 'fours' which weighed approximately 1 cwt.

Examining the freight traffic in greater detail, there was an abundance of coal traffic for both power station and domestic use. The (horse and foundry) nails, previously mentioned, would be sent out in wooden boxes conveyed by van from the factory to the station. Cables were dealt with in the goods yard, as were various heavy items of machine tools required by the construction of the

The goods yard at Portishead Old Station in September 1963. A rather nice 'around the corner' view showing the usual goods yard bric-a-brac,

Mr Bennett

Again a rather different view of Portishead from that normally seen in railway photographs. The main line to Bristol can be seen swinging away to the right and the old station is directly ahead with the docks on the right. The connection to the goods yard runs in from the left. The picture was taken in 1953 during the quiet period before this area changed completely.

Mr Bennett

new power station. Parcels traffic was fairly heavy and deliveries were made to the surrounding districts twice weekly. Wednesday was a good day in that the station received a weekly consignment of Worthington Beer for the town on that particular weekday.

One anecdotal story, recalled by Tom Pugsley, concerned an especially well worn set of crossings in the sidings leading into the dock property itself. On one occasion, a 'Dean Goods' engine ran over the crossing and was completely derailed; all the wheels came off the track and so the re-railing equipment was called for. This arrived, the engine was re-railed and the vans returned to Bristol. Hardly had they reached Pill when they received the news that the engine had come off the track at the same set of points and would they please return and do the job again!

One interesting aspect of the, by now, long disused Pier Station was that the GWR and British Railways owned the water rights at the pier itself and their Dock Master had the job, each day of sweeping and cleaning the steps that ran down to the water level at the pier, after high tide had occurred here. He would also sell fresh water to the pilot boats which called there. These practices were still in use during the final days of the old station and did, in fact, continue into the early life of the new. But change was on the way and a marked change it was to be at that.

By March 1953, a new quay, South Wharf No. 2, had been built to replace the old timber wharf. At the same time, work was well under way with South Wharf No. 3. In the dock itself regular shipping was provided by Messrs Osborn & Wallis' fleet of colliers bringing coal from Barry, Cardiff and Penarth to the 'A' power station.

Alongside the 'A' station, preliminary work was being undertaken for the construction of the new giant 'B' station. This had been authorized in 1949, was first commissioned in 1955 and was completed ten years after work had started, in 1959. The new power station was to be equal in size to the 'A' station. Much of the current it was to generate was to be absorbed directly into the then embryonic factory of Albright & Wilson Limited.

The actual site for the power station lies between Portishead 'A' and the dock itself, and the area of the site was actually 26½ acres. Before access to the site could be obtained, the original B & PP & R Company's original 1867 station had to be demolished, and a new station, with its associated sidings, had to be built about half a mile to the south. Interestingly, the station's new site was almost identical with that proposed in the plans for the 1862/3 branch terminus. Transit sheds and the PBA granary also had to be demolished to make way for the 'B' power station, while three 132,000 volt overhead transmission line circuits, and several 33,000 volt underground cables had to be diverted.

The new terminus station was formed of a two sided platform, 754 ft. in length, with run round loops off each of the two platform roads. On the Up side the large goods yard had ten sidings. For the staff who moved from the old to the new stations on 4th January 1954, the station's official opening date, the changes in working conditions were dramatic. The new station was luxurious compared with the conditions that had existed in the old. As soon as you entered the booking hall from the High Street there were two ticket windows facing the traveller. These windows were supposedly draught proof for the ticket clerks! The latter had their own kitchen and toilet. The floor of the office was tiled, while there were other offices for the porters and for the stationmaster, of course. Conditions for the passengers were much improved and there was a General waiting-room, a Ladies' rest room and Ladies' and Gentlemen's toilets. The waiting-rooms had marble effect Parkray stoves.

The new station's fluorescent lighting was dazzling: so much so that, when the first electricity bill arrived, it was decided by the railway authorities to take every alternate tube out of use. Obviously all that lighting was one of the ways in which the Electricity Board could get back some of the £250,000 it had paid to have the station built in the first place. After all, it was they who wanted the old station's site for their new power station!

On the Clevedon side of the station, two long coaching sidings had been laid in. It had been planned to outstable passenger coaches in these but, because of changed circumstances, they were rarely used for their original purpose. However, they were used to store stock overnight, and one set of coaches was stabled here for the Up 8.18 a.m. passenger in the 1950s. The engine off the first Down freight of the day, having shunted the yard at Portishead, would then work the 8.18 back to Bristol. Since the engine was often low on steam by the time the shunting was completed, (this often being the case on cold winter mornings), it would have some difficulty in heating the empty coaching stock that had been left at Portishead overnight.

The practice of using the engine off the first Down freight continued into diesel days, when the highly unreliable D63XX class engines were seen at Portishead. They would come down in tandem on an early coal, and then one engine would run back with the 8.18 or its equivalent in the timetable, since the times varied slightly from year to year. Incidentally, these engines were always breaking down: no wonder they soon disappeared from the railway scene!

car, along with Nos. 23, 24, 35 and 36 were all stationed at St. Philip's Marsh Depot.

H. Ballantyne

Standard 2-6-2T, No. 82039 arrives at Clifton Bridge Station with a Bristol to Portishead passenger train. The carriage sidings used for stabling stock can be seen in the background beyond the footbridge. The photograph was taken on 3rd March 1962, two years before the branch lost its passenger service.

In the massive goods yard, which had been laid by private contractors from South Wales, there was a small goods shed, a shunters' cabin, a weighbridge and the usual hand crane. Pride of place, however, went to the new, and highly acclaimed signal box. Sited a fair way from the station itself, this was an extremely original design of box and it is believed to have been the first on the Western Region to have a lever frame that looked into the box rather than out over the tracks. Very comfortable for the staff who worked it, the box was heated by gas.

With the opening of the new station the passenger traffic increased quite considerably. This was not at all surprising in that it was much more comfortable and much more central to the town than the old one, with its long walk down Station Road, had been. The station's two booking clerks, one on early and one on late shift, handled the brisk passenger traffic. The day at the booking office would start around 6.00 a.m. with the workmen's traffic. The full fare and season ticket holders would keep the line busy around 8.00 a.m. and 9.00 a.m., while the cheap day returners and shoppers would come into their own after that. All these groups made greater use of the line once the new station had opened.

Portishead old into new — 4th January 1954. The last trains to use the old station were the 8.10 a.m. from Bristol and the return service at 9.05 a.m. Diesel railcar No. W28W was used for these journeys and it left the old station to the accompaniment of exploding detonators. There were around fifty passengers on board, the majority of whom were railway enthusiasts. The station staff then transferred equipment from the old to the new station. The first ticket issued from the new booking office, a single to Portbury, numbered 2303, was purchased by Mr D. G. Farr. The first train to arrive at the new station was the 12.11 p.m. from Temple Meads. Moving from Portishead Old Station to Portishead New on the morning of 4th January 1954, the staff in the picture, from left to right, are as follows:
G. Richards, stationmaster; Peter Stonestreet, lorry driver; Alex Shoreland; Albert Spencer, porter; Cyril Hayman, (carrying box); Tom Pugsley, (behind Cyril Hayman); Fred Willmott and Norman Jelley.

Tom Pugsley

The station would really come alive on Bank holidays as had its predecessor in the 1920s, 1930s and early 1950s. Filled with day trippers, trains were still packed to capacity on the way down from Bristol. They were often more crowded on the way back because, on may occasions, passengers who had come to the resort by bus found them full for the return journey. The 'overflow' paid a special 1/- fare for the single journey back to Bristol. Over Bank holidays, Tom Pugsley reckoned that, on average, roughly 500 people went back on the train having come down by bus.

Not long after the station had opened, subsidence started to let the place down. Doors would not shut properly where the building had moved out of true, while the stove in the booking office started to take on a rather strange angle that was not too close to vertical! The booking clerks eventually had to move out into a 'Portakabin' for around six or seven months while the problem was corrected. The subsidence was brought about by the fact that the station had been built on ashes which were, in turn, laid upon reclaimed ground, the land having once been part of the old Pill at Portishead. By 1955 the problem had, officially, been 'solved' although, in reality, the subsidence problems continued until the end of the station's working life in 1964.

As we have read, there was also a marked increase in traffic on the freight side, particularly for the 'B' power station and the then developing factory of Albright & Wilson. Both sites required a large amount of steelwork in their construction. This traffic was handled by mobile cranes working in the new goods yard, there often being two cranes in use to handle the large volume of traffic then on offer. The loads would be road-hauled to the power station and to deal with this, and other traffic, there was a parcels van, three articulated lorry units and five or six trailers.

Pipe and platework for yet another development in the 1950s also went in by rail. This project involved the development of a Ministry of Fuel & Power Depot for fuel storage on the Down side of the main line into the new station. This, and other similar depots, provide oil storage facilities in time of war. A similar depot exists at Flax Bourton on the former GWR main line between Bristol and Weston-super-Mare. During the 1952—4 period, there had been several proposals to construct a British Electric Authority coal stacking ground on the Up side of the main line into Portishead with exchange sidings on the Down side leading into new sidings serving the Ministry of Fuel Depot. Unlike the former, the latter was built and was brought into use on 22nd April 1956, a much simplified affair with six sidings, unlike some of the other plans prepared by BR. The depot's connection to the main line was taken out of use on 21st July 1958, and the private siding agreement was terminated on the last day of December 1967.

126

The new station was built in pre-stressed concrete and local limestone and was deliberately designed to blend well into its surroundings. In the seven months that it took to build, the station was not without its problems. It was impossible to get a mason to tackle the undressed rubble and so, finally, a wall mason undertook to train bricklayers. By the time the project was finished, eight previously untrained men had qualified as masons. An early example of 'job creation'! This photograph shows Portishead New Station under construction and pictures the station buildings and main forecourt.

OPC Collection

Portishead New Station showing the platform buildings. From left to right the various facilities were as follows: Men and Womens' toilets, ladies' waiting-room and general waiting-room. A very interesting article in *The Architect* for March 1954 says that ' . . . The seats in the waiting-rooms are of resin-bonded moulded plywood, mounted on pressed metal cantilever brackets and are designed for maximum comfort, consistent with rough usage usually encountered on the railways.' The authorities were obviously expecting the vandals to arrive!

OPC Collection

The new signal box at Portishead Station, 1954.

As can be seen from the photographs, the signal box at the new station was original and somewhat unconventional in design. Built in pale yellow brick with a slanting aluminium roof, it had windows on three sides. These were canted at an angle of 9½ degrees to cut down reflection. Inside the box, the lighting consisted of low intensity spotlights mounted on the ceiling and directed at the instrument shelf. The lever frame had 47 working levers, 24 spare levers and 12 spaces. Signals were (unusually for the Western Region) of the upper quadrant type, although the platform starters were colour light. The whole building was constructed on a raft because of the very low load bearing capacity of the soil.

Returning to the early 1950s, the chemical firm of Albright & Wilson chose a site at Portishead for the construction of its new factory. A closer examination of this provides great interest for the railway enthusiast. The reasons for the firm's choice of a site at Portishead were simple. It had good harbour access, while energy supply was plentiful with the construction of the 'B' power station on the north side of the dock. Indeed, the factory had four feeders direct from the CEGB to provide it with the high power that the processes carried out at Portishead required.

Phosphate for the plant came in by ship, the first to arrive being the *SS Areti* which berthed in the early evening of 8th October 1953. The following year the first load of phosphorus to be carried by rail left the factory in February 1954 when four of the company's rail tankers were put on to the Portishead line. At 2.45 p.m. on Monday, 22nd February, the firm despatched tank cars Nos. 4, 9, 11 and 16 loaded with crude yellow phosphorus. These wagons caught the 3.20p.m. goods to Bristol. At the end of December 1956 the first load of phosphates were taken by rail to the firm's Oldbury Works in Birmingham.

Within the works, the rail system included a weighbridge and wagon tipper assembly. During the company's production days it received, direct from the South Wales coalfields, approximately 1,000 tons of anthracite per week. This all came in by rail. At the same time, approximately 1,200 tons of silica pebbles also came in by train from Budleigh Salterton in Devon. The other raw material required by the firm, phosphate rock, came in, as we have already seen, by sea, and was discharged into silo facilities. There were, however, occasions when this material was also despatched by rail to the firm's factory in Birmingham.

The company had its own fleet of 24 liquid phosphorus tankers and these shuttled between the Portishead Works, the factory in Birmingham and two factories on Merseyside. In those days, the premises at Portishead were turning over between 36 and 40 tankers a week. All the rail traffic was delivered by British Railways to the company's exchange siding by the firm's own shunting locomotives. These provide a whole story in themselves.

To handle the rail traffic within the works at Portishead, in 1956, Albright & Wilson hired an 0-4-0 diesel-mechanical shunter, (5000), from the Bristol firm of Peckett. This was one of the very few diesel locomotives produced by the firm. It was returned to them the following year. This was followed by another diesel-mechanical, (5002), from Peckett. Bought new, this locomotive worked at Portishead until it was scrapped in Birmingham around 1971. However, the firm had trouble with these diesel locomotives and hired an 0-4-0 saddle tank from Peckett to help them out.

This locomotive, (1611), was built in 1923 and was hired from Peckett in 1959. In November 1961 Albright & Wilson bought the locomotive. It was withdrawn from service in 1961 and for a time was displayed on a plinth outside the works. It eventually went, on permanent loan, to the Cornish Steam Locomotive Society, at Bugle in Cornwall, on 29th July 1978.

In 1969 the firm acquired No. D2001 *Norman* second-hand from the PBA. This was an 0-4-0 diesel-mechanical locomotive, (D774), built by Hudswell Clarke of Leeds in 1950. However, the firm had trouble with this locomotive in that the Paxman engine gave problems due to cracking cylinder heads. In 1971 Albrights bought, for £3,500, an 0-4-0 diesel-electric, (381753), built by Ruston & Hornsby Limited. This came in May of that year from Thomas Ward of Sheffield and seems to have earned itself a good reputation at the plant. With the cessation of rail traffic in 1978, the locomotive went to the firm's Birmingham Works where, at the time of writing this section (June 1981) the locomotive was still running.

The above mentioned discontinuance of rail services to the Portishead plant, came about in the following way. In the 1970s, the wagons used for the firm's traffic were nearing life expiry and so the firm had to consider two options regarding future transport needs. The first option was to go over to road transport and have traffic completely carried by road tankers. Alternatively, they could purchase a new fleet of rail tankers. Unfortunately for British Rail, they decided on the former course of action, since any replacement rail wagons would be large bogied vehicles and the curves on the factory site were too tight for these. In addition, the loading platform would not have been strong enough, and so the traffic was lost to road; yet another nail in the coffin of rail's trade with Portishead. Incidentally, since we are looking at Albright's facilities at Portishead, it is well to mention that in order to service their locomotives, the firm had built a locomotive shed. This consisted of a straightforward building of suitable size to hold one locomotive and one of the firm's fleet of rail tankers. A floor pit was provided and fuel, water and pressure testing facilities were also available.

Albright & Wilson's traffic provided a good deal of work for the staff of the new station at Portishead. Phosphorus ore was dealt with at the works, and since the chemical had to be kept dry, all the loads had to be sheeted and, in some cases, double sheeted. Sheeting frequently took place 12 hours a day, 7 days a week and this gives some idea of the amount of traffic handled through the

Portishead area. In addition, the liquid phosphorus, despatched by rail to Oldbury in tankers, needed considerable care in handling. Sleepers caught fire due to leaking valves on the phosphorus tanks, while, on one occasion, a lorry, that had recently returned from Albrights, was driven into the station goods yard, its tyres ablaze from phosphorus picked up on the firm's premises.

Incidentally, as a final note, just before Albrights came into full production they looked around for reliable staff to work their new plant. For some of these they looked no further than British Railways. The railway staff were offered better salaries and, consequently, some of them did indeed transfer. One exception to this was the stationmaster, Mr Richards, who was too much of a railwayman to let money interfere with a lifetime of railway working!

Pictured on South Wharf, is 200 b.h.p. prototype Peckett diesel locomotive, No. 1956. The proud driver is Mr D. Webber. At this time, the locomotive was on hire to Albright & Wilson Limited, and in the following year it was returned to Peckett. Note the concrete sleepered track contrasting with the rather less modern wagons. The power station site can be seen in the background.

Albright & Wilson Limited

A view of South Wharfs Nos. 2 and 3 serving the new factory of Albright & Wilson Limited. A ship is being unloaded using the new suction equipment. The whole scene looks as if it has been cleaned by one of those 'whiter than white' cleaners.

Albright & Wilson Limited

In the mid-1950s, the railway and the dock were well and truly working together. In 1955, for example, eighteen ships had arrived with a total of 16,000 tons of timber. All of these timber imports were handled by the PBA from the ship's rail. The ships would come in alongside the South Wharf No. 1 and from here the timber was lifted to the deck of the ship by the ship's own gear. From here it was moved by ancient, but reliable, steam cranes, put in when the wharf was originally built back in the 1905 period. These cranes had their own rail tracks which ran at right angles to the dockside lines. The slings of timber were then either loaded directly on to road or rail vehicles, or were taken, by the cranes, to the rear of the stacking ground for storage. The rail goods workings for this traffic were generally handled by 0-6-0 pannier tanks once the trains were out on the BR line. Timber which was to be stored under cover at the rear of the piling ground was put into BD wagons, the port's internal user wagons, of which, at that time, there were around 70, and roughly half were small bogie bolster type vehicles.

In the dock itself the generating station was served by colliers and these workings involved seven ships in and out on every tide. Handling of this traffic was entirely by mechanical means. Staff working at PBA (Portishead) worked as follows: at the start of every afternoon, the following day's requirements for railway wagons, locomotives, workers, etc., were worked out. A small staff handled a large amount of tonnage and trade was good.

One final point very worthy of note was that, at this time, the PBA operated a 100 b.h.p. diesel-mechanical locomotive at Portishead. This particular engine, *Gordano*, (D894), was built in 1954 by Hudswell Clarke and was purchased new from the manufacturers. In addition,there was also a stand by steam locomotive. Both locomotives were kept in excellent external condition. They were mainly used on the timber trade, and spent the majority of their time hauling BDs to the timber storage sheds. They were also used to marshall trains of timber when the latter were ready to go out on to the main line. Occasionally Albrights also made use of PBA locomotives if they were having trouble with their own.

More developments were taking place inland when, in 1958, two new sidings were installed at Clifton Bridge Station, on the Up side. These sidings, which connected into wartime sidings that had been added here, were controlled by Ashton Junction West ground frame and were brought into use on 3rd October 1958. As this connection was going in, slightly further up the line another Ashton connection was being removed. The old colliery connection at Strachan & Henshaw's Ashton Works was severed in 1958. The firm was required to maintain the rail/road crossing outside the works at Ashton Vale Road and since, by 1958, minimal use was being made of the rail connection, the firm decided not to continue with it. For many years an old flat wagon was used to move plate from one engineering shop to the other, but even that practice has now ceased. All that remains is a set of rails in the ground that testify to relics of a bygone age, a reminder of a long established connection with the Bristol & Portishead railway.

Also in 1958, on 9th September to be exact, Portishead Dock was closed to shipping in order to allow essential and urgent repairs to be carried out to the entrance lock. Because of this closure, the CEGB had to arrange for an increase of rail deliveries of coal, while Albright & Wilson had its imports of phosphate rock delivered and discharged at Avonmouth and, from here, it was fowarded to Portishead by rail. Timber for Portishead was discharged at the City Docks. The work, carried out by the firm of J. Laing, contractors to the Portishead 'B' power station, was

It is interesting to note that the Portishead Branch, like many, but not all, GWR branches, was double track to the first station along it, Clifton Bridge, so that Staff/Key changing was carried out away from the main line. Still in GWR livery, one of the pre-war AEC diesel twin units approaches Clifton Bridge Station on 18th July 1953. These units were well-known on both the Portishead and Cheddar Valley lines in the 1950s.

C. R. L. Coles

completed by spring of the following year. The dock re-opened to shipping on 1st March 1959 when arrangements returned to normal.

Once the building of the second power station and the Albright & Wilson factory were completed, rail traffic levels dropped, particularly since a second stage of development for the latter firm never developed. Through the late 1950s and into the early 1960s, however, the yard at Portishead dealt with traffic for Albrights, coal traffic for the power stations, (this was still heavy), some scrap traffic and some general goods. Indeed, one estimate suggests that 1,000 wagons a week were using the branch in those early years of the 1960s. The yard at Portishead was still busy, and a pilot engine was put down there all through the week. On Saturdays and Sundays the pilot dealt with CEGB coal traffic only, and for this, the CEGB reimbursed BR for the cost of providing both pilot engine and crew. In addition, fish traffic for local traders, and the occasional human corpse, were also dealt with. There was obviously no end to the variety of work provided for the BR staff down at 'Posset'!

At the same time as all this was taking place, BR still handled some stone traffic from Black Rock Quarry, traffic which had formerly been handled by the GWR through its link with the WC&PLR. By the mid-1950s the traffic was road-hauled to Portishead and then loaded on to rail from there. The staff at Portishead encouraged the railway authorities to take extra traffic then on offer, but BR was slow off the mark in accepting it, and today all the stone from this particular quarry is handled by road. The possibilities of this traffic are endless, especially when one considers the developments that have taken place at quarries in the Frome area, such as those at Cranmore and Whatley, by Foster Yeoman and ARC respectively. However, the line's link with the stone re-occurs in the next chapter, so more of this later.

In the first few years of the 1960s, the passenger traffic gradually changed over from steam-haulage to being, mainly, handled by the then diesel multiple units. At the same time, and with the onset of the Beeching era and the ensuing economies to local branch lines, the passenger service was thinned out. First, the line lost its mid-morning and mid-afternoon shoppers' services, in much the same way as its Severn Beach to Temple Meads counterpart did in the mid to late 1970s. Fares went up, the bus service to town was improved, and the lack of railway services after 9.00 a.m. hastened, even more, the line's demise.

Ironically, however hard the railway authorities tried to kill the line off, the Bank holiday traffic levels remained obstinately high.

For example, in 1963, only one year away from the line losing its passenger services, Whit Monday still produced very creditable traffic loadings. For example, the 11.40 a.m. special train from Bristol produced 400 passengers, the 1.15 p.m. from Portishead to Bristol had 200 passengers while the 2.30 p.m. Bristol to Portishead added another 180 passengers to the holiday influx.

On the same Whit Monday, the 5.15 p.m. from Portishead to Bristol Temple Meads took 350 passengers back to Bristol. This train then formed the 5.55 p.m. to Bournemouth West, via Bath (Green Park) over the now, sadly, defunct Somerset & Dorset line. Incidentally, BR did provide through services to both Bath stations (Green Park (LMR) and Spa (WR)) and, usually, by this time in the line's story, at least, those through to Green Park were provided by BR Standard 82XXX 2-6-2 tanks and coaches. However, the rot continued and the Portishead branch lost its special fares and its other through workings, such as the locally known 'Coast to Coast' workings from Portishead to Severn Beach. The passenger service to Temple Meads would, itself, be the next to go.

Ex-GWR pannier tank No. 7729 draws away from Portbury Shipyard on 17th February 1962.

H. Ballantyne

Miles	Week Days only	am	am	pm	pm	pm	pm	pm	pm P	pm U
—	Bristol (Temple Meads) dep	6 47	1017	1 30	2 53	5 20	6 15	7 45	9 45	1035
2	Brislington	6 55	1025	1 38	3 0	5 27	6 22	7 51		
4½	Whitchurch Halt	7 3	1032	1 45	3 7	5 34	6 29	7 58	10 2	1049
6½	Pensford	7 10	1039	1 53	3 16	5 41	6 36	8 5	1010	1056
10	Clutton	7 22	1048	2 3	3 25	5 50	6 45	8 14	1019	11 5
11½	Hallatrow	7 29	1052	2 7	3 29	5 54	6 52	8 18	1023	11 9
12½	Farrington Gurney Halt	7 34	1056	2 11	3 33	5 58	6 56	8 22	1027	1113
14¼	Midsomer Norton & Welton	7 39	11 0	2 17	3 37	6 3	7 0	8 26	1031	1117
16	Radstock West K	7 46	11 5	2 21	3 41	6 10	7 4	8 30	1035	1121
19	Mells Road	7 55	1113	2 29	3 49	6 20	7 12	8 36	1043	1129
24½	Frome arr	8 7	1124	2 40	4 0	6 31	7 22	8 45	1053	1139

K Adjoins Radstock North Station
P Except Wednesdays and Saturdays

U Wednesdays and Saturdays only

For OTHER TRAINS between Bristol (Temple Meads) and Frome, see Table 62

Table 75 BRISTOL and PORTISHEAD

Miles	Week Days	am (2) Through Train from Stapleton Road	am	am	am	am	am	am	am	am	am (2)	am
—	Bristol (Tem. Meads) dep	5 27	6 55	6 58	7 25	7 48	8 5	8 20	8 42	9 0	9 30	1030
1	Bedminster	5 30	6 58	7 1	7 28	7 51	8 8	8 23	8 45	9 5	9 33	1033
1½	Parson Street	5 34	7 0	7 4	7 30	7 54	8 11	8 25		9 8	9 36	1036
3	Ashton Gate			7 7			8 14				9 39	1039
3½	Clifton Bridge	5 39		7 10			8 16				9 41	1041
7	Ham Green Halt											
7½	Pill	5 48		7 19			8 29				9 50	1050
9½	Portbury						8 35					1056
11½	Portishead arr	5 58		7 27			8 40				10 0	11 1

Week Days—continued	am	am (2)	am	am	S pm	pm (2)	E pm	S pm	S pm	E pm	S pm
Bristol (Tem. Meads) dep	1042	1130	1138	1153	12 8	1230	1240	1257	1 0	1 10	1 22
Bedminster	1045	1133	1143	1157	1212	1233	1244	1 1	1 3	1 14	1 25
Parson Street	1049	1136	1146			1236	1247	1 3	1 6	1 16	1 27
Ashton Gate		1139				1239			1 9		
Clifton Bridge		1141				1241			1 11		
Ham Green Halt						1248					
Pill		1150				1250			1 22		
Portbury						1256			1 31		
Portishead arr		12 0				1 1			1 36		

Week Days—continued	pm	pm	pm (2)	pm (2)	E pm	pm	pm	pm	pm	E pm
Bristol (Tem. Meads) dep	1 30	2 0	2 30	3 30	3 50	4 0	4 35	4 42	5 15	5 20
Bedminster	1 33	2 3	2 33	3 33	3 53	4 3	4 38	4 48	5 18	5 23
Parson Street	1 36	2 6	2 36	3 36	3 56	4 6	4 41	4 51	5S20	5 26
Ashton Gate	1 39		2 39	3 39	3 59		4 44			
Clifton Bridge	1 41		2 41	3 41	4 2		4 46			
Ham Green Halt			2 48				4 53			
Pill	1 50		2 50	3 50	4 11		4 55			
Portbury	1 57		2 56				5 1			
Portishead arr	2 1		3 1	4 1	4 29		5 6			

Week Days—continued	pm	pm	E pm	E pm	pm	pm (2)	pm	pm (2)	pm V	pm	pm A
Bristol (Tem. Meads) dep	5 30	5 32	5 42	6 4	6 10	6 30	6 33	7 30	9 30	9 43	11 0
Bedminster	5 33	5 36	5 46	6 7	6 14	6 33	6 37	7 33	9 33	9 48	11 3
Parson Street	5 36	5 39	5 48	6 10		6 36	6 40	7 36	9 36	9 51	11 6
Ashton Gate	5 39			6 13		6 39		7 39	9 39		11 9
Clifton Bridge	5 41			6 15		6 41		7 41	9 41		1111
Ham Green Halt	5 48										1118
Pill	5 50			6 24		6 50		7 50	9 50		1122
Portbury	5 59					6 56					
Portishead arr	6 3			6 36		7 1		8 0	10 0		1132

Sundays	am	am (2)	am	pm	pm	pm	pm	pm	pm (2)	pm	pm (2)
Bristol (Tem. Meads) dep	9 0	1030	1052	1230	2 25	2 30	3 50	5 12	6 30	7 45	8 35
Bedminster	9 4	1033	1055	1233	2 28	2 33	3 54	5 16	6 33	7 49	8 38
Parson Street	9 7	1036	1058	1236	2 31	2 36	3 57	5 18	6 36	7 52	8 41
Ashton Gate		1039		1239		2 39			6 39		8 44
Clifton Bridge		1041		1241		2 41			6 41		8 46
Ham Green Halt				1248		2 48					
Pill		1050		1250		2 50			6 50		8 55
Portbury		1055		1256		2 56			6 55		
Portishead arr		11 0		1 2		3 1			7 0		9 4

For Notes, see page 167

Miles	Week Days only	am	am	am	pm	pm	pm	pm	pm
—	Frome dep	6 26	7 37	1050	1 10	4 5	5 55	6 5	9 25
5¼	Mells Road	6 38	7 49	11 1	1 22	4 17		6 20	9 37
8½	Radstock West K	6 45	7 56	11 8	1 30	4 24	6 11	6 27	9 44
9¾	Midsomer Norton & Welton	6 49	8 0	1112	1 34	4 28		6 32	9 48
11¾	Farrington Gurney Halt	6 53	8 4	1116	1 38	4 32		6 38	9 52
12½	Hallatrow	6 57	8 8	1120	1 42	4 40		6 42	9 56
14¼	Clutton	7 1	8 12	1124	1 46	4 44		6 46	10 0
17¾	Pensford	7 12	8 20	1132	1 54	4 52	6 32	6 58	10 9
20	Whitchurch Halt	7 19	8 27		2 1	4 59		7 8	1016
22½	Brislington	7 24	8 31	Ss	2 6	5 4		7 15	1021
24½	Bristol (Temple Meads) arr	7 31	8 38	1148	2 12	5 10	6 52	7 30	1027

K Adjoins Radstock North Station

Ss Stops on Saturdays only at 11 42 am to set down

For OTHER TRAINS between Frome and Bristol (Temple Meads), see Table 62

Table 75—continued PORTISHEAD and BRISTOL

Miles	Week Days	am	am (2)	am	am	am	am	am	am	am (2)	am	am	am	am	am	am
—	Portishead dep									6 44				7 55		8 18
2	Portbury									6 49				8 0		8 23
3½	Pill									6 54				8 5		8 28
4½	Ham Green Halt															
8	Clifton Bridge									7 3				8 14		8 39
8½	Ashton Gate							6 45		7 5				8 16		8 41
9¾	Parson Street	5 16	5 50		6 25	6 33	6 37	6 49	6 58	7 9	7 11		8 10	8 20	8 31	8 44
10½	Bedminster	5 19	5 54	6 1	6 29	6 36	6 41	6 52	7 1	7 12	7 14	7 49	8 13	8 23	8 34	8 47
11½	Bristol (Tem. Meads) arr	5 23	6 0	6 4	6 32	6 41	6 45	6 55	7 5	7 15	7 19	7 52	8 16	8 26	8 38	8 51

Week Days—continued	am	am	am	am	S pm	pm (2)	E pm	pm	pm (2)	pm	S pm
Portishead dep		9 0	1015	1115		1215			1 15		1 45
Portbury			1020			1220					1 50
Pill		9 10	1025	1125		1225			1 25		2 0
Ham Green Halt		9 12				1227					2 3
Clifton Bridge		9 21	1034	1134		1236			1 34		2 12
Ashton Gate		9 23	1036	1136		1238			1 36		2 14
Parson Street	9 4	9 27	1040	1140	12 9	1242	1255	1 16	1 40	2 12	2 17
Bedminster	9 7	9 30	1043	1143	1212	1245	1 0	1 19	1 43	2 15	2 20
Bristol (Tem. Meads) arr	9 11	9 34	1046	1146	1215	1248	1 5	1 26	1 46	2 18	2 23

Week Days—continued	pm	pm	pm (2)	E pm	pm (2)	pm	pm	pm	E pm	pm	pm
Portishead dep	2 15		3 15		4 15		5 15		5 47		6 15
Portbury	2 20		3 20				5 20				
Pill	2 25		3 25		4 25		5 25		6 0		6 25
Ham Green Halt	2 27				4 28						
Clifton Bridge	2 36		3 34		4 36		5 34		6 9		6 34
Ashton Gate	2 38		3 36		4 38		5 36		6 11		6 36
Parson Street	2 42	3 9	3 40	4 31	4 41	5 28	5 40	5 48	6 15	6 27	6 40
Bedminster	2 45	3 12	3 43		4 44	5 31	5 43	5 51	6 18	6 30	6 43
Bristol (Tem Meads) arr	2 48	3 16	3 46	4 36	4 48	5 36	5 46	5 56	6 21	6 34	6 46

Week Days—continued	pm (2)	S pm	E pm	pm	pm (2)	pm	pm	pm	pm V	pm	H night (2)
Portishead dep	7 15				8 15				1015		
Portbury	7 20										
Pill	7 25				8 25				1025		
Ham Green Halt											
Clifton Bridge	7 34				8 34				1034		
Ashton Gate	7 36				8 36				1036		
Parson Street	7 40	7 50	8 4	8 19	8 40	8 59	9 38	1018	1040	1110	1242
Bedminster	7 43	7 54	8 7	8 22	8 43	9 2	9 42	1021	1043	1113	
Bristol (Tem. Meads) arr	7 46	8 1	8 11	8 28	8 46	9 5	9 46	1028	1046	1116	1248

Sundays	am (2)	am	am	am	am (2)	pm	pm	pm	pm (2)	pm	pm	pm (2)	pm
Portishead dep					1115	1 15	4 30		7 15			9 30	
Portbury					1120	1 20	4 35		7 20				
Pill					1125	1 25	4 40		7 25			9 40	
Ham Green Halt							4 43						
Clifton Bridge					1134	1 34	4 50		7 34			9 49	
Ashton Gate					1136	1 36	4 53		7 36			9 52	
Parson Street	1242	6 37	8 39	1033	1140	1 40	4 57	6 6	7 40	8 7	9 52	9 56	1027
Bedminster		6 41	8 43	1036	1143	1 43	5 0	6 9	7 43	8 10	9 55	9 59	1030
Bristol (Tem. Meads) arr	1248	6 45	8 47	1040	1147	1 47	5 3	6 13	7 47	8 13	9 58	10 2	1034

A Second class only Mondays to Fridays. First and Second class on Saturdays
E Except Saturdays

H Saturday nights only
V Second class only on Saturdays

S or S Saturdays only
(2) Second class only

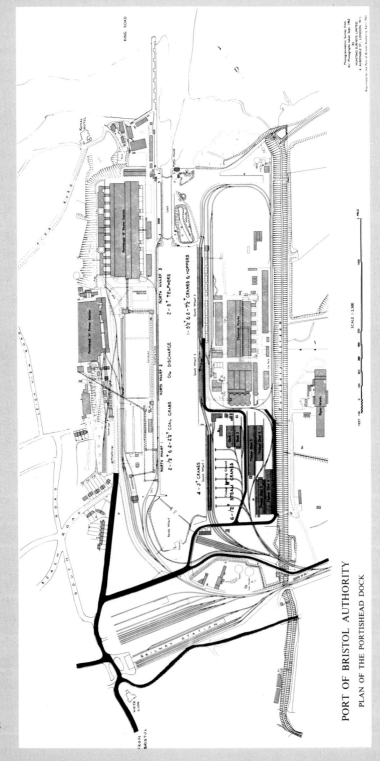

PORT OF BRISTOL AUTHORITY

PLAN OF THE PORTISHEAD DOCK

Clifton Bridge Station, on 25th August 1980, looking towards Bristol. The Avon & Somerset Constabulary premises are to be seen on the right.

Martin C. Smith 139

Chapter Eight

In the late 1950s and early 1960s the standard of permanent way maintenance was extremely high on the branch, and this was especially evident near Nightingale Valley where the grass verges were always kept in beautiful condition, where grew the wild orchids and where there was an example of a fairly rare species, the Bee Orchid. Unfortunately, in the line's latter years the annual weed-killing train did not discriminate between the weeds and the flowers, and so all were killed.

In the 1950s, permanent way gangs Nos. 146, 147 and 148 were responsible for the Clifton Bridge, Pill and Portishead lengths respectively. The regular members of the Clifton Bridge gang were Ganger Wensley, Sub-Ganger Bert Jackson, Ernie Wilson, Harold Bratchell, George Baker, Bill Livings and Mr Clarke. In charge of this motley collection was Inspector Ralph. Whilst not forgetting the worthwhile contribution made by others, special mention needs to be made of Ganger Wensley. He was a ganger at Clifton Bridge for 22 years, but in 1922 he left the railways to take up a position in charge of the engine house of the bascule bridge at Bathurst Basin, in the City Docks. (See Chapter 9 for more on this). A Devonian by birth, he started life working on a farm and for this was paid the princely sum of 6/- (30 pence) per week. For years he lived in a riverside cottage on the Somerset side of the Avon opposite the Hotwells pontoon.

He was a real character, building a catwalk under the line at Clifton Bridge to allow his cats to cross the line safely! However, do not in any way be mis-led, for he was no fool! He wrote several papers on railway subjects and was a Silver Medallist of the Permanent Way Institution. Sadly, the only visible signs, today, of those interesting days of yesteryear, are the ruins of the gangers' cottage at Clifton Bridge.

In the Pill area, permanent way work was carried out by Ganger Wager, Sub-Ganger Pugsley and platelayers Joe Haworth, Stan Simmons and Charlie Mail. Walking down the line past Portbury Station, with its large station house and offices, the gangers would check the short sidings into the cattle dock. These sidings, large enough to take only two or three wagons, were taken out of use in 1963. They handled cattle traffic for the cattle market which was regularly held at Portbury. Potatoes were also handled here. They were brought in to provide pig food, and were stained blue to show that they were, indeed, only fit for pigs, and were not for human consumption! The station staff, in later years, consisted of a stationmaster and one general factotum. This factotum, the

In the 1930s, there were three permanent way gangs working on the track from the station at Clifton Bridge to the line's terminus at Portishead. Mr Gibson's gang, made up of three men and a ganger, worked from Nightingale Valley as far as the station site at Portbury Shipyard. The work included packing joints and replacing sleepers and worn rails. The grass at the track-side was kept tidy by the use of scythes while the fencing had to be kept in good repair to keep the cattle off the track. In those days, of course, all the work was done by hand. The men worked from 7.00 a.m. until 5.00 p.m. on weekdays and from 7.00 a.m. until 12 noon on Saturdays. The weekly pay was £2 2s 0d. The worst jobs in the winter were fogging and snow sweeping, but the men were pleased with the extra cash, even though the jobs were often awful to do.

Photograph Martin C. Smith and text Fred Gibson

late Harold Skelley, had one arm and a hook, and has already been mentioned in our narrative. He kept a beautiful station garden, overgrown and wild these days, but, at its height, something really special. One of his specialities was topiary, the art of shaping privet etc., into various shapes such as birds and army tanks. There was also a goldfish pond to add to the station's beauty.

At Portishead the permanent way work was heavy, with much maintenance being required in the goods yard, on the power station connections and on the lines into the docks, etc. Busy in the summer with the holiday crowds and their children in push-chairs and prams, the Portishead gang was kept pretty busy. The gang was made up of Ganger Gibson, Sub-Ganger Osmend and platelayers Harry Derrick, Danny Costello, Jack Broad, Ted Newton and Burt Warren. By all accounts when the contractors were excavating the site at Portishead for the new (1954) station, they came across some old wooden piles. They had obviously been there for years and their upper parts were in pretty poor condition. However, once the lower parts were uncovered, the piles proved to be completely intact, preserved, and as good as the day they had been put in.

By 1980 the line needed far less careful attention and maintenance, and one patrolman walked the Ashton Gate to Ham Green section while one other covered the Ham Green to Portishead end. This is a very different story from the pre-1964 state of affairs, when passenger trains were still using the line. At that time, inspections were carried out three times a week, on Monday, Wednesday and Friday, while in hot weather, these were increased to a daily routine. On a Sunday, a ganger would walk all three lengths covered by the Portishead, Pill and Clifton Bridge gangs. Having walked the line myself, with the kind consent of British Rail, I can admit to the line's beauty and interest. Even today the line has a very rural feeling. Although surrounded by new developments such as the Royal Portbury Dock and the M5 motorway, there are stretches of the line which still seem to belong more to the 1950s than to the 1980s.

One new development on the branch in its declining years, worth mentioning, was the provision of a new civil engineering depot at Ashton. This depot, built in 1960 at Ashton Gate and sited close to the sidings at Ashton Meadows, was to cover activities previously carried out by depots at Pylle Hill and St. Phillip's Marsh, and by bridge depots at Bath Spa and Bathampton. It consisted of a large, concrete, portal frame building with brick walls and a pitched roof to accommodate workshops and stores. It was served by a new rail siding and paved roads. Other smaller buildings, containing offices and a messroom, were erected, together with a sawmill, cement store, plant store and garage. In addition, a stacking area was provided adjacent to two new sidings and paved roads.

However, in spite of this new project, the line's course was still very much downward. In March 1962, the train service on the branch suffered a drastic cut. The previous service of 14 trains daily was viciously reduced to only 6 peak hour services. The 5 each way Sunday services were withdrawn completely. This was a real blow, in that Sunday trains were exceedingly popular during the spring and summer months, when the days were bright and warm, although it could not be denied that it was very much a case of summer profits not covering winter losses that led to the removal of the Sunday trains. On 30th April 1962, Portbury Station was closed completely, while on 26th August 1962 part of the goods yard loop, at the Bristol end of Pill Station, was removed.

From 29th October of the same year, the platform at Ashton

A diesel multiple unit enters Ashton Gate Platform from the Portishead direction in the early 1960s. Special workings, for which the Portishead line will be remembered, were the traditional football specials to Ashton Gate for Bristol City's ground. Most winter Saturdays would produce a crop of three or four trains which would come from within the Bristol area, for example, from Avonmouth, and from further afield. Signalmen on the branch were often asked to work at Ashton Gate on a Saturday afternoon, collecting tickets and closing carriage doors. The empty coaching stock would later be taken to the carriage sidings at Clifton Bridge where the engine would run-round ready to move the crowds away at the end of the match. Quite often, the part-time ticket collectors would themselves disappear off to the ground to watch the game as well!

Arthur Day

Taken in the late 1950s, this picture shows a BR standard 2-6-2T approaching Ashton Gate Platform, with the carriage sidings at Clifton Bridge in the background. The train, running from Portishead into Bristol was, along with workings formed of GWR diesel railcars, typical of the Portishead branch line scene in the 1950s.

Arthur Day

Gate and the station at Clifton Bridge both became unstaffed. These were swift sure signs that the line was in serious decline. In 1963, late in the year on 1st November, the remainder of the goods loop was removed at Pill. The end was in sight. By the winter of 1963 the WR issued proposals to withdraw the Bristol—Portishead passenger service. This they had originally intended to do on 3rd February 1964. At that time, traffic levels were around 160 people travelling daily (Monday to Friday) with between 60 and 110 making use of the service on Saturdays. According to figures presented by the WR in its closure proposals, however, the picture was far less healthy. Revenue directly attributable to the line stood at £6,100. On the cost side £4,700 was incurred in terminal costs while £11,400 was incurred in movement costs. In addition, the railway authorities estimated that, in the period 1963—1968, renewals on buildings would cost £5,200. Interestingly enough, no major expenditure was foreseen for permanent way renewals.

Even the dock workers had deserted the line! When the National Dock Labour Board was consulted about the closure they replied, that, when dock workers were required at Portishead they travelled there by road. However, although the end seemed and was, in fact, inevitable, a reprieve was obtained. The, then, Minister of Transport, the late Ernest Marples, told the House of Commons, in February 1964, that he would delay the proposed closure of certain lines to holiday resorts in order to avoid uncertainty about holiday travel. Included in these were the railways from Taunton to Barnstaple and Minehead and the Bristol—Portishead branch. The proposed closure date of 3rd February was postponed and, in spite of all the usual protests, the final blow was all too clearly on the cards and the Minister set the date for the loss of the line's passenger service as 7th September 1964.

In April 1964 the crossing loop at Pill was taken out of use. The end was drawing closer. At Portishead, the decision to close had been patiently awaited by railway staff. In 1962 a relief stationmaster had been appointed and the station, which had cost thousands of pounds, was allowed to decay. The waiting-rooms gleamed behind locked doors, their tables and chairs neatly set out. In the latter days they were inaccessible to passengers unless a request was made for them to be unlocked. Here was the station, built in modern pre-stressed concrete and traditional local limestone, that was designed to blend in with local surroundings. In the seven months of its construction it had had its problems. Finding it impossible to get a mason to tackle the undressed rubble, a wall mason finally undertook to train bricklayers and, by the station's completion, eight untrained men had qualified as masons. To make way for the new station building, the local Labour Exchange, a British Legion hut, a Boy Scouts' HQ., a blacksmith's forge and a jeweller's shop had all been pulled down and the marshland had become a marshalling yard for 300 wagons.

At 3/- return, the fare, at closure, was still 1/- less than the bus and, with the running time of 28 minutes, compared to that of 55 minutes by bus, the rail service should have been the logical answer to those who were seeking a speedy service. But with falling receipts, the line, at closure, carried about 450 passengers a week, in each direction and the death knell was rung. Even though the appalling winter of 1963 had shown how important the railway could still be, it was doomed. The A369 had been blocked by snow, but the railway, a lifeline to the community, kept going. However, it was not to see the winter of 1964! Like so many branches at this time, the Portishead line saw the, now, all too familiar, last rites. The last train from the ten year old £250,000 station, the crowded coaches and the railway staff, sad in the knowledge that their own masters had killed the line off.

WEEKDAYS ONLY : WINTER 1963/1964

		a.m.	a.m.	(2) p.m.	p.m.	(E) p.m.
Bristol (T.M.)	dep.	5.27	6.58	8.15	4.37	5.45	6.45
Bedminster	dep.	5.32	7.02	8.18	4.40	5.48	6.48
Parson Street	dep.	5.34	7.04	8.21	4.43	5.51	6.51
Ashton Gate Halt	dep.	—	7.08	8.24	4.46	5.54	6.54
Clifton Bridge Halt	dep.	5.39	7.10	8.26	4.48	5.56	6.56
Ham Green Halt	dep.	—	—	—	4.55	6.03	—
Pill	dep.	5.48	7.19	8.35	4.57	6.05	7.05
Portishead	arr.	5.58	7.28	8.46	5.07	6.17	7.16
Portishead	dep.	6.30	7.53	8.23	9.15	5.15	6.25
Pill	dep.	6.39	8.03	8.38	9.25	5.25	6.36
Ham Green Halt	dep.	—	—	—	9.27	—	—
Clifton Bridge Halt	dep.	6.48	8.12	8.47	9.36	5.34	6.44
Ashton Gate Halt	dep.	6.50	8.14	8.49	9.38	5.36	6.46
Parson Street	dep.	6.54	8.18	8.53	9.42	5.40	6.50
Bedminster	dep.	6.57	8.21	8.56	9.45	5.43	6.53
Bristol (T.M.)	arr.	7.02	8.24	8.59	9.49	5.46	6.56

(2) Second Class Only
(E) Except Saturdays

One of the staff on that last day, 5th September 1964, was the late Mr David Trudgian. He had started at Portishead forty five years earlier, in 1919, and had seen the station grow sufficiently in stature for him to be promoted to signalman. He then watched as traffic declined to the point where he once again became porter and general factotum. It was told that he could remember well the old station with its trains coming in over the wooden viaduct, which was discussed earlier in the book. He had seen the last train out of the old station in just the same style as he had seen the last train out of the new; in best dress suit and silk topper. In April 1964 he was 70 years of age and, when the last train pulled out of the new station, he retired.

Whatever else happened, there can be no doubt that in the years just before the removal of passenger traffic, there was a good deal of variety in the motive power used on the branch. It seemed that it was a railway that the authorities would 'throw anything down'. The passenger service had its GWR railcars, BR diesel multiple units and pannier tanks. The BR diesel multiple units worked in two or three car sets, but single units were also used, particularly as closure drew near. D63XX class locomotives and coaches were also regularly seen. On the freight side there were 'Castles', 'Halls', 'Granges' and 2-8-0s of both the GWR and LMSR variety, the latter being employed on the phosphate trains to Oldbury. The pannier tanks of classes 37XX, 57XX, 77XX and 94XX were also regular performers. BR Standard class 3MT 2-6-2 tanks of the 82XXX series were also in evidence. The freight services were dominated by 'Westerns', 'Hymeks', 'Peaks' and Type 2s, once the freight side was dieselized.

Like the former gasworks at Portishead, the power station had always received coal from mines in the Radstock area of North Somerset. By the early 1960s the traffic still required two trip workings to the Radstock area. The first trip went to Radstock itself, while the second went to Old Mills Colliery. This latter mine was situated on the north side of the former GWR line from Radstock to Bristol and had standard gauge sidings serving the screens. These workings, diesel-hauled, usually by 'Hymek' class engines as far as Bristol East Depot, were then tripped by steam locomotives, often pannier tanks of the 77XX class, to Portishead. These steam workings were often double-headed and this gives some idea of the length and weight of these trains. Coal trains from Old Mills were discontinued early in 1966 when the private sidings there ceased to be used.

Once the coal had arrived at Portishead, the sidings at the power station would be shunted and empty wagons from here, and from the gasworks, would be formed into another train, often around 50—60 wagons in length for the run back between 9.00p.m. and 12.30a.m. Even at this point in the line's history, the coal traffic was heavy enough to justify special 'Q' workings in the timetable. However, after being heavy in the early years of the 1960s the traffic became more and more intermittent, and once the line lost its passenger traffic it started to take on a neglected look.

The timber traffic was not heavy in the early 1960s but the later building of the M5 motorway provided some additional cement traffic. This did not last long, although, at the time, it justified the provision of booked trains from West Depot.

By the spring of 1965, Portishead Dock was being mainly used for the supply of coal and oil fuel to the two power stations, the import of phosphates for Albright & Wilson and for the Baltic timber trade. On the railway, 5th April 1965 saw all passenger loops, sidings and the signal box being taken out of use at Portishead. In early May 1965 the line through Clifton Bridge was singled. By August, proposed plans were put forward to convert the station buildings at Portishead into a petrol filling station. The plans envisaged using the booking hall, along with other buildings and the extensive forecourt. Amid controversy, the plan was finally approved in March 1966.

Once permission had been won for the conversion of the former (new) station into a garage, and this was carried out only after there had been a tremendous amount of local opposition to the plan, work proceeded apace. Nine months had been spent in the campaign to convert, but the conversion itself took little time and occurred during July 1966. The conversion, supervised by Mr Bryan Hill, the then General Manager of the original firm of Messrs Green, meant the installation of tanks, pumps, etc. and showroom conversion. Officially opened on 26th August 1966, the opening was attended by the Lions of Longleat, who were, fortunately for the public at least, suitably drugged and sluggish! At that time new cars were stored on the station's former platform. Although one may bemoan the fact that the station is now serving its major rival, the motor car, the conversion was well carried out and the present structure is still very attractive to look at.

One of the reasons for opposition to the garage scheme was, that during January 1966, Portishead Council had been pressing for the re-opening of the town's rail passenger link with Bristol. Representations had been made to the council concerning the unsatisfactory nature of the replacement bus service. Various other local councils later joined this campaign, hoping that a railcar service could be reinstated. Pointing out that the line which, of course, was still being used for freight traffic, was in good condition, the councils concerned asked the Transport Licensing Authority to make provision for at least an emergency service, even if a full time one could not be provided.

However, all the effort was to no avail and, even worse, further facilities were soon stripped from the branch. In November 1966 further rationalization took place at Clifton Bridge Station when the signal box there, and the ground frame at Ashton Junction

Portishead New Station in 1981. It has been well adapted to serve the railway's main competitor. Note the new light industries springing up on railway land around the site.

Bryan Stanley, Station Garage

West, were closed. The wartime sidings here were also removed at this time. In 1967 the line closed to public goods traffic. It was kept open only for private siding traffic, such as Albright & Wilson, CEGB and PBA timber traffic, with 'one train only' working in operation. At long last, however, in the late 1960s and early 1970s things took a slight turn for the better.

On the passenger side, Ashton Gate Platform, which had been closed along with the rest of the line's stations at closure, re-opened for football specials, the first train to use the revived station arriving from Birmingham on 29th September 1970. However, its use was short-lived for, in 1977, Parson Street Station took over Ashton Gate's role and since that time the Ashton Gate Platform has been out of use yet again.

On the freight side in the early 1970s there was also good news. In 1913 a paperboard mill had been opened at St. Anne's in Brislington. This mill was supplied with woodpulp via Bristol City Docks and, from here, it was taken by boat through the feeder canal to the mill's site at St. Anne's where it was off-loaded into large storage sheds. This practice continued until the late 1960s, since this was regarded as being the most efficient and economical way of handling the woodpulp although it did, in fact, involve transhipping the cargo into lighters for the latter part of their journey.

However, with the imminent closure of the City Docks to commercial traffic, the firm decided that it must look around for a storage site, adjacent to a quay, to which woodpulp could be directly discharged. The mill's requirements could then be met direct from store. It was decided that Portishead Dock was just such a site, and an area of nearly five acres was leased to the St. Anne's Board Mill Company to be used for their new woodpulp terminal. From here the woodpulp was to be loaded directly into rail wagons to form block trains to Marsh Ponds. This latter site, east of Temple Meads, was conveniently close to the Board Mill at St. Anne's and had formerly been the location for a set of carriage sidings.

And so, early in June 1971, the woodpulp terminal at Portishead received its first cargo of pre-stropped woodpulp, when 700 tons arrived in the *M V Jan Laurenz*. The cargo was discharged direct to rail and was conveyed to Marsh Ponds. The second vessel to arrive at this specialized terminal was the *Gerda Bres* followed, in quick succession, by other ships employed in the Baltic trade, and during July alone ten vessels discharged woodpulp at the terminal. Woodpulp and the Western Region were well on the way!

With the opening of the new woodpulp terminal, an 0-6-0 diesel-mechanical locomotive, (D916), built in 1956 by Hudswell Clarke, was transferred to Portishead from Avonmouth on 1st June 1971 to help out with the extra work. This locomotive, named *Dubglas*, worked for the PBA until 1973 when it went to Romford Scrap Metal Company. It was later purchased by a Belgian firm. The woodpulp traffic, which lasted until 1977, was essentially handled for British Rail by Mr Garfield Trudgian. He tells of how, in one year alone, this traffic amounted to somewhere in the region of 55,000 tons. At the start of the trade there was a fleet of 52 specially built timber wagons to handle the bales of woodpulp, but by the end, this total had increased to 57. The bales were never roped. They were either wire whipped, as in the early days of the traffic, or steel banded, as became the practice in later days.

The wagons built to deal with this traffic were vacuum-fitted and had roller bearings. If there were 26 wagons in a train this was handled by almost any diesel locomotive except a Class 31; these engines were limited to around 19 or 20 wagons. The traffic was hauled by a real mixture of motive power including Class 31s in tandem, 25s alone and in tandem and 45s, 46s, 47s and 50s on their own. All this traffic was handled in the remaining sidings of the former (new) station. This traffic ceased early in 1977 and at Portishead the rail connection into the docks is now fenced off.

At around the same time as the above traffic, bitumen and (Tunnel) cement traffic were also being dealt with at Portishead. The cement company had, until recently, a distribution centre at Portishead which included a large storage tank in the goods yard. Occasional scrap metal consignments were also handled. The last cement train went into Portishead on Monday, 30th March 1981. It returned as the last cement out on Friday, 3rd April. Sometimes Freightliner trains would also be worked to Portishead to handle containers, which had been road-hauled, out of Royal Portbury Dock. Twenty car sets have been handled at Portishead, admittedly with difficulty; normally ten has been the maximum, these being split into two five car sets for running round purposes at Portishead. More will be said of Freightliner developments later in the chapter.

Having walked the line, one thing I noticed was that many of the wooden sleepers were marked as if something had derailed at some stage in time. The mystery was why the marks extended so far along the length of the line. The answer was obvious when I was told that, on 29th December 1969, one of Albright & Wilson's tank wagons, forming part of the 15.20 from Portishead, came off the rails. To be strictly accurate, only one pair of wheels actually derailed and from Portishead to Ashton Junction this particular wagon ran with one set on and one set off. At 16.35, control received a phone call from the train's driver informing them of the situation. It is sad to think that this incident may hasten the line's complete closure in that where the wagon marked the sleepers the rain has penetrated and they have started to rot through. In later years the goods yard at Portishead was worked by Garfield Trudgian and Bernie Jordan, he known as 'Bernie the Bolt'. Later all the work of weighing and shunting was handled by Mr Trudgian.

On 6th December 1971, in connection with the MAS resignalling of the Bristol area, the signal box at Parson Street Junction was closed. On the same date the associated signal box at West Depot was also closed as was the connecting chord from the main line at West Depot to the Portishead line at the former West Loop North

Portishead New Station yard, 25th August 1980.

Martin C. Smith

Junction. No longer could trains off the Portishead line run direct to the West Country as the former 'Wapping to Wookey' specials had done. Reversal via Parson Street was now the order of the day. The truncated chord was converted into sidings.

In 1973 further attempts to revive passenger services on the branch were made by Portishead District Council. The hope was that the line would be temporarily reopened to passenger traffic during the difficult period when the Somerset section of the M5 had opened to traffic but the Avon Bridge section was not then completed. Traffic was being diverted on to the narrow and difficult A369 and the council hoped that the line's reopening, to commuters only, would help ease the chaos on the roads. Unfortunately, the reopening did not take place, even for a temporary period!

However, in the 1970s, railtours occasionally ventured over the Portishead branch. Recent ones include the Oxford Railway Circle's tour in the autumn of 1976, when a chartered six car diesel multiple unit came on to the line. In October 1977 a local school chartered a diesel multiple unit for a day's outing to Bath. On Friday, 7th October 1977, Doug Evans, the last driver to bring a pannier-hauled passenger train into Portishead in 1964, once again took a diesel multiple unit passenger train over the branch, when he drove a three car unit from Portishead to Bath. A school party from Gordano School had chartered a special for a day trip and they invited Doug to go with them. The youngsters were also joined by former Portishead signalman Mr Jack Trigg, Panel Supervisor Don Hardwood and former Gordano schoolteacher, Mr John Martin, who had launched, at that time, an unsuccessful campaign to buy the line.

On 22nd October 1977 the 'Toffeeapple Farewell' railtour included the Portishead branch in its itinerary, and the signal box at Ashton Junction was specially opened for the occasion since this was a Saturday working. The locomotives were two Class 31s from the Eastern Region. Incidentally, a few months after this tour, the old crossing at Ashton Junction was replaced by a half-barrier type with flashing lights and, at the same time there was some removal of track. This work, carried on in the spring of 1978, brought a large crane to the branch and this Sunday working, the first for many years, brought a Class 47, hauling the permanent way train used in the operation, on to the line. Another link with the past disappeared in 1978 when the final section of the old wooden viaduct leading into the original B&PP&R Company's passenger station at Portishead, was demolished by divers using underwater chain saws.

What of the line's future? Does it even have one? Possible future traffic would seem to centre on three sources: container traffic from the Royal Portbury Dock, opened 8th August 1978; the proposed Avon Metro and incoming stone traffic through Royal Portbury for the firm of Foster Yeoman Limited of East Cranmore near Shepton Mallet in Somerset. Let us finish our story of the Portishead branch by reflecting on each of these possible traffics.

Immaculate Eastern Region type 31/0 diesel locomotives, Nos. 31005 and 31019, from Stratford Depot, London, leave Portishead with the Railway Pictorial Publication's 'Toffeeapple Farewell' 08.03 (charter) Paddington to Portishead and Tytherington (1Z10) on Saturday 22nd October 1977.

G. Roy Hounsell

Class 31 diesel locomotive, No. 31273, emerges from Bath Road Bridge, Bristol, with a Presflo train from Lawrence Hill to Portishead on 10th December 1976. The wagons originated from Tring Cutting.

B. J. Nicolle

Class 37 diesel, No. 37206, rumbles into Bristol (Temple Meads) with a rake of hoppers, including three 24 tonners. The train is destined for Wapping Wharf.

B. J. Nicolle

The original intention of Freightliners Limited was that the present (mini) depot at South Liberty Lane, opened in 1974, should be no more than a temporary set-up, so that when the developments at the PBA's Royal Portbury Dock were in full flight and rolling, there would be a complete move, to that maritime site, by Freightliner. However, due to recent changes in legislation, any terminal on dock land has to be worked by dockers, and so if Freightliners had implemented a full move to Portbury their domestic traffic would have been lost to other agencies. Freightliner's present plans (as at 1981) are now to keep South Liberty Lane open as a terminal in addition to any new terminal that may be built in the future at Portbury. The method of working at the port would entail the use of shunt vehicles from the ship being loaded or unloaded to the Freightliner trains. Once loaded at Portbury, the trains would run down the branch to West Depot where they would 'tie up' with existing Freightliner trains from West Depot.

The present situation seems to be that of the classic 'chicken and egg' syndrom, namely that new traffic is expected to develop when the new container operators move in and build their depots at Portbury. Once built, these will encourage further operators to move in and, hopefully, further traffic will follow. Certainly one thing in the line's favour for the development of container traffic is that all the tunnels on the line will take an 8 ft. 6 in. 'box'.

There are, as we have already read, precedents for working containers over the branch in that, during 1979 for example, several Freightliner trains were carried over the branch in connection with the sailing of a Dafra Line ship. The 'boxes' came in via Portbury. They were then road-hauled to Portishead where a temporary depot had been set up with cranage facilities, etc. The containers were loaded on to rail sets here and they then went out, via the Portishead branch, to Manchester. The traffic was handled through ACL, who were the agents, on behalf of Dafra Line. One can only hope that isolated workings such as these will become far more frequent in the future.

One very interesting but, unfortunately, not very likely possibility, for the future use of the line, is its inclusion in a new Metro system which has been proposed by Richard Cottrell, Member of the European Parliament for Bristol. In November 1979 an initial study was published and laid before all the local authorites in Avon and, indeed, before almost anyone else who was professionally involved in the transport arena. Five Metro lines are suggested and these are all based on parts of the existing Bristol suburban railway network; essentially the Avonmouth/Severn Beach 'Avon Link' line, various closed lines, for example, parts of the now defunct Midland network around the city, such as the former Lawrence Hill/Fishponds/Staple Hill/Mangotsfield/Yate section of the former MR and, lastly, a central section, essentially in tunnel, that leaves the present Clifton Down Station, in the new plan this is renamed Whiteladies Gate, to plunge under Clifton, burrowing under the city centre, to re-emerge into daylight at the main interchange which would be based on the currently quietly mouldering station at Lawrence Hill.

This interchange, now simply the first halt out of Temple Meads on the Avonmouth/Severn Beach service, would be transformed, under the Metro plan, into a major focus for the entire system, since all five lines would meet here. They would then be 'tied together' for the whole of the central underground section to Whiteladies Gate. The line that concerns us in this book is the Metropolitan line. This would start at Yate running through to Lawrence Hill, using the former Midland approach into Bristol. Going underground at Lawrence Hill, it would pass through stations at Old Market, Broadmead, the Centre, Haymarket, Colston and Exhibition. It would branch off here from the Brunel and Plimsoll lines to tunnel, with the Imperial line, under the river with stations at Albion (for the industrial museum at Prince's Wharf) and Baltic (for *SS Great Britain*) linking in with the Portishead line itself at Ashton Gate.

On the rejuvenated section of the branch there would be stations at Ashton Park, Pill and Portbury, where a car-park would be provided for 'park n' ride' facilities, and at Portishead, which would be the coastal terminus of the Metropolitan line. The Avon Metro scheme is strongly embedded in the thinking of the Tyne & Wear Metro project which is almost certainly one of the very few good examples of new and integrated urban transit systems in Britain. Whether its Avon counterpart will ever be built remains conjectural, there are too many vested interests against it. Nevertheless, the beneficial effects it could have on a wide area of Bristol and Avon are self evident. This is probably one reason why it will never be built. I hope that I am proved totally wrong.

One final proposal for the Portishead line, combining both passenger and freight traffics, has only very recently been in the news for, although the last cement train may well have disappeared, there are still those who believe that the line has a future. In March 1982 Portishead town councillors made yet another plea for the reinstatement of the Portishead to Bristol passenger service. They are expecting the line to be repaired and improved, to carry millions of tons of crushed granite from Royal Portbury Dock which the major Somerset firm of Foster Yeoman are hoping to bring in, by sea, from Scotland in 1984.

The councillors believe that if this exciting development takes place, a passenger service from the town to Bristol could again become a viable proposition. The town is expanding and, with growing congestion on what has always been a difficult road, the A369 to Bristol, a rail service might grab enough of the commuter traffic to make it profitable or, at least, cover its costs. Will the line survive yet another period of slump and see itself into the 21st century? It deserves to. It has hung on so determinedly in the past, and in 1982, with some exciting possibilities for the future, it would seem a good time to pause and linger over some reflections on the Portishead branch.

A Class 31 diesel heads back to Bristol with an empty cement train on 21st August 1980. It was photographed on the site of Portbury Shipyard loop and shows the access road to the Royal Portbury Dock in the background. The section of continuous welded rail was installed when the loop and associated sidings were taken out of use here.

Author

ENGINE RESTRICTIONS—continued

Section of Line	Route Colour	Engines Authorised	Local Prohibitions
Portishead Branch	'Dotted Red' Parson Street Junction and West Depot to Clifton Bridge.	Parson Street Junction and West Depot to Clifton Bridge. All except 47XX. All 'Red' engines not to exceed 20 m.p.h. between Parson Street Junction and West Depot to Clifton Bridge. Southern Region modified 'West Country' class engines may work between Parson Street Junction and Clifton Bridge. (This includes permission for two engines to work coupled or coupled to any other permitted engine.)	Ashton Sawmills-Siding—All engines not to work into Sidings in Timber Yard beyond the road Level Crossing.
	'Yellow' Clifton Bridge to Portishead	Clifton Bridge to Portishead. 'Uncoloured' and 'Yellow' engines 94XX (singly, coupled, or coupled to any other permitted engine.)	Clifton Bridge—Great care to be exercised in working B.R. STD 75XXX, 73XXX, 70XXX and 78XX, 79XX, 70XX, 68XX, 10XX into Down Siding Loading Bank Portishead end of Station.

GOODS LINES, ASHTON BRIDGE SIGNAL BOX TO CANON'S MARSH AND WAPPING.

1.—INTERMEDIATE SIDINGS.

There are Sidings communicating with the Running Lines between Canon's Marsh and Ashton Bridge Signal Box, and between Wapping Wharf and Ashton Bridge Signal Box as shewn below:

Name of Siding.	Connection with Up or Down Line.	Distance from Canon's Marsh Goods Depot.	How worked.
Cumberland Sidings	With Wapping Wharf single line at Ashton End (Key on Token)	—	By pilot service or trains appointed to call.
Merchants Dock .. (Heber Denty's & Osborn & Wallis)	Up (Worked from Avon Crescent South Ground Frame)	About ¾ of a mile	Traffic for this Siding to be taken to Canon's Marsh and worked back from there. Traffic from the Siding to be picked up direct by Up Freight trains.
Merchant's Road .. (Heber Denty's)	Down (Wheel-stop to be kept padlocked)	About 1,000 yds.	Traffic for this Siding to be put off direct by Down Freight trains and traffic from the Siding to be taken to Canon's Marsh to return from there.
Poole's	Up (Lever working catch point to be kept padlocked)	About 900 yards	Traffic for this Siding to be taken to Canon's Marsh, and be worked back from there. Traffic from the Siding to be picked up direct by Up Freight trains.
Gas Works	Up Line and Canon's Marsh Yard (Wheel-stop to be kept padlocked)	At Canon's Marsh Yard	By Canon's Marsh shunting engines. Traffic to work to Canon's Marsh in each direction.

WORKING TIMETABLE 16th SEPTEMBER 1957 TO 8th JUNE 1958

SHUNTING ENGINES

Station	Engine No.	Starting Time	Authorized Hours							Total per week		Particulars of work
			Mon	Tues	Wed	Thur	Fri	Sat	Sun	Hrs.	Mins.	
PORTISHEAD	1	5.35a.m. Weekdays	2½	2½	2½	2½	2½	2½	—	15	0	Works 5.00 a.m. West Depot to Portishead (arr. 5.35 a.m.) and 8.18 a.m. Passenger Portishead to Bristol (T.M.)
	2	10.00a.m. Weekdays	5	5	5	5	5	5	—	30	0	Works 8.15 a.m. West Depot to Portishead (arr. 9.36 a.m.) and 3.25 p.m. Portishead to Stoke Gifford
	3	6.45p.m. SX	1¼	1¼	1¼	1¼	1¼	—	—	6	15	Works 4.50 p.m. Henbury SX Passenger, Avonmouth to Portishead (arr. 6.35 p.m.) and 8.30 p.m. SX Portishead to Ashton Meadows

Engine Restrictions — Branches

Section of Line	Route Colour	Engines Authorized	Local Prohibitions
Portishead Branch	Dotted Red — Parson Street Junction and West Depot to Clifton Bridge Yellow — Clifton Bridge to Portishead	Parson Street Junction and West Depot to Clifton Bridge: All classes except 60XX, 'King', 47XX, BR standard Class 8 (4-6-2) and Gas Turbine locomotives Nos. 18000 and 18100	
		All Red engines not to exceed twenty miles per hour between Parson Street Junction and West Depot to Clifton Bridge	Ashton Sawmills Siding: All engines not to work into sidings in Timber Yard beyond the road level crossing
		Trigger Cock Gear Lever to be removed from 61XX Class engines	
		Southern Region 'West Country' and 'King Arthur' Class engines may work between Parson Street Junction and Clifton Bridge subject to the following stipulation	
		'King Arthur' Class engines must not exceed twenty miles per hour. (This includes permission for two engines of either class to work coupled together or coupled to any other permitted engine)	
		Clifton Bridge to Portishead: Uncoloured and Yellow engines and BR standard Class 2 (2-6-0) (84XX and 94XX singly, coupled together, or coupled to any other permitted engine)	Clifton Bridge: Great care to be exercised in working BR standard Class 4 (4-6-0), Class 5 (4-6-0), Classes 6 & 7 (4-6-2), and 78XX, 40XX, 49XX, 59XX, 69XX, 79XX, 4073, 50XX, 70XX, 68XX, 10XX, Classes into Down Side Loading Bank Portishead end of station

SUMMARY OF BR LOCOMOTIVES SEEN ON THE PORTISHEAD/CITY DOCKS LINES
1975—1979

Class	Type	Traffic Handled
03	204 b.h.p. diesel shunter (0-6-0)	Hauled works train when one set of rails was taken up over Ashton Swing Bridge in the spring of 1976
08	350 b.h.p. diesel-electric shunter (0-6-0)	Hauled coal trains from Ashton Meadows to Western Fuels Depot, also handled all shunting at depot, until July 1976. Occasionally hauled BR works train and handled shunts at Ashton Meadows
25	1,250 b.h.p. diesel-electric Bo-Bo	Worked lighter coal trains and empties to and from Ashton Meadows sidings and also works trains. Occasional freight to Portishead also handled. Grit/road salt trains and empty wagon workings were also under their control
31	1,470 b.h.p. diesel-electric A1A-A1A	Very rarely seen. Hauled light coal trains, and sometimes empties. Most often seen on works trains. Occasionally handled empty woodpulp wagon workings to Portishead. Almost exclusively handled Portishead freight and empty wagon workings in the line's final days. In October 1977, two hauled the 'Toffeeapple Farewell' railtour to Portishead. The locomotives used were Nos. 31005 and 31019, both from Stratford (ER) Depot
37	1,750 b.h.p. diesel-electric Co-Co	Handled heavy morning coal trains exclusively, also most afternoon workings and return empties
45 & 46	2,500 b.h.p. diesel-electric 1Co-Co1	Seen on coal trains and this class has handled works trains. Hauled woodpulp trains alternating with Class 47s until early 1976 when Class 45, and less often Class 46s, handled these trains almost exclusively. Have hauled Portishead freight in lieu of Class 31s on at least one occasion
47	2,600 b.h.p. diesel-electric Co-Co	Handled afternoon coal trains and empties. Used to appear frequently on works trains. Handled most of woodpulp workings until 1976, then less frequently. Sometimes hauled Portishead freights
52	2,700 b.h.p. diesel-hydraulic C-C	Hauled some coal trains until early 1975. *Western Venturer* handled one day's woodpulp working in June 1976*

Also seen on the line were Western Fuel's *Western Pride*, since July 1976 and an ex-PBA Hudswell Clarke 0-6-0 diesel-mechanical shunter. Since April 1978, *Henbury*, an 0-6-0 Peckett steam locomotive was also seen and is now at Bristol Industrial Museum

NB * Believed to be the last time a 'Western' worked over the branch. When returning with the first loaded woodpulp train at 12.101p.m., Class 47 *Vulcan* on a Portishead bound cement train, passed the 'Western' at Ashton Junction level crossing. Paul Holley thinks that this may have been the last occasion on which two trains ever passed at this location.

Text: *Paul Holley*

Chapter Nine

SUMMARY

The following two chapters cover the history and development of the Wapping (Bristol Harbour Railway) and Canon's Marsh (Bristol Harbour Lines 1897) lines respectively.

In 1841 the Great Western Railway opened throughout between Paddington and Bristol, but it was not until 1872 that the city's Floating Harbour had rail connected docks and wharves. On 11th March 1872 the Bristol Harbour Railway to Wapping Wharf opened for freight traffic. An expensive line to contruct, because it was over developed land, it was owned jointly by the Bristol & Exeter and the Great Western Railway. Nearly thirty years were to elapse before more major railway works were constructed in the City Docks area.

In 1906 two new railway links were established under the Bristol Harbour Lines Act of 1897, and both were connected to the main Portishead branch at Ashton Gate. The first route left Ashton Junction signal box and, by means of a double track line, crossed the River Avon on the bottom deck of a new, hydraulically operated, double deck swing bridge. A single line then swung off this main line to run alongside the New Cut, this branch making an end-on junction with sidings of the Bristol Harbour Railway at Wapping Wharf.

The second branch ran on from the first at Ashton Swing Bridge North Junction. This important double track section crossed Cumberland Basin by yet another swing bridge and headed on to a large, newly constructed, goods depot at Canon's Marsh. This was built on a site close to the city centre near the Cathedral.

The Bristol Harbour Railway (via Redcliff) was closed to traffic in January 1964, although a connection still remains (via Ashton Swing Bridge) into the Portishead branch at Ashton. One year later the Canon's Marsh extension also closed.

In 1866, a Bill passed through Parliament allowing the construction, by the Bristol & Exeter and GWR companies in partnership with Bristol Corporation, of the Bristol Harbour Railway and Wharf Depot. To be precise, the corporation exercised their powers to construct the wharf itself, with a depot at that wharf, while the companies naturally built the connecting railway. The scheme was put forward in order to alleviate heavy road traffic through what were, even then, overcrowded city streets. Goods that were being transferred by road from the harbour, then still not rail connected to the main line companies' tracks at Bristol, would be able to move directly from ship to rail, and vice versa, at dockside.

The cost of the scheme was estimated at £165,000 and was to be equally divided between the Bristol & Exeter, the GWR and the corporation, and considering that the line was only three quarters of a mile in length one can see just how expensive it actually was. It was engineered by Charles Richardson and work began in August 1868. Its construction forced the demolition of the old vicarage at the church of St. Mary Redcliffe, plus nearly all one side of Guinea Street. It involved the construction of a 282 yard long tunnel under the churchyard at Redcliff; for this the church received £2,500 in compensation. With the money received, some land, at Arno's Vale in Brislington, was purchased and many bodies were reburied there. The railway gave access to a district that was generally poorly known to Bristolians. In laying out the line the surveyors had come across a considerable bed of 'withies' (which is a kind of willow particularly common on the Somerset levels) growing in the area between Redcliff church and the station at Temple Meads. In addition, much local interest was aroused by the (re)discovery of a comprehensive network of caves under Redcliff Hill during the line's construction.

In 1869 the railway companies decided to increase the size of the wharfage provided for in the scheme. They applied for further Parliamentary powers while the corporation agreed to a 400 ft. extension of the wharf, west of Princes Street Bridge.

The railway was opened on 11th March 1872 but not before the Inspecting Officer, Colonel Yolland, had examined it on 26th February 1872. Precise as ever, the report gives the following details of the line's construction and route. According to the report the line was double throughout with the exception of the first 6½ chains where the single line joined, end-on, a goods line of the Great Western Railway. The width of the line at formation level for the double line on the viaduct was 27 ft., on the embankment it was 30 ft., while in the tunnel it was 27½ ft. In the two cuttings it was 29½ and 35 ft. respectively. The line was broad gauge.

The permanent way consisted of flat bottomed Siemens steel. It was laid on cross sleepers of creosoted Baltic Redwood timber. The rails were secured to the cross sleepers by four ¾ in. fang bolts in each sleeper, except for the sleepers next to the joints which had six of these bolts. The ballast was of broken stone below and

Central Bristol, showing the route of the Bristol Harbour Railway.

furnace ashes above. It was stated to be 11 in. deep. The sharpest curve on the line had a radius of 15 chains and the steepest gradient was 1 in 100.

There were five under and two over bridges in addition to an opening bridge over a lock connecting Bathurst Basin with the Floating Harbour. There was an arched viaduct 346 yards in length and a tunnel 282 yards in length. Four of the under bridges had brick abutments and wrought iron girders, while the other, and one of the over bridges and the viaduct and the tunnel, were brick built. The remaining over bridge was a footbridge at Guinea Street and was stated to be in place of a private level crossing. The wrought iron girders of the under bridges and of the drawbridge were regarded as being sufficiently strong.

Colonel Yolland thought that the whole of the works were very well executed and the line was in good order, but it was not intended, at that time, to be used for passenger traffic. Thus there were no passenger platforms or stations. The signalling was in an incomplete state and there were no connections between facing points and signals. He suggested a catch siding should be put in near the top of the 1 in 100 incline to prevent vehicles running backwards down the incline and across Guinea Street level crossing. One was warranted, he felt, connected with signals at the Manure Works siding! There was no lodge at Guinea Street crossing as the law required, and Yolland felt, that the gate should be moved by a lever at the side. In this way the keeper would not have to go into the middle of the road, a dangerous activity since there was a good deal of traffic using it.

One of the items particularly mentioned by Yolland in his report was the bascule bridge at Bathurst Basin. He suggested arrangements should be made for cutting off the supply of steam when the bridge was nearly horizontal or vertical. This the engineer, Mr Richardson, stated he would do. In fact, the bridge engine has had a very interesting history for, being removed on the line's closure in the 1960s, it is now resident at the new industrial museum at Princes Wharf. A simple twin cylinder type, it was always kept in immaculate condition. Making about 110 r.p.m. to open or close the bridge, the latter was so well balanced that it needed roughly the same effort on the engine's part to raise or lower the bridge.

In November 1888 a schooner carrying petrol blew up in Bathurst Basin, covering the waters of the Basin with flames. Under the extreme heat the bridge warped slightly. Operating the bridge was a little more complicated than at some of the other City Docks' bridges, in that the bascule bridge was both a road and rail bridge while the water main supplying Wapping Goods Yard also ran across it, and this had to be disconnected. Two sets of gates and the operation of signals protecting rail traffic, all added to a more involved procedure. Interestingly enough, as late as 1961 an express goods from Temple Meads to Penzance, the 8.30 a.m. Down, was put down the Harbour Railway over the bridge.

Returning to Yolland's report, he states that the line was to be worked with the assistance of the telegraph on the absolute block system, and that arrangements were being made similar to those then existing at Swansea Docks. The arrangement was such that electrical contact would be broken when the bridge was open and no telegraphic communication would be able to take place. In addition, Yolland suggested that the Up line, on the western side of the bridge, should have facing points running into a blind siding whenever the Up signals were at danger and, since there was a good deal of shunting going on in the GW goods yard at Temple Meads, Yolland also recommended that similar provision be made on the Down line there to prevent trucks being kicked over the top of the incline. These works were subsequently carried out. Yolland's conclusion was that although he could not recommend the opening of the line to passengers, since the railway companies had no intention to prepare the line for passenger use, there was really no major stumbling block and so, on 11th March 1872, the Bristol Harbour Railway opened for freight business.

The line was an immediate success, so much so that in 1873 Parliamentary permission was obtained for further constructional work. This involved the building of two additional wharves, one on either side of Princes Street Bridge, while a third, over 1,400 ft. in length, was built further down river at Wapping. The rail extension to Wapping was opened in June 1876 by which time the Harbour Railway had become the exclusive property of the GWR.

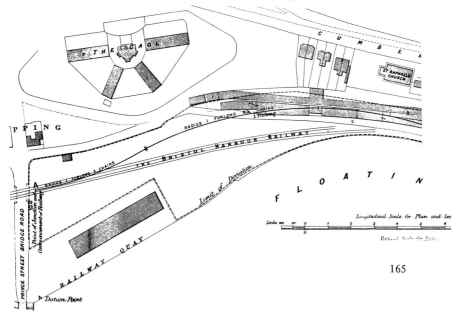

As we have read, and amazing as it is now to relate, it was not until the opening of the Harbour Railway that the City Docks in Bristol were actually connected to the main GWR network. This is particularly surprising when one considers that the GWR main line between Paddington and Temple Meads had opened some 31 years earlier on 30th June 1841. However, there had been high hopes of the docks becoming rail linked in 1863 when the Bristol & North Somerset Railway Company was incorporated with the aim of linking Bristol with Radstock. As part of the scheme, it was planned to construct a 'dock tramway' from Temple Meads down along the New Cut to a suggested quay on the south side of the Floating Harbour below Wapping. The line's precise route was to have been on the north side of the Avon along Clarence Road terminating in the area beyond Wapping Road. *(See map on page 163)*.

In spite of the fact that only around £16,000 of the £275,000 capital needed for the project had been subscribed at the time, work on the project began on 8th October 1863. On that date the Mayoress of Bristol, Mrs Sholto Vere Hare, 'laid' the first rail of the Dock Tramway. This is how the event was reported in the *Illustrated London News* of 17th October 1863.

'The first rail of the tramway connecting the North Somerset Railway with the Floating Harbour at Bristol was laid by the Mayoress, Mrs Sholto Vere Hare. The ceremony took place on a piece of ground on the towing path behind St. Raphael's Church, where a platform had been erected for the accommodation of invited guests. The shipping was also well filled with spectators, and from Mr W. Terrell's rope-walk to the edge of the water, with the exception of a small space reserved by the police, there was one dense mass of human beings. Rows of flags from various buildings, the rigging of vessels in the floating harbour, and, in fact, every salient point, imparted animation to the scene. The company was welcomed to the spot by the cheery strains of the artillery band and the merry peals of the bells of glorious old St. Mary Redcliffe. The work allotted to the Mayoress — which consisted of the filling of a highly ornamented barrow with earth, lifted with a silver spade, and wheeling it along a plank and overturning it — was efficiently performed, and was completed amid the applause of a large assemblage which the event had brought together. A large party afterwards adjourned to Mr Hyde's sail loft, which had been decorated for the occasion, and where an elegant dejeuner was served, and several speeches delivered.

The silver ornamentations . . . on the barrow and spade (used by) the Mayoress of Bristol, . . . were the work of Messrs Mappin Brothers of London Bridge . . . Mrs Hare's spade bears the crest of the Hare family, and underneath 'Presented to Mrs Elizabeth Hare, Mayoress of Bristol, Oct 8, 1863'. To which is to be added, 'In commemmoration of laying the first rail of the tramway of the Bristol & North Somerset Railway'.'

Mrs Hare, then Mayoress of Bristol, lays the first rail of the Bristol Harbour Tramway in connection with the construction of the Bristol & North Somerset Railway on 8th October 1863.

Author's Collection

However, the company's financial commitment proved to be overwhelming and some of the company's directors were ruined. In 1869 the company obtained a new Act in order to finish the works but this was not to be and, in May 1871, the proposed tramway to the Floating Harbour, which even then was still unfinished, was abandoned.

In 1880 the Bristol Tramways Company applied for powers to construct tramways on the quays in connection with the Harbour Railway, but the city council, after initially approving of the plan, subsequently reversed its decision. Some development did take place, however, in the spring of 1888 when four more sidings were brought into use at Wapping Wharf. These sidings remain in use today at the coal concentration depot.

However, many interested parties still felt that the City Docks should be better served by rail and so, on 8th October 1889, the council approved an extension of the Harbour Railway to the Cumberland Basin, with sidings for the timber wharves and the Irish cattle trade, and an experimental coal tip at the Cabbage Gardens, Cumberland Basin. The estimated cost of the extension was to be over £10,000. It was agreed that a Bill should be promoted leaving final details to be made with the GWR while the Bill was actually in Parliament. In June 1890, Mr Charles Wills told the council that the Bill had passed one Parliamentary committee with little opposition. However, since the Bill was due to go before the next Parliamentary commitee in a few days time, and no arrangements had been agreed with the GWR, Mr Wills proposed that the Bill should be withdrawn. This the city council agreed to.

The grain sheds and granary at Prince's Wharf, City Docks, in the early 1900s.

Author's Collection

In 1892, at a council meeting on 11th October, the chairman of the Docks Committee, Alderman Low, pledged the council to promote a Bill for the construction of a similar railway to the one of 1890. This again had its route from the Bristol Harbour Railway down to the Cumberland Basin and then over a bridge across the Avon to the Portishead line. The Bill, however, never reached the statute books for, in the following year, the corporation did an about-turn on the issue. After the Bill had been introduced into Parliament, Alderman Proctor Baker, on holiday when the October meeting took place, returned to fight the new Bill tooth and nail.

At a special meeting on 20th June 1893 the council was called to decide whether or not the Bill should proceed. Due to some difficulties concerning aspects of the Bill relating to work at Avonmouth Dock, Alderman Baker then recommended that the section of the Act relating to Avonmouth should be withdrawn. This was agreed to. He then went on to say that the clauses relating to the Harbour Railway extension should also be withdrawn and this too was agreed. And so, in spite of popular support for the Avonmouth and Harbour Railway aspects of the Bill, nothing was done about these two projects.

On 27th September 1895, the council recommended the construction of a wharf over 1,500 ft. in length from the Harbour Railway to the Cumberland Basin. The project was going to cost £120,000 and included £36,000 for the purchase of part of Messrs Hill's premises. The GWR had also undertaken to give another £20,000 towards general improvements. The wharf was to be built essentially to aid the development of the timber traffic which, it was suggested, was leaving the port. The work included a railway from the Harbour Railway to the Portishead line, with a swing bridge over the Avon. This plan too was a non starter.

On 16th October of the same year the council met, yet again, to discuss the issue. Indeed, Alderman Baker, now chairman of the Docks Committee, put forward the proposal that the above mentioned wharf and railway scheme should be carried out. This plan was not agreed upon. It is very interesting to note, incidentally, the way that Proctor Baker put forward and supported a scheme that, only two years before, he himself had violently opposed! Two years was a short time in politics, even then!

The process to build the long overdue railway dragged on until, at a meeting in July 1896, Proctor Baker proposed that the 1895 plan should be turned into reality. This the council firmly agreed to do. However, at a statutory meeting of Bristol citizens, on 29th September 1896, the proposed Bill was rejected by a large majority! Eventually, however, under the Bristol Harbour Lines'

Act of 1897, the GWR obtained powers to connect the Bristol Harbour Railway with the Portishead branch.

Work began on this project in September 1897. Construction work centred on two sets of lines. The first of these left the Bristol Harbour Railway at Wapping Wharf and ran westwards parallel with the New Cut of the River Avon. It then curved southwards to cross the Avon by a new swing bridge, the Ashton Swing Bridge, before joining the Portishead branch at Ashton Junction signal box. (The second line, considered in much greater detail in chapter 10, left the Wapping branch near Ashton Swing Bridge, passed eastwards along the north side of the Floating Harbour to terminate in a new goods yard and depot at Canon's Marsh).

In detail, the line from the Harbour Railway ran for a distance of 53 chains between the New Cut of the River Avon and the Cumberland Road, the latter having been diverted in order to make room for the railway. Incidentally, roughly 20,000 cubic yards of soil were removed to 'fit' the line in between road and river, the majority of this spoil being used to fill in a portion of the former Merchants' Dock which lay on the route of the Canon's Marsh extension on the other side of the harbour.

Some interesting new bridges were constructed on the Wapping—New Cut—Ashton Swing Bridge North signal box section. At 5 chains from the junction with the Harbour Railway, a new bridge was built to carry the Cumberland Road over the new railway. This bridge, with its skew span of 55 ft., was built with a steel superstructure formed of two main girders and trough flooring. The abutments were of masonry and, owing to the nature of the ground, were built on 12 in. x 12 in. timber piles. A second bridge, very similar to this first one, carried a new road over the line near Ashton Swing Bridge itself. The Wapping Wharf—New Cut—Ashton Swing Bridge North section was brought into use on 4th October 1906. Two months later, on 17th December 1906, the line connecting the corporation cattle pens at Cumberland Basin with the New Cut section was brought into action. This particular piece of railway bisected the main double track line of the Canon's Marsh extension at Ashton Swing Bridge North signal box.

By 1908 the GWR had berthing rights for 1,600 ft. of quay served by the depot at Wapping, and a very extensive grain traffic from ship to rail was dealt with here. By this time the corporation had also erected a large granary adjoining the depot and in addition there were two spacious transit sheds. All were rail connected with the depot. There was a large mileage traffic, principally of coal, timber and flour, while as many as 350 wagons were occasionally loaded from the depot in one day.

Redcliff Yard was also a mileage depot which daily handled a large number of wagons. There was a large amount of flour and feeding cake traffic loaded at Redcliff from mills in the vicinity, while inwards a regular, and heavy, coal traffic was also dealt with.

Once World War I came along, the Harbour lines were very busy with increased traffic in various commodities. Additionally, ships

Midland Railway Depot, St. Philip's, circa 1904, showing the wealth of traffic on tap. The view also shows one of the Midland Railway barges that plied between St. Philip's and the City Docks.

Author's Collection

An aerial view of the City Docks showing, from left to right, the line from Ashton Swing Bridge North curving around to the left, past Merchant Dock, along Hotwells Road and Mardyke Wharf, where two of Campbell's paddle steamers can be seen. In the upper right hand corner of the photograph is the crowded wharf at Wapping. On the extreme right can be seen the Ashton Swing Bridge North to Wapping Wharf section running along the New Cut.

Port of Bristol Authority

sunk by enemy action had to be replaced and Hill's Albion Dockyard played its part in building wartime, 'standard', ships. The railways of the City Docks played their own part in carrying vital war supplies.

Post-war, in the early months of 1925, the signal box at Junction Lock was rebuilt, re-opening as a ground frame on 18th March 1925. At Avon Crescent, a new signal box had also been built and this was in a more favourable position in relation to the crossing and the various interlocking arrangements. This too was brought into use on 18th March 1925. More warehouses were built during 1929 at Wapping Wharf to deal with the traffic then being handled. In addition, in order to improve the tempo of working the goods traffic between Temple Meads and Wapping Wharf and Ashton Swing Bridge North signal box, electric train token working was installed during the latter half of 1929. This replaced the wooden train staff working previously in use. The new system was in operation by January 1930. Two sections were necessary, namely Redcliff sidings to Bathurst Bridge and Wapping Wharf to Ashton Swing Bridge North. The Cumberland Basin ground frame, which had previously been locked by Annett's Key, was now locked by token, as was Moredon siding.

Incidentally, one of the incentives for the GWR to substitute electric train token working along the New Cut may have been the future and foreseeable use of the route as a diversion, while work was taking place on the main line in connection with the 1930s quadrupling between Filton Junction and Portishead Junction. In the following year additional siding room and other accommodation was provided for the coal traffic at Wapping Wharf. These were, indeed, busy days.

One of the railwaymen working both Portishead and City Docks lines in the 1930s was the late William James R. Pollard. After being a telegraphist (Booking Boy) at Bristol East signal box, he started as a Grade 2 porter at Pill on 29th August 1927 at the age of 20. During his time at Pill he applied for promotion several times but for some reason was never successful. One day, whilst he was cleaning and tidying up the stationmaster's office, he pulled out a drawer and found, to his surprise, all his applications neatly bundled inside — they had never been sent off! The next time he applied for promotion, the application was sent directly to Bristol, thus by-passing the stationmaster. Shortly afterwards an Inspector got off a Down train and demanded, from Mr Pollard, an explanation, which was duly given. It later came about that the stationmaster received a private rebuke!

Promotion came by the normal channels and, on 3rd July 1930, William Pollard started as a porter/signalman at Pensford. He returned to Bristol on 8th August 1931 as a Class 5 Goods signalman at West Depot/Swing Bridge North. (According to his notebook he was learning on the 8th, appointed on the 12th and 'on nights' on the 13th! Interestingly, only the 8th August appears on his staff record). While working at Swing Bridge North the following incident occurred. Mr Pollard had a Down train 'on line' from Ashton Junction to Wapping and had been offered an Up goods from Avon Crescent which he could not accept. Then came an urgent phone call from Avon Crescent; could he accept and give the road to the Up goods as there was a ship under way down the harbour and the Up goods was standing on Juncton Lock Swing Bridge? No doubt urged on by the thought of the ship colliding with the bridge, William Pollard returned the boards to normal behind the Down goods. He then pulled over the Down facing points for the Canon's Marsh line in order to release the Up trailing points. However, he was a second too soon, for the rear wheels of the brake van just caught the ends of the point blades as they moved across and they derailed. As the couplings of the goods grew taut around the curve towards Wapping, so all the wagons came off the road. However, at Avon Crescent, they had solved their dilemma by splitting the train, leaving the rear portion on the Canon's Marsh side, the forward portion drawing clear on to the Avon Crescent side. Very soon after, an Inspector arrived to question Mr Pollard about the incident, but as far as Mr Pollard's son is aware no disciplinary action was taken.

During the 1930—35 period engineering work on the main line brought passenger trains on to the Ashton—Wapping line. Indeed, this practice continued after this time when, for example, during World War II, bombing near the signal box at Bedminster, on the Temple Meads—Parson Street Junction section, blocked the main line for between 12 and 24 hours on 3rd January 1941. Once again in the Bristol Harbour Lines' history, passenger trains were seen traversing City Docks' metals. Mr Pollard eventually left Swing Bridge North and moved to Filton West signal box, where he started on 11th March 1935.

Leading on from what was said in the last paragraph, the traffic from the Canon's Marsh and Wapping areas was immense during World War II with pilots on duty 24 hours a day at both places. At those times when convoys were in dock, trains were formed at Ashton Meadows through to destination. There was no remarshalling etc. for these trains within the Bristol area, this practice ensuring the rapid clearance of these vital freights from the City Docks.

Bristol had to put up with occasional bombing attacks throughout the summer of 1940. However, the real blow fell on 24th November when the City Docks area was badly damaged and 200

REDCLIFFE GOODS YARD

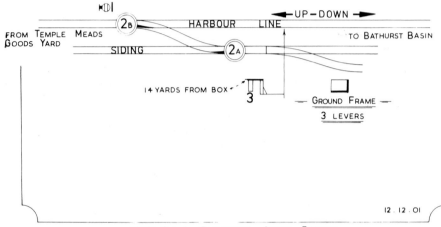

G.W.R. SIGNAL ENGINEER'S OFFICE READING.

people died. Charles Hill's shipyard was hit, as it was, yet again, in the next major raid on 2nd December 1940.

One incident during the war, recorded by D. J. Fleming in his railway reminiscences, concerned the Redcliff pilot. On this particular working, the small signal box at Redcliff was generally used for shelter when bombing became particularly bad. One night when bombing took place, the shunter had a brake van pushed inside Redcliff Tunnel for greater protection. Coincidentally, the box was hit that night and after that the tunnel, like others in the area, became regularly used as an air raid shelter. Once the war was over, port and railway activities soon returned to normal at Wapping and Canon's Marsh.

'To the returning servicemen in 1945, the Port of Bristol seemed much the same as the one they had left six years before. The busy self-confident life of the docks was vibrant as ever. Coasters called in at the City Docks again, and cargoes came and went as before from Princes Wharf, Canon's Marsh and Wapping. The Scandinavian timber boats were back at Baltic Wharf and joy of joys, the *Ravenswood* took Campbell's first post-war excursion out of Hotwells . . . Albion Dockyard was busy with new orders . . . Typical were a Trinity House light and buoy, a light-ship for Ireland, numerous dredging craft . . . and a variety of tugs'.

Text: *F. Shipsides and R. Wall*

174

The late 1940s and the decade of the 1950s were good years for the City Docks and before closure to commercial shipping, Wapping Wharf handled a variety of traffic including coal, esparto grass, wood and alcoholic beverages such as sherry and Guinness. The latter would come in on Guinness boats such as *Juno* and *Cato*, while another common cargo was sherry. Sometimes casks in transit would 'spring' or split and workers in the vicinity might go home that day with a little 'unofficial' sherry to their name. Meat traffic was also handled. For example, on Sunday evenings there would be railway meat specials to London. These trains, often hauled by 49XX 'Hall' Class engines, would be loaded with produce brought in by the meat boats which were also a regular sight in the City Docks.

The late 1950s produced two rather interesting railtours of the City Docks area. The first took place in 1957 when the RCTS organized a tour from Paddington to branch lines in the Bristol area. The tour had Class N15, No. 30453 *King Arthur* at its head from Waterloo to Reading. Here No. 3440 *City of Truro* took over for the leg, via Trowbridge, to Bristol. Ivatt 2-6-2 tanks Nos. 41202 and 41203 took the special over the dock lines along the New Cut to Ashton Junction, West Loop North Junction and the former GWR main line west to Wrington, Highbridge and Burnham. The special then returned to Bristol where No. 3440, ably assisted by 55XX class No. 5528 from Bristol to Westbury via Radstock, took the train back to Paddington.

In 1959, on Sunday 26th September to be exact, another special covered several of the goods only lines in the Bristol area. The three coach special, headed by an ex-works condition panner tank, No. 9769, visited Wapping Wharf, Canon's Marsh, Avonmouth, Yate and the branch to Thornbury. New ground was broken by the special's visit to Canon's Marsh goods depot. The coaches used were 57 ft. in length and great care had to be taken on the severe curves near Cumberland Basin Swing Bridge. The buffers almost locked in places, the railway staff having to loosen couplings for the sake of safety as well as ensuring that all points on the route were clamped.

On more ordinary, everyday, workings an interesting run was to be had on the single line from Temple Meads to Wapping Wharf through Redcliff Tunnel. Ron Gardner, a former GWR and BR (WR) driver, clearly remembers driving freights out over Victoria Street Bridge, past the yard at Redcliff goods to the General Hospital and Guinea Street. Trains would rumble on over the bascule bridge, which frequently caused delays, eventually reaching the level crossing at Prince Street and the Wharf at Wapping. Memories of the shunting staff in the line's later days, Joe Marton, 'Tiger' Lewis and Bill Rowlands, soon come drifting back!

175

Ex-LMS 2-6-2 tank engines, Nos. 41202 and 41203 haul an RCTS special on the Bristol Harbour line on 28th April 1957.

R. J. Leonard

An RCTS special, hauled by Nos. 41202 and 41203 rounds the sharp curve leading from the Wapping line on to the main Canon's Marsh line at Ashton Swing Bridge North. This train had been hauled by ex-SR 4-6-0, No. 30453, *King Arthur* from Waterloo to Reading, where ex-GWR, No. 3440 *City of Truro* had taken over for the Reading to Bristol, via Trowbridge, leg. Nos. 41202 and 41203 had handled the trip over the City Docks lines in the Bristol area. *City of Truro* hauled the train back to Paddington, with assistance from ex-GWR '4575' class, No. 5528, between Bristol and Westbury, via Radstock. The trip was organized by the RCTS and ran on 28th April 1957.

R. J. Leonard

There were complaints on many occasions from people living around Wapping because of noisy shunting at night and early in the morning. Ron believes that the complaints came mainly from the (then) vicar of St. Raphael's Church who lived in the nearby vicarage! The train most responsible for these complaints was the 5.40 a.m. transfer from Temple Meads to West Depot (via Wapping). Now, like the 23XX standard goods locomotives that used to haul these trains, the line under Redcliff and the extension to Canon's Marsh have gone. Indeed, with the 1960s came the run down of the City Docks and the beginnings of the decline and fall of the Bristol Harbour Railway.

From 1960 onwards the rot truly set in. In December 1960 the line over the Victoria Street Bridge was singled while two years later the once busy yard at Redcliff goods was closed on 1st June 1962. The entire line from Temple Meads Goods Yard to Prince Street was closed completely on 11th January 1964. Subsequently the closed section was lifted from Prince Street back to Temple Meads and today, with the major exception of Redcliff Tunnel, the alignment has all but disappeared under a new hotel, a road flyover and various industrial and commercial premises. Further removals took place at the Ashton end of Wapping Wharf in November 1966 when the siding to the timber firm of Wickham & Norris was closed.

However, all was not lost! Wapping Wharf was, and still is, served from the Ashton end. Today there is still, generally speaking, one daily coal train to Ashton Meadows sidings where a private owner locomotive from Western Fuels Limited takes the train along the New Cut to the coal concentration depot at Wapping Wharf. The locomotive normally involved in this working is the company's Hudswell Clarke diesel-mechanical 0-6-0 shunter, No. D1171, built in 1959. It was formerly used at both PBA Avonmouth and Portishead until Western Fuels Limited purchased it for their own use.

In the later days of steam haulage, most of the workings on the City Docks' lines were handled by ex-GWR 0-6-0 pannier tanks. In early diesel days, 0-6-0, Class D9500 diesel-hydraulic shunters often shunted the coal trains. These were supplemented by 0-6-0 diesel-electrics, Class 08, but larger diesels such as 'Westerns', 'Peaks' and 'Hymeks' were often seen on coal trains. As for traffic on the Ashton Junction/Wapping line in its later years there was still some variety.

Below is reproduced a typical Monday working during the September 1975 and July 1976 period as seen by Paul Holley.

'Around 8.00 a.m. a coal train, made up of both 21 and 24 ton

Wapping Wharf and Canon's Marsh in their heyday. Note the large number of railway wagons at Wapping and the timber being unloaded into barges for delivery to paper and cardboard mills further up the river. During World War II, the harbour lines were very busy indeed. When bombing raids occurred, all swing bridges were swung open in order to minimise damage to them. All trains came to a halt, the crews staying with their engines. It must have been a harrowing experience with the wagons, would arrive with coal for Western Fuels Depot at Prince Street. The engine would deposit the train at Ashton Meadows, run round and leave the branch light. After waiting some time at the level crossing at Ashton Junction, it would then proceed towards Parson Street around 8.50 a.m./8.55 a.m. Shortly afterwards, (the times varied) a diesel shunter would arrive. This would haul the full coal train to Whapping Wharf coal depot where it would do some shunting. It would return with the empties which it would leave in the sidings at Ashton Meadows. Shunting engines were sometimes seen leaving the branch as late as 4.30 p.m.'

'Later in the morning, often just after 10.30 a.m., a works train for BR's civil engineering depot at Ashton Gate would arrive and leisurely shunt an odd mixture of antiquated rolling stock in the sidings. After having formed a train with stock from the BR depot the train would depart, usually between 12.15 p.m. and 12.45 p.m. Sometimes departure was not before 1.30 p.m. and, exceptionally, much later if the morning arrival was late. At about 11.00 a.m./ 11.15 a.m. a train of woodpulp empties for Portishead Dock would pass through Ashton Junction. There would be a short stop at the temporary level crossing used for contractors' vehicles working on the flood alleviation scheme, near the headquarters of the Mounted Police. Incidentally, the latter had, by now, been built on the site of Clifton Bridge Station. The driver would open the gates for the train to proceed. By about 12.10 p.m. it would have returned loaded with woodpulp. It would wait alongside the Clanage playing field for the crossing gates to open and by 12.20 p.m. the train would proceed to St. Anne's Board Mill.'

'On rare occasions a short freight, made up of cement wagons bound for Portishead, would pass through Ashton Junction at around 12.30 p.m. while during the afternoon, usually between 2.30 p.m. and 3.30 p.m., another coal working would often run. Occasionally, a light engine would arrive, but more often than not this was usually a loaded coal train. Whereas the morning train might consist of up to 50 hopper wagons, the afternoon train often had fewer than 20 wagons, often 16 ton mineral, and on one occasion, Paul remembers only six in the train. The locomotive would then depart with the empties more often than not, although he can remember that once or twice there were full coal wagons in the train! Departure was around 3.30 p.m./ 4.00 p.m., sometimes later. Often as late as 4.30 p.m. the pulp train would return empty from St. Anne's to Portishead for the second working of the day. It would return again around 5.30 p.m. and the same locomotive would handle both the day's workings. Very occasionally, cement hoppers would be worked with the woodpulp wagons'.

Ex-GWR 0-6-0 pannier tank, No. 9729, swings around the curve near Ashton Swing Bridge North signal box and heads towards Wapping along the New Cut with a freight train in 1960.

D. J. Pollard

The lines to Wapping and Canon's Marsh were, generally speaking, both well used. The City Docks were always busy with such traffic as the Guinness boats from Dublin and the esparto grass boats from Spain and North Africa. This particular grass was used for making bank notes at a paper mill near Wookey Station on the line from Yatton to Witham, the Cheddar Valley line. Special trains were run carrying this grass and they were known to railwaymen in the local area as the 'Wapping and Wookey Specials'. These would leave Wapping Wharf, travel to Ashton Meadows and then on to the GWR main line to the West Country at West Loop North Junction. They would then travel on down the main line, the esparto grass being unloaded from ship to rail in the City Docks to Yatton where they would join the Cheddar Valley line for their journey to Wookey.

Photograph Port of Bristol Authority and text R. Cook

'During this period Tuesdays and Wednesdays were normally quieter, with coal and woodpulp workings only. On Thursdays a short freight for Portishead would pass through Ashton Junction at about 11.15 a.m. This usually consisted of four to seven Presflo wagons, and sometimes mineral wagons and box vans were included. This train later appeared more often on Fridays, often early in the afternoon. The return works train for the BR depot at Ashton Gate also ran on Fridays. Other workings during this period included rakes of empty wagons for storage at Portishead and road salt trains, the latter often being stored in a siding near the *SS Great Britain*. By late 1976 only one woodpulp train per day ran. By early 1977 the workings had become sparse and erratic and soon they ceased completely. During the summer of 1977 some 26 of the woodpulp wagons were stored at Ashton Gate alongside the Clanage.'

By 1980, although the coal workings continued, the shunting was now handled by *Western Pride*, the engine belonging to the Western Fuels Company. Portishead freight workings, basically cement, were far fewer and were handled, generally speaking, by Class 31 locomotives. Wagons, including new Railfreight vans, sometimes appeared at Portishead, presumably being in storage there. Occasional road grit trains still appeared and the works trains still continued in the Ashton area.

In the autumn of 1981 the ex-PBA 0-6-0 shunter *Henbury* (Peckett 1940) successfully completed a three week contract hauling 450 tonne loaded coal trains from Ashton Meadows to Wapping Wharf. The locomotive, preserved by the Bristol Magpies, a steam preservation group attached to the Bristol Industrial Museum, had received a full overhaul in the Port Authority's locomotive sheds at Avonmouth the previous winter. Once the 3 week contract expired another PBA locomotive, this time Rolls-Royce Sentinel No. 41 (10220), replaced the steam locomotive. Both engines were required as replacements while the firm's own locomotive was being overhauled.

Further activity occurred, in July 1981, on the Wapping/Ashton Junction section, when a serious collapse occurred on part of the Cumberland Road which had slipped into the New Cut. City of Bristol engineers had to relay track ballast on the Wapping line since, at one stage, the track was left suspended in mid air after the landslip. However, after a good deal of work by the City Council's engineers and PBA staff, the line was subsequently reinstated. Wapping Wharf remains linked to the main BR system by a spider's thread of a connection, the last remaining section of railway to reflect on in the City Docks.

Wapping Wharf, looking west on 25th August 1980. The loop to Cumberland Road/Ashton can be seen on the left of the picture.

Martin C. Smith

Chapter Ten

'Strangely enough, the GWR, whose foundation in the 1830s was conceived in Bristol, rarely showed any initiative to develop the port trade by rail facilities in the closing decades of the nineteenth century. They were virtually local monopolists and concerned to keep the MR from too close contact with any of Bristol's docks. Monopoly men wear leather suits.'

Text: *W. G. Neale*

In 1888 a Bill was introduced to put into effect a plan for connecting the Port & Pier line at Hotwells with the area around Canon's Marsh. It was not a new idea and the difficulty and expense of joining the district around Canon's Marsh to the railway systems to the east and south of the city had, for years, led people to think of the Port & Pier as the means to do this. The new line would have started from the Port & Pier Station at Hotwells and, after running through the rocks, along the back of St. Vincent's Parade, it would have emerged in Clifton Vale near Cornwallis Crescent, where there was to have been a station. It would then have continued underneath Clifton Wood, Jacob's Wells and Brandon Street emerging into College Street. There would have been a terminus on the site of Green's Dock which was almost exactly where the goods shed was finally built at Canon's Marsh in 1906. There would also have been branch lines to the gasworks and the, then, new wharf, both at Canon's Marsh. From there the line would have crossed the Floating Harbour, by means of a swing bridge, to the Grove and Welsh Back. This scheme came before Bristol Chamber of Commerce. In principle, it approved of the line but felt that certain sections of it should be under the control of the city council. This view was put forward to the council and the House of Commons. Indeed, they also sent a deputation to the directors of the Midland Railway urging them to support the project. It was, however, all in vain and nothing further was done.

In 1890, when the Port & Pier came into the joint possession of the GWR and the MR, people again began to ask if something could be done to connect it with the City Docks. The Chamber of Commerce encouraged both railway companies to support the scheme which was then being revived. Success looked more likely and the Midland Railway drew up the notice of its intention to apply for Parliamentary powers. The line was included in the Omnibus Bill then being promoted by the company.

This new scheme would also have started at Hotwells Station. It would have terminated on the eastern side of the Butts, opposite the then George Hotel, near today's Exhibition Centre at Canon's Marsh. The General Manager of the Midland Railway wrote to the Secretary of the Chamber of Commerce, on 17th November 1891, saying that the directors of the company intended to go ahead with the line. Later that same year, however, the Midland directors then declared that they were not prepared to take on a project involving so much capital expenditure. It was found, for example, that the amount of tunnelling involved would have pushed the total sum needed to build the line up to around £400,000 and so the proposal was reluctantly abandoned. In addition, a number of private citizens put forward a plan to build railway facilities to the north side of the Floating Harbour and to connect them, again by means of a tunnel, to the CER at Montpelier Station but once again the cost was found to be prohibitive.

A plan showing the proposed route of the railway from the Port & Pier Railway to the Grove : 1888 Act.

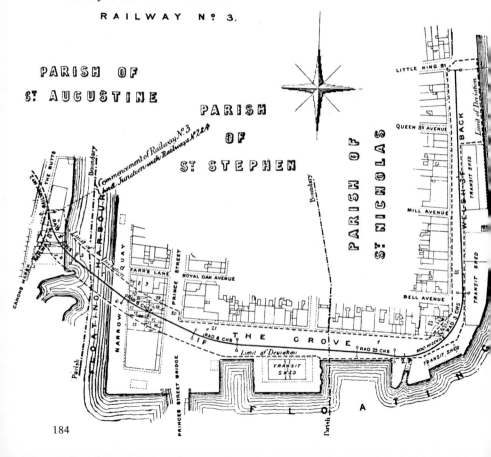

In 1892, the Chamber of Commerce again urged the Midland Railway to take action. They reasoned that the Bill that had been previously dropped, tacitly admitted the need for a rail connection to the north side of the harbour and that the construction of deep water berths at Canon's Marsh had increased the need for a railway connection. The Midland Railway promised to keep the matter in mind and, to make sure that they did, a large deputation of Bristol citizens saw the directors in November 1892. Again the company was favourably disposed to the plan and agreed to issue Parliamentary notices. The preparations for applying the Bill to authorize the line from the Port & Pier to Canon's Marsh were entered into. The project looked distinctly hopeful but, unfortunately, the matter was again dropped.

Yet again the Chamber of Commerce wrote to the Midland Railway, but to no avail. In order to maintain the momentum of the campaign to build a line, Mr (later Sir) George White laid before the city a plan to construct a line from the Port & Pier to Canon's Marsh with a station at Cumberland Basin. The scheme, prepared in September 1892, allowed for an extension from Hotwells Station avoiding most of the tunnelling put forward in the other proposals. The cost was to be around £140,000 but when the scheme was put to the Midland, it was rejected.

It seemed as if Canon's and Deans Marsh wharves would never be rail connected either with the Great Western or the Midland railways. The city council continued the struggle and they put forward plans, in 1892, for extending the Harbour Railway. This extension would have served the timber yards on the south side of the Floating Harbour, the line continuing down Cumberland Road and on across the Avon to join up with the Portishead branch across Ashton Fields. However, this line was not built after a strange turn around in council policy in 1893. The route to Canon's Marsh was tortuous but gradually history shows the build up to the route finally chosen.

In December 1895, the Chamber of Commerce once more intervened. It petitioned for a railway following almost exactly the route later adopted in 1896. This ran via the Cabbage Garden, Cumberland Basin, across various bridges over various locks, past the Merchants' Dock, Mardyke Wharf and then on to Canon's Marsh. In 1897, the GWR finally co-operated with the corporation in the building of a goods depot at Canon's Marsh. This was finished in the autumn of 1906. After all this preparatory work it seems ironic that considering the involvement, from the late 1880s onwards, of the Midland Railway, the construction of the line to Canon's Marsh was finally carried out by the GWR.

— BRISTOL TEMPLE MEADS GOODS YARD —

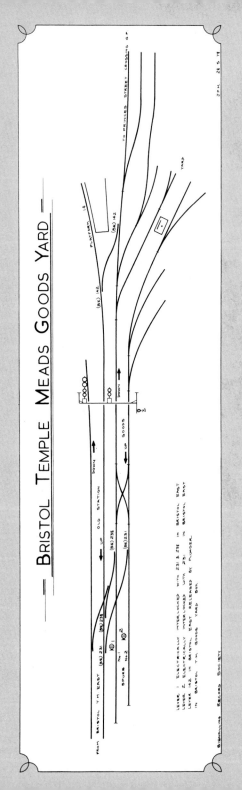

LEVER 1 ELECTRICALLY INTERLOCKED WITH 231 & 232 IN BRISTOL EAST
LEVER 2 ELECTRICALLY INTERLOCKED WITH 231 IN BRISTOL EAST
LEVER 142 IN BRISTOL EAST RELEASED BY PLUNGER
    IN BRISTOL T.M. GOODS YARD BOX.

SIGNALLING RECORD SOCIETY

SECOND EDITION, 1905.

GLOUCESTERSHIRE................SHEET LXXV. N.E.
SOMERSET................PART OF SHEET................VI.
BRISTOL CO. & PARLY. BORO.

All these plans and proposals suggest that the area around Canon's Marsh was rich in traffic potential for the railways. The reverse was, in fact, the case. Canon's Marsh itself was, at one time, Cathedral property and consisted of marshy meadows stretching from the precincts of the Cathedral down to the Avon, which later became part of the Floating Harbour. Before the railway came there was very little here; a gasworks, a marble and slate works, a few timber yards; so why did the GWR decide to build an expensive line to this fairly quiet part of Bristol right on the doorstep of the city centre?

The main aims of the project were as follows:

1) to give, for the first time, rail access to the deep water wharves on the north side of the Floating Harbour

2) to develop the advantages of Canon's Marsh as an industrial part of the city

3) and, by dealing with all West of England general goods at the new Canon's Marsh Depot, to relieve the congestion of traffic at other important goods stations, for example Temple Meads and Pylle Hill

On the branch to the new depot it was necessary to support the line alongside the Floating Harbour by constructing a retaining wall 500 ft. in length, and of an average thickness of 10 ft., built in concrete and faced with brick above water level. Beyond this was Mardyke Wharf, where provision had been made for unloading goods direct from ship to rail. The length of the wharf and the adjoining St. Jacob's Well Wharf was 19 chains. Ten chains further on was the entrance to the 'piece de resistance', the new goods depot itself, an impressive building served by an impressive yard of no less than 320 chains of sidings.

The shed was built of reinforced concrete on the Hennebique principle. It had warehouses, offices and the shed proper. The warehouse was 270 ft. long by 133 ft. wide, was 35 ft. in height and contained a floor area of over 35,000 sq. ft. There were two platforms 20 ft. wide running the entire length, and on these were eight cranes and three hoists all electrically operated. Four lines of track ran through the shed. The contractor for the building was Mr Robertson of Bristol, while the work was carried out under the supervision of Mr P. E. Culverhouse, architectural assistant to the new works engineer.

In connection with the new railway works at Canon's Marsh was the associated work carried out under the 1897 Bristol Corporation Docks Act. Under this Act the corporation increased the deep water wharfage at Canon's Marsh by 935 ft., making a total length of over 2,500 ft. They also laid railways around the quays at Canon's Marsh and these connected with the new GWR lines. The corporation also built two new transit sheds, one being 275 ft. by 113 ft., the other slightly smaller at 200 ft. by 93 ft. Both were double storied and were equipped for the most up to date and efficient transhipment of cargoes.

One notable result of the Canon's Marsh extension was to give the Bristol Gasworks at Canon's Marsh direct rail communication with the company's principal plant. It also provided direct rail access to the two tobacco warehouses which were then being constructed, by the corporation, close to the swing bridge over the Avon at the Cumberland Basin end of the Floating Harbour. One of these warehouses was 300 ft. by 100 ft. and had six floors, the other being 200 ft. by 100 ft. with nine floors. Close by were the lairage, cattle pens and sidings which had been provided chiefly for the Irish traffic. With the new developments the Cork and Waterford steamers were able to discharge their livestock within a few yards of these, thus avoiding a drive of one or two miles to the nearest railhead. Cumberland Basin and New Junction lock were both spanned by steel bridges, the latter being a swing bridge worked by hydraulic power.

Further description needs to be given of the Ashton Swing Bridge. This structure, built by Bristol Corporation, was unique in construction and controversial in cost. The bridge had originally been estimated to cost £36,500 and the GWR had agreed to contribute roughly a half share (£18,000 to be precise). In fact, the bridge eventually cost over £70,000 and, since the GWR had agreed to pay half, there was a good deal of public outcry when the true cost was revealed, especially as the GWR's contribution was specifically mentioned as £18,000 in the Act. The Docks Committee was accused of bungling the whole issue. Apparently the additional cost had been engendered by alterations to the location and construction of the bridge, while the Docks Committee had felt it undesirable to make the GWR pay a larger contribution because the committee were very keen to see Canon's Marsh rail connected. However, when work was completed, pressure was put on the GWR to contribute a larger sum to the cost of the bridge. This they did, £22,000 being the sum agreed and this was in spite of the fact that the Canon's Marsh railway project had cost the GWR £130,000 more than had been originally estimated.

The bridge, along with the rest of the Canon's Marsh/Wapping scheme, was opened for traffic on Thursday, 4th October 1906, by the Mayoress, Mrs A. J. Smith. The length of the bridge was

Ashton Swing Bridge.
National Railway Museum

THE WORKINGS OF ASHTON SWING BRIDGE

'. . . When the bridge-master wishes to swing the bridge for river-traffic, he rings, from the machinery-tower, a bell in each of the railway signal cabins, and as soon as the signalmen have withdrawn their bolts he receives a reply signal. The withdrawal of the railway bolts mechanically releases the lever by which the bridge bolts are actuated, and he withdraws these bolts. This movement back locks the railway bolts and electrically releases the lifting-press lever, which he then pushes over; and as soon as the ends of the bridge are lifted correctly, the sliding-lock lever is electrically fixed. When the sliding blocks are properly withdrawn, the ends of the bridge can be lowered and the action of lowering frees the starting valve handle, enabling the bridge to be swung open. When the bridge has been turned to its open position, one of the screens can be raised by means of a lever to obscure the red light for one direction only.

In order to close the bridge the screen must first be lowered so that the red light is again shown; then the bridge is turned to the railway position and the shooting of the automatic locking-bolts electrically frees the lifting-press lever; this lever is then pushed over, and the lifting of the ends of the bridge frees the sliding-block lever; the sliding blocks are then inserted and the lifting-press lever is pulled over to lower the ends of the bridge; this electrically releases the interlocking-bolt lever which is moved over, thus electrically locking the turning, sliding-block, and lifting-press levers, and mechanically releasing the railway bolts, which being shot put an electric lock on the interlocking lever.

Electric indicators fixed in the machinery-tower give the following information to the bridge-master.

1.   Railway bolt : shot or withdrawn
2.   Lifting-presses : up or down
3.   Sliding blocks : in or out
4.   Automatic locking-bolt : shot or withdrawn
5.   Bridge set for road or river

Of the first four indicators, there are two sets, one for the nose end and the other for the rear end . . .'

Text: Savile in 'Swing-Bridge over River Avon' Inst. C.E. Vol. CLXX

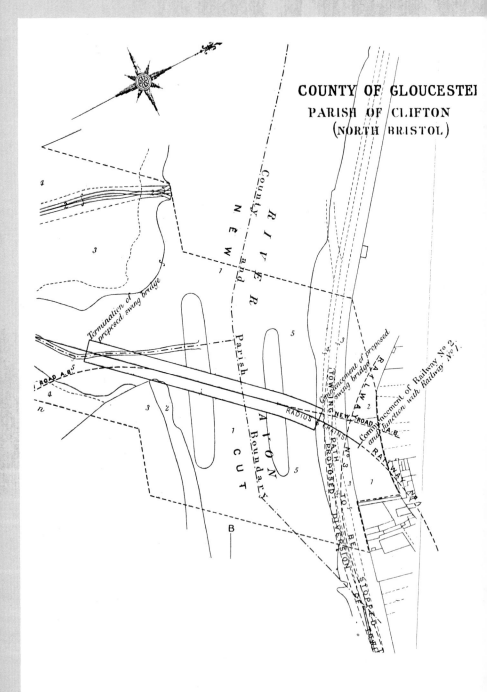

582 ft. and it contained 1,500 tons of steel in its original condition. Opened and closed by hydraulic power, it was worked from a central control tower, the swinging portion of the structure weighing 1,000 tons and being 202 ft. in length. Bristol made, the bridge was built by John Lysaght & Co.

The river traffic, for which the bridge was designed to swing, consisted, for the most part, of small coasting vessels and barges which, at that time, entered the docks via Bathurst Lock and Basin. Larger vessels used the deeper lock at Cumberland Basin and, even at its time of construction, there was some doubt as to whether there was any real need for a 'swinging' bridge at Ashton. Indeed, by 1912, it had been discovered that the decline of traffic up the New Cut meant that the Ashton and Vauxhall swing bridges did not really justify their being kept as opening bridges. However, there were problems in closing them and although the matter came up from time to time, it was not until the 1930s that the Ashton Swing Bridge was finally swung for commercial traffic, 3rd February 1934 being the exact date of this event. The bridge was eventually made a fixed bridge under the 1951 Bristol Corporation Act. The control cabin and top road deck were removed as part of a comprehensive road and bridge rebuilding scheme that was completed in 1965 at a cost of over £2½ million.

Returning to 1906, and the construction of the line between Ashton Swing Bridge and Ashton Junction, the route passed through Ashton Meadows and here siding accommodation had been provided for the storage of wagons en route to and from Canon's Marsh. Near the junction of the new line and the Portishead branch a bridge, carrying the former Ashton Road over the railway, had been constructed in order to give clearance for the additional tracks of the Canon's Marsh/Wapping lines. Once under this bridge the new tracks joined the old at Ashton Junction signal box, which was opened 20th May 1906. Incidentally, the branch to Canon's Marsh had other signal boxes at Ashton Swing Bridge South, Ashton Swing Bridge North (junction for the Wapping line) Avon Crescent, Junction Lock and Canon's Marsh.

Before leaving the new works altogether, we need to mention the new construction work that had been taking place at West Depot, on the GWR main line to Weston-super-Mare, near Portishead Junction. Here extensive siding accommodation had been provided along with two relief lines laid in for a distance of 63 chains. A double track connecting loop had also been laid in from the Exeter direction joining the Portishead branch at West Loop North Junction. The Up relief line was brought into use on 8th April

1906, the Down relief on 6th May 1906 while the West Loop curve itself came into use on 4th October 1906 along with all the other Bristol lines' works. All of these works were designed and carried out under the supervision of Mr W. Y. Armstrong, the new works engineer for the GWR. The contractor for the portion of the line from Merchants' Dock to Canon's Marsh, including the new depot, was Mr Strachan of Cardiff. The rest of the work was carried out by Messrs Nuttall of Manchester.

The Bristol lines soon settled into efficient operation. One way that this had been achieved was the fact that the Inspector in charge at Wapping and Canon's Marsh was made directly responsible for the supply and berthing of empty wagons. He alone was responsible for the working away of traffic and this helped to facilitiate traffic working generally. One interesting point to note here was that the Inspector on the Harbour line was supplied with a uniform trimmed with gold braid. The reason for the admiral-like uniform was that the GWR considered it gave the Inspector greater authority over the dockmen. By all accounts, there had been few delays over the various swing bridges during the first year of operation and the corporation had co-operated fully with the GWR in moving the traffic on offer.

Early in 1924 authorization was given to improvements in the lifting appliances then in existence at Canon's Marsh. The scheme consisted of the extension of two of the existing electric platform cranes, in order to get a greater height of lift when dealing with bulky loads. A 30 ton electric gantry crane was to be provided in the yard to replace a 12 ton fixed crane then in use. The new electric cranes were brought into use by January 1926.

A former GWR and BR (WR) man, Ivor Phillips, reflects upon his experiences as fireman and later as driver in the Canon's Marsh area from the late 1930s onwards. He remembers when Canon's Marsh Goods Yard handled beer, imported Guinness, imported steel and crated general goods and cargo. The yard itself was partly surrounded by an iron fence. Approaching the goods yard from the city centre, one came across a pair of gates at the bottom of Canon's Road and these led into the yard. First you passed the goods shed and just beyond this building was the shunter's cabin. This was long and narrow, one half of it being reserved for the foreman and the other for the shunters. The iron fence mentioned above ran up the right hand side of the yard and on the other side of this fence was Anchor Road and beyond this was the Cathedral back. The fence also ran along the bottom of the yard to another set of gates. These led out on to the City Docks and were locked when not in use. On the left hand side looping up the yard was

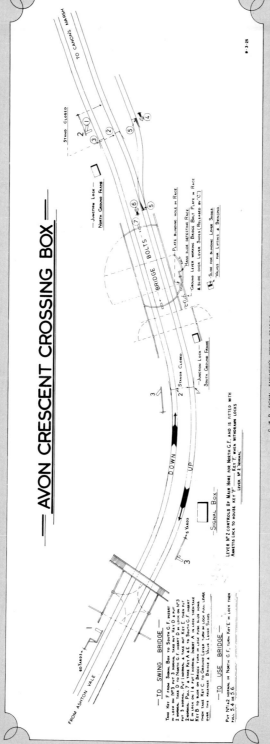

─ AVON CRESCENT CROSSING BOX ─

─ TO SWING BRIDGE ─

Take Key F from Signal Box to South G.F. insert
in lock on N°3 put 3 normal, take out N°1 D & put
2 normal, take D to North G.F. insert D in lock on N°3
put 3 normal, put 1 normal, & take out Key E then put
2 normal. Put 7 & take N°1 A & E to South G.F. insert
E in lock on 1 & put 1 normal, Insert A in lock then take
Key B to slide on Bridge, turn in lock push slide home,
then take Key C to Ground Lever turn in lock pull lever
over releases Bridge & Valve Lever Shoes.

─ TO USE BRIDGE ─

Put N°1 & 2 normal in North G.F. turn Key E in lock then
pull 5, 4 or 5, 6.

Lever N° 2 controls Up Main Home for North G.F. and is fitted with
Annett's lock to house key "F". Key "F" when withdrawn locks
lever N° 2 normal.

G. W. R. Signal Engineer's Office Reading

one wall of a large tobacco warehouse. This wall enclosed the yard on that side.

At the top of the yard was a crossing leading from Anchor Road to Gas Ferry Road. This, naturally enough, led on to the ferry which plied across the Floating Harbour. It was a dangerous crossing because so many people used it. There were lorries going to the gasworks, seamen going to their ships and people on their way to the ferry. There was a signal box at this crossing called Canon's Marsh signal box and this controlled two banner signals, one for trains going out of the yard and the other for trains going in. The small levers operating these signals were about 1 ft. in length.

The remarkable thing about Canon's Marsh box was its size. It was only about 12 ft. long and 4 ft. wide. Indeed, it was so small that two men could not pass one another inside without turning sideways. Many spent years of their working lives in such a confined space. The staff had to be very accustomed to trains for wagons passed very close by and there was very little room to spare. It only needed one truck to jump the road when passing the box and the men inside would have been 'goners'. Still, throughout Ivor's years on the railway, he told me that nothing untoward had ever happened at this spot.

Gas Ferry crossing proved difficult in other ways in that, with this type of yard, trains had to be kept on the far side of the crossing on the Down road until room could be made for the trains from Temple Meads to pull into the yard itself. An additional problem was that since Canon's Marsh was a mileage yard where wagons were loaded, sheeters on the day turns were always sheeting loaded wagons. These men carried the sheets on their heads and with them they climbed up ladders on to the top of wagons. Drivers always had to be on the look-out for these sheeters when shunting. Other obstacles were the horses with their carts drawn up against the wagons. Going out on to the dockside, a shunter always walked in front of an engine to stop any traffic coming along the road which led from the city centre. Mention of the docks leads us on to another interesting aspect of traffic working at Canon's Marsh. At the time Ivor knew the branch, Class 15XX, 17XX and 20XX tank engines were using the yard, their lightweight also allowing them to go out on to the quayside. However, their lightweight was also a serious disadvantage since they slipped so much when shunting the yard.

Being very near the edge of the dock, there was always danger from so many obstacles all around. There were ropes from cargo ships, items such as boxes fouling the railway tracks and, on many

The late Mr W. A. Jupp, pictured with his shunting crew at Canon's Marsh on 25th July 1935. In the distance Brandon Hill and Cabot Tower can be seen.

Paul Holley

occasions, it took quite a time to shunt the network of tracks around the docks. Sadly, one of the old foremen was killed stepping over one such rope leading from one of the ships, moored at the quay. This rope was looped over one of the bollards which are always to be found on the docks and when the ship moved slightly, the rope, being a little slack, tightened, came up and caught the man. The injury he received cost him his life.

Another similar incident occurred one night when shunting was taking place along Gas Lane. A Polish seaman, coming from his ship, saw a row of wagons stop on the crossing. He started to crawl under the wagons just as the shunter called the engine back. Unfortunately the seaman's legs were severed. A young shunter held the pressure points on the man's legs until the ambulance came, and then he returned to his work. Ivor feels that the shunter should have been shown some appreciation from the GWR, but this did not happen. This shunter is now deceased, but Ivor reckons he was the sort of person that he will always remember.

It was almost impossible to avoid this type of accident when shunting, for it was obvious that the crossing keeper, or the shunter, could only be on one side of the rake of wagons at any one time. This could easily lead to trouble, particularly when seamen came back from a night out, some of them a little the worse for drink! Often they would take chances just as the Polish seaman had done.

Working a transfer freight which, in Ivor's days, was generally worked by 0-6-0s of the 23XX, 24XX and 25XX series, from Temple Meads into Canon's Marsh, had its interesting side. Once across the Basin Swing Bridge, the freights passed along the backs of shops, the latter's fronts facing out on to the Hotwells Road. Roughly between every five shops there was an entrance way from the shops out on to the railway tracks, and more than once collisions occurred between trains using the line and cars and lorries.

WORKING AT CANON'S MARSH ON SUNDAYS — In accordance with an undertaking given by the British Transport Commission, no train or engine must run between Lower College Green Avenue and the road known as the 'Butts'; nor must any shunting or moving of any train or wagons be carried out during the hours of service at the Cathedral on Sundays in a manner which is likely to be audible in the Cathedral.

No sounding of the whistle of any engine between the points shewn above must take place during the hours of service in the Cathedral on Sundays.

Having talked a little about freight working on the Canon's Marsh let us now take a trip on the line. We have already seen how the 15XX, 17XX and 20XX classes were commonly used on the line. The 17XX and the 20XX had their rear sand boxes on the footplate and this was a real nuisance for the firemen who had to prepare them. They often skinned their knuckles when filling the boxes with sand or when they were firing the locomotives. These engines were stabled at St. Phillip's Marsh and drivers were allowed 45 minutes to prepare them for the road. One of the turns Ivor worked to Canon's Marsh Goods Yard was as follows:

He used to book on duty at 6.15p.m. and departure 'off shed' was roughly 45 minutes later at 7.00p.m. During this time the engineman did any oiling required, filled the lubricator, examined the engine for any defects and tried both vacuum and steam brakes. The fireman prepared the fire until he had a good head of steam, examined the smokebox and ensured that the smokebox door was screwed up tight. He also tried the sanding equipment, front and rear, and checked that they both delivered sand right down on to the rail. He topped up the sand boxes when empty, trimmed the headlamps and ensured that the rear lamp was complete with its red shade. With the help of the driver, he filled the tank with water and then, when all was done, the footplate crew were ready to leave the shed which, in Ivor's case, was generally around 7.00p.m. Leaving the shed, bunker first, locomotive and crew travelled, via the loop line at St. Phillip's Marsh, out under Bath Road Bridge, down through Bedminster, on to Malago and then to Parson Street box and over the branch to Ashton Junction box. Taking the Wapping and Canon's Marsh line we would head up toward Swing Bridge South box, would cross the Swing Bridge itself, arriving at Ashton Swing Bridge North signal box. Trains for Wapping would pick up the single line staff here, although it was double track for us to Canon's Marsh!

From Ashton Swing Bridge North box we continued on to Avon Crescent Crossing, where the signal box operated the road gates and also the signal for the Swing Bridge over the Basin. Once over the bridge the train squealed round the curve past Merchants' Dock, on again past Pooles Wharf, until we finally reached the black and white banner signal protecting Gas Ferry Road crossing and the yard at Canon's Marsh. Once the signal was in the 'off' position we went into the yard, but not before we had received an additional signal, by hand, from the crossing keeper. We arrived at the yard around 7.45p.m. the timing depending on whether the Swing Bridge was open for rail traffic. The pilot, until our arrival, shunting the yard, would then couple on to the front of the train it had been forming and leave the yard as the 8.00p.m. transfer freight to West Depot. Once the train was put off at West Depot, men and engine went off to shed, again via the loop at St. Phillip's Marsh. It was very rare to go to shed through Temple Meads.

Having seen the journey Down, let us quickly catch the 8.00p.m. transfer back. This train ran all week except Saturdays. It was worked by the pilot engine which had been shunting all day at Canon's Marsh. As soon as the relief pilot engine arrived in the yard, at around 7.45p.m., the pilot went on to the train it had already formed, which, incidentally, was usually made up of wagons carrying mixed traffic. The guard would come up, give details of the load and take the name of the driver and the number of the engine. With the banner signal in the 'off' position and, at night, the green light from the crossing keeper, you gave a touch on the whistle and started to move out of the yard. When you felt you had a tight chain on the couplings and saw the guard's van moving off, (at night the guard would wave his lamp when this happened), you could touch the whistle to acknowledge this. As you left the yard the Floating Harbour would soon come into view on your left. Lying alongside the quay was the training ship *Flying Fox* and as you approached it you could often see cars, owned by the officers on board, fouling the Down road. Stopping the train you would walk aboard and inform those in charge that they would have to come and move them. Once this had been done and you had received the signal from the guard, you would be clear to set off again. You had to be always on the look-out along this stretch to make sure all your train was on the move and in one piece, for the youngsters around this area of Hotwells would sometimes slip between the wagons and uncouple them. A guard would often see his train disappearing into the distance after it had been delayed for some reason. The regular guards who worked these transfer freights knew when the Swing Bridge would be swung and how long it would take to get into Canon's Marsh. While waiting for the bridge to move back for rail traffic, they would slip around the corner to their favourite drinking house, have a quick one and then quickly get back into their van. After all, if by the time they returned from the pub their train had gone, it was only a short walk to the yard at Canon's Marsh!

The section of the line between Ashton Swing Bridge North and Canon's Marsh was always full of incidents, and something was always going on. There was the traffic along Hotwells Road, the ships berthed on the Floating Harbour, while across the Harbour was Heals Dockyard and, as you passed by, your attention was sometimes distracted by the launching of some ship. This line was truly part of old Bristol. It reminded Ivor of the old tram days. It had so much character and it is sad to think that it is now only a memory. Ivor's final comment was, that in those days, a railwayman's life was very demanding and he worked all the hours that God sent. However, like many other railwaymen I have talked to, Ivor gave me the impression that he enjoyed the work, that time passed quickly and that he would be quite happy to see those days again.

Ronald Gardner, whose name cropped up in the previous chapter, worked the lines to Portishead and Bristol City Docks from 1936 until the cessation of steam from St. Phillip's Marsh shed in the early 1960s. I'll let him reflect on some of the events and places mentioned earlier in the text.

'A fairly typical day would begin at 7.05 a.m. when we would book on duty at St. Phillip's Marsh shed. In the early days we would prepare engine No. 1538, while from the 1940s onwards, the chances would be that we would have a member of the 22XX or 36XX classes. In the 1950s, engines of the 94XX class were allowed to work to Portishead and over the Wapping Wharf line.

Ex-GWR 0-6-0T, No. 9769, is seen with the RCTS special on the Bathurst Basin Swing Bridge, (Bristol Harbour line) on 26th September 1959. This bridge and line have long since been dismantled.

R. J. Leonard

Ex-GWR 0-6-0T, No. 9769, crosses Cumberland Basin Swing Bridge with an RCTS special on the branch to Canon's Marsh Goods Depot on 26th September 1959. This bridge and line have long since been dismantled.

R. J. Leonard

They were subsequently allowed to work the Canon's Marsh road.'

'Off shed by about 7.50 a.m. we would then run light engine to West Depot Up side. Here we would pick up our goods train and this we would propel from the yard towards South Liberty Junction signal box. Then, making our way to West Loop North Junction, we would travel on through Ashton Junction to Clifton Bridge, Oakwood, Pill, Portbury Shipyard loop, Portbury Station and on down to Portishead. Here we shunted the yard as required, the usual traffic being coal, timber and, from the 1950s onwards, phosphorus. Once the shunting was over the engine was turned on the turntable adjacent to the old power station, Portishead 'A'. We then had a cup of tea and at about 12.20 p.m. our reliefs came on duty and we worked a passenger train back at 1.34 p.m. Our arrival at Temple Meads was 2.05 p.m. Here we were relieved, walking back to St. Phillip's Marsh to book off duty at around 3.05 p.m.'.

'A couple of points to note here, the first being in connection with the turntable at Portishead. It was of a rather different design to that to which I was accustomed on the GWR. It was large enough to take a 22XX or a 23XX standard goods engine and you actually went round with the table, since the turning mechanism was operated from the table itself. As mentioned previously, once we had shunted the yard we worked the 1.34 p.m. passenger back to Bristol. The engine for this turn was usually a Class 55XX 2-6-2T and it was often my luck to get engine No. 5577! This was always my favourite (!) since it was a locomotive that never steamed freely. Unfortunately, I seemed to have more than my fair share of this engine. Other locomotives I can remember working the line included Nos. 5512, 5535, 5547, 5548 and 5561. Sometimes we would get engines of the 37XX or 46XX classes, depending upon the general availability of the locomotives on shed.'

'As far as the personalities, I can still remember some of the shunting staff then at Portishead. People like 'Tot' Callard and Ron Hayman, while the refreshment rooms on the station platform were, of course, run by Mr & Mrs Howe. It was very easy to remember her; she was lovely, with golden plaited hair, lovely skin and very good looks, all the locomotive men will tell you the same. Still, I had better move on, I think! The chaps in the signal boxes, and the shunters helped to make their job so enjoyable, and memories of driver, fireman, guard and shunter having a quiet five minute nap, before leaving Portishead around midnight on a late freight or light engine, still come to mind.'

There would sometimes be operating problems on the line but these were rarely serious and were due, mainly, to the single line working which, of course, involved having to wait for trains at the various crossing points, such as Pill. Occasionally, some delay was caused by the felling of trees in Leigh Woods, between Clifton Bridge and Oakwood loop, while at other times problems were sometimes encountered with the very wet rails in Pill Tunnel. All were fairly minor in nature!'

'On the traffic side, I think it should be mentioned that the Portishead, Wapping Wharf and Canon's Marsh lines were feeders to the former marshalling yards at West Depot, Temple Meads and Stoke Gifford. For example, the 3.05p.m. train from Portishead conveyed traffic for Albright & Wilson of Birmingham. This was conveyed to Stoke Gifford yard for the 11.20p.m. Stoke Gifford and Oxley sidings freight. Also it must not be forgotten that the Saturdays only transfer from Canon's Marsh conveyed traffic to West Depot for the 10.55p.m. West Depot and Plymouth (Laira) while the 7.20p.m. transfer from Temple Meads to West Depot contained certain traffics for Plymouth, Taunton, Exeter and Barnstaple. There was also a transfer from Temple Meads at 8.45p.m. to West Depot for the 10.55p.m. West Depot and Barnstaple. This conveyed an occasional wagon for Taunton. In addition, there was also a transfer at 8.10p.m., Stoke Gifford to West Depot, for traffic to Taunton, 11.45p.m. and Exeter, 2.30 a.m. Another late night transfer was the 11.10p.m. West Depot, Wapping, Temple Meads and Stoke Gifford, this conveyed traffic for Gloucester and Worcester. Finally, in the period from the 1930s to 1948, another transfer would start from Ashton Meadows at 11.30p.m. This conveyed coal empties to Pengam sidings, Cardiff!'

'On the Canon's Marsh line it was very common for trains to be stopped on several occasions, due to the swing bridge being in operation or when people left cars fouling the line in the proximity of the RNVR ship *Flying Fox* and, of course, it needed action on the part of the engine crews to remove the offenders. Other problems often arose when crews were shunting the private sidings, due to the number of public footpaths crossing the line at various places including those at Heber Denty's timber siding and at Osborne & Wallis' coal siding.'

Also along this stretch, an incident of special note occurred around 1937. Number 5 transfer was leaving Canon's Marsh around 8.30a.m., engine and van, for Ashton Meadows and the engine, a Class 23XX, was travelling tender first. As was the usual procedure, the fireman had made a cup of tea and both he and the

No. 1 Tunnel, as seen looking towards the former station site at Clifton Bridge. Running under the Suspension Bridge, the tunnel is 59 yards in length and, as can be seen from the photograph, is generous in its proportions. This view was taken in August 1980 when the author walked the line. At that time, the line was still carrying the occasional freight working. Generally, these were cement trains bound for the depot of the former (new) station at Portishead.

Author

The Port of Bristol Authority engine, *Lionel*, an 0-6-0ST built by Peckett in ▷ 1889 (No. 466). This engine worked for a time at Portishead, eventually being sold by PBA in 1951. This photograph was probably taken when the locomotive had been delivered new from the Bristol works of Peckett in 1889. At that time, Portishead was served by two PBA engines, namely *Harold* and *Alexander*. However, *Lionel* was used initially at the Avonmouth installations.

Courtesy D. Cross

driver were trying to snatch a bite to eat, breakfast having been fried on the shovel, as was the custom in those days! At a point some half-way along Hotwells Road, a lorry pulled across the rails and started to unload its cargo of beer on to P. & A. Campbell's pleasure steamer *Glen Usk*, which was tied up alongside the harbour wall. What happened next was unbelievable in that neither driver nor fireman saw the lorry, belonging to D. M. W. Bullock Limited of Canon's Marsh, bottlers of Bass etc!, and before any evasive action could be taken, the lorry and its contents were pushed into the Floating Harbour. A subsequent enquiry into the accident, not surprisingly, laid a considerable amount of blame on the driver. Fortunately, no lives were lost.'

'As a young fireman, I was working at Canon's Marsh on the evening turn one very dark, winter night. It had been pouring with rain for several hours when, walking along Anchor Road I saw three of the ladies of 'easy virtue' who were always much in evidence in those days in the dock area. Of course, if there were no ships in port there was 'no work' and times were hard! This particular night, these three laides were soaked to the skin due to the heavy rain, and I remember the keeper at Gas Ferry Crossing telling them to go a little way down towards the gasworks and there they would find a nice fire in the watchman's hut so that they could dry their clothes. You can imagine the railwaymen's curiosity to walk down to the watchman's hut and see three ladies as naked as the day they were born! You can just picture the amusement this caused to the half a dozen men who were on duty at the time!'

'One other thing about Canon's Marsh that deserves mention was the method of shunting out on the dockside. When trains went out over the dockside roads the foreman, in my time it was 'Fanny' (Fred) Wheeler, would walk in front of the locomotive with a red flag in order to warn the dockers of the locomotive's movements. However, most shunting was done when the dockers were at meals, or during the night when the dockers were not working. Wagons were put out on to the docks during the night for loading the following day.'

'In conclusion, I remember one particular point of interest about one of the signalmen at Ashton Swing Bridge North signal box. Mr Ball (senior), signalman in this box at the time when I was a young fireman on the line, had lost one of his legs in an accident. Some years later, Mr Ball's son, who worked in the locomotive department, also met with an accident in which he, too, lost a leg and had to leave that particular department. He became a signalman at Ashton with his father, a real family concern indeed!'

During World War II the City Docks were the target during Easter 1941 for what came to be called the 'Good Friday Raid'. Canon's Marsh and Broad Quay were hit and nearly 200 people lost their lives. Throughout the war Albion Dockyard, Charles Hill and the railways in the City Docks were all busy.

The end of the war brought changes. On the docks' railways in the late 1940s, engines Nos. 2031 and 2035 were regular performers on the Wapping and Canon's Marsh lines, but these were later replaced by locomotives of the 16XX class. However, as with the Wapping line, after the boom years of the 1950s, the demise of the City Docks in the early 1960s led to cut backs on the neighbouring railways. On 1st July 1958 Ashton Swing Bridge South signal box was closed. This was replaced by a new ground frame at Ashton Meadows which was brought into use at the same time. On the same date, Ashton Swing Bridge North box was renamed Ashton Bridge. The decline of both the dock and the dockside railway and depot continued and, on 14th June 1965, the Canon's Marsh extension was closed with less than 60 years service to its name. The whole scheme was, perhaps, built far too late in the first place?

Some idea of the way in which the line to Canon's Marsh was worked in its final years was kindly given to me by Mr Colin Weeks who, during 1963, worked as signalman at Avon Crescent. By this time the only remaining signal boxes left open on the line were the boxes at Ashton Swing Bridge North, Avon Crescent and Canon's Marsh. Colin describes his own box at Avon Crescent as follows:

'It was a ground floor box and it was very much like a large garden shed. It had three levers, two block bells and two block instruments and lighting was by a single gas light. A single gas ring was also supplied for cooking purposes and heating was by coal fire. The box did not have electricity or running water, and any water required had to be collected, by the Avon Crescent signalman, from Ashton Swing Bridge North signal box.'

The Ashton Swing Bridge itself, incidentally, was unlocked by the signalman at Avon Crescent and was swung by lock keepers provided by the Port of Bristol Authority. This 'grand opening' was known as 'the ceremony of the keys' and Colin suggested that the only man who could really swing the bridge properly was Mr William Buck of the PBA. He alone seemed to have the 'knack'. The swing bridge was worked by two hydraulic rams connected by a heavy chain wound around a large pulley wheel on the spindle of the bridge. Shipping took precedence over rail traffic,

A view of Ashton Swing Bridge Junction in October 1965. At the fork, the lines to the left go to Canon's Marsh and the lines to the right, to Wapping Wharf.

R. J. Leonard

The Ashton Swing Bridge in October 1965.

R. J. Leonard

and if a ship lost the tide because the rail bridge was blocking the ship's passage, the railways were responsible for the payment of demurrage.

There were two shifts for working the box at Avon Crescent; the first of these ran from 6.00 a.m. until 2.00 p.m. whilst the second ran from 2.00 p.m. until 10.00 p.m. General traffic workings over these two shifts were as follows:

EARLY TURN — 6.00 a.m. until 2.00 p.m.

6.00 a.m.	(Monday mornings only). At this time the week's pilot engine would come off shed and run to Canon's Marsh, while the engine that had been employed there during the previous week should have returned to shed the previous Saturday night.
8.30 a.m. until 9.30 a.m.	(Monday to Saturday). About this time a transfer freight worked to Canon's Marsh. The signalman at Avon Crescent would give the guard of this train the keys to unlock the sidings at Merchants Road and at Poole's Yard.
11.00 a.m. until 11.30 a.m.	The above transfer would return from Canon's Marsh and would, if required, shunt Poole & Co's. siding, again under the control of the guard. It would also deal with traffic at Heber Denty and Osborn Wallis sidings, these points and signals being controlled by the Avon Crescent signalman working in the ground frame at Junction Lock North. After the guard had returned the keys of the sidings to Avon Crescent signal box, the train would leave for West Depot.

LATE TURN — 2.00 p.m. until 10.00 p.m.

2.00 p.m. until 2.30 p.m.	During this time, a transfer trip to Canon's Marsh would run.
4.30 p.m. until 5.00 p.m.	A return working of the above transfer would take place.
5.30 p.m. approx.	Another transfer would run up to Canon's Marsh.
7.00 p.m. until 8.00 p.m.	Finally, the last transfer of the day would run from Canon's Marsh to West Depot. This train was scheduled to follow the 7.30 p.m. Wapping to West Depot transfer on from Ashton Swing Bridge North signal box.
Approx. 10.00 p.m.	On Saturdays only, the pilot engine from Canon's Marsh would run on to shed.

At this point in the line's history, there were various interesting special workings. For example, during the autumn of 1963 a fair number of timber ships arrived in Merchants Dock and this gave an increase in the rail traffic handled. Indeed, the morning transfer had a fairly busy time of things shunting empty wagons in and full wagons out of Heber Denty's siding. Some of these shunts involved crossing the road at Avon Crescent. One particular load worthy of note was that attached to a morning West Depot—Wapping transfer. This was a ship's diesel engine bound for the Albion Dockyard.

One amusing incident occurred during the evening rush hour at the end of a hot summer day. A goods train was waiting to leave Avon Crescent for Bristol East Depot. However, road traffic was blocking the level crossing and so the gates could not be opened. As signalman, Colin asked the motorists to pull clear of the crossing, which all but one promptly did. This allowed him to open two of the gates. For the second time he asked a motorist to move clear of the crossing. However, he still met with a refusal. On hearing this the locomotive driver said that he would soon change the motorist's mind. He gave a long blast on the engine's whistle and started to move the train. At the same time he opened the locomotive's cylinder drain cocks, and sprayed the car with steam! When the steam had cleared the motorist looked out of his car window to see a pannier tank towering high above him. This seemed to bring about a change in the attitude of the motorist who quickly moved clear. The remaining two gates were opened and the train departed without further ado!

Locomotives used at this time included pannier tanks of the 57XX and 96XX varieties and they were used on the transfers along with diesels of the D63XX type. Naturally any diesels used on the Marsh line had to have a short wheelbase in order to negotiate the very tight curves encountered on the route. In diesel days, the Canon's Marsh pilot engine was usually a 204 h.p. diesel-mechanical of the 03 ('Noddy') type although 0-6-0 Class 08 ('Growlers') were also to be seen. In general, nothing heavier than the 2251 class 0-6-0s and pannier tanks were allowed over the Harbour lines and, in reality, the panniers had virtual monopoly. Fairly heavy panniers, for example the 94XX class, were allowed into Canon's Marsh but, if the sidings on the dockside were to be shunted, lighter versions, for example the 16XX class, were used instead.

And so, in June 1965, the line closed to traffic and all the remaining signal boxes were closed. The goods yard at Canon's Marsh was later converted into a corporation car-park. Such then was the Ashton Swing Bridge North Junction/Canon's Marsh line in its declining years. Today, even the route of the line is fast disappearing under new housing and commercial development. It was a most interesting, busy, inner-city, dockside branch that has, unfortunately, vanished forever.

Ashton Junction — Canon's Marsh.

LEVEL CROSSINGS.

The following Level Crossings are protected by fixed signals and Crossing Keepers are in charge by day and night, except Sunday nights after 10.0 p.m., when the Boxes are closed and gates are across the railway giving free user to road traffic.

(1) Ashton Crossing (worked from Ashton Junction Signal Box), (2) Avon Crescent, (3) Gas Works Lane.

N.B.—Gas Works Lane Crossing and Avon Crescent Crossing are worked by the respective Signalmen.

The undermentioned Level Crossings are not in charge of Crossing Keepers nor protected by fixed signals:—

(1) Cumberland Sidings, (2) Nova Scotia, (3) *Tongue Head, (4) *Cattle Lairs, (5) Denty's Timber Yard (6) *Merchants Dock, (7) *Blackhorse Lane, (8) Dock Gates Lane, (9) Poole's Siding, (10) Canon's Road.

Gates at Level Crossings.— Gates are provided at the Crossings shewn above, and in the case of the Crossings marked with an asterisk (*) there are small side gates as well as the large road gates; they will be open for the passage of traffic across the line, but are arranged that they can be fastened so as not to obstruct the running lines.

Gas Works Lane Level Crossing.—This Crossing leads from Anchor Road to the Gas Works and is a busy thoroughfare. It is of the greatest importance that the Crossing should be kept clear for the public as far as possible. Guards and Shunters must see that no undue occupation occurs, and trains must be brought to a stand clear of the Crossing, and not be allowed to stand on or foul it except for shunting purposes.

Speed when approaching Level Crossings.—Drivers must approach each Level Crossing shewn above at a speed not exceeding 4 miles per hour, and they must keep a good look-out to satisfy themselves that the Crossing is clear before passing over, and at Gas Works Lane the man in charge must shew an all-right signal to the Driver, viz.: a green flag by day and green light by night, if the Crossing is clear for the train to proceed.

Denty's Timber Yard Crossing.—This is to be used only by Denty's Limited, for the purpose of hauling their traffic across the running lines to and from their timber depots. The gates on each side will be shut and locked by the Employees of Denty's, Limited, after each user and the Firm will retain the key of the gates. When hauling across the level crossing, vehicles must never be allowed to stand on or foul of the running lines, or interfere in any way with the passage of trains, and the users of the crossing are responsible for ascertaining the position of trains approaching, before attempting to cross the lines. The crossing is not to be used during fog or falling snow, or in any way to endanger or delay the traffic on the lines of the Commission.

DOCK LINES AT QUAYS AND SHEDS AT CANON'S MARSH AND DEAN'S MARSH.

The Dock Lines serving the Quays and Sheds at Canon's Marsh and Dean's Marsh are laid on Corporation property adjoining public thoroughfares, and are approached from the Canon's Marsh Depot by a double line connection which crosses Canon's Road on the level.

Engine power and Staff for working traffic on the Dock Lines will· be provided by the British Transport Commission, and the following instructions must be observed in carrying out shunting operations:

1. Before moving wagons on Dock Lines, Enginemen must give notice by whistling once, and Shunters and others, before giving the signal to the Engineman to move such wagons, must always walk the whole length of the wagons and personally caution each individual who may be engaged on or near the line, and at the same time make him understand at what time it will be safe to resume his work. Shunters and others when at work on the Dock Lines with engines are required to instruct the Drivers verbally, as far as possible, with respect to the movements of the engines, and not to trust to hand signals.

2. When it is necessary to pass over Canon's Road Crossing in either direction, the Foreman must see that a man is stationed there with a red flag by day and a red light after sunset, to keep foot passengers and road vehicles clear of approaching trains, and he must further satisfy himself that no road vehicles or other obstruction is foul of any of the line over which the shunting movements are about to be made. When the movement over the crossing has commenced he must proceed to carry out his duties in the Docks.

The train or engine must stop before passing over the Crossing.

3. When a light engine, or an engine **drawing** vehicles, is working over Dock Lines, the Under Shunter must walk in advance of the engine, at such a distance from it as will ensure the train or engine stopping short of any obstruction, and when an engine is **propelling** vehicles the Head Shunter must walk in advance of the first moving vehicle taking the same precaution. The Foreman must see that, when necessary, men are so placed as to be able to repeat the Head Shunter's signals to the Driver.

4. Under no circumstances must vehicles be loosely shunted on the Dock Lines, but they must remain attached to the engine when moving.

5. Not more wagons than can be readily controlled must be drawn or propelled over the Dock Lines during the shunting operations.

6. Drivers of engines working over the Dock Lines must exercise the greatest vigilance, and be prepared to stop short of any obstruction. In no case must the speed exceed 4 miles per hour.

PBA LOCOMOTIVES USED AT PORTISHEAD

Engine name and number (PBA)	Works Number	Maker and date taken over by PBA	Date/place scrapped
Alexander	280	0-6-0 ST (o.c.) Fox Walker 1875	Portishead 1937
Harold	459	0-6-0 ST (o.c.) Peckett 1887	Portishead 1949
Lionel	466	0-6-0 ST (o.c.) Peckett 1889	1951
Leslie	1371	0-6-0 ST (o.c.) Avonside 1898	South Wales 1933
Kenneth	808	0-6-0 ST (o.c.) Peckett 1900	Avonmouth 1959
Murray	1006	0-6-0 ST (o.c.) Peckett 1904	Came from Avonmouth in 1947. Had returned there by August 1952. Scrapped in 1958
Alfred	1679	0-6-0 ST (o.c.) Avonside 1914	Came to Portishead around 1943. Returned to Avonmouth and scrapped on site by Pugsley in 1959
William	1725	0-6-0 ST (o.c.) Avonside 1915	Went new to Portishead. Subsequently returned to Avonmouth. Scrapped about 1964
Gordano	D894	0-4-0 diesel-mechanical Hudswell Clarke 1954	Went new to Portishead. Transferred to Avonmouth in May 1966. Later in the same year it was returned to Portishead. Scrapped at Romford in 1973
Norman	D774	0-4-0 diesel-mechanical Hudswell Clarke 1950	Went new to Avonmouth. Sent for trials to Portishead in 1953. Returned to Avonmouth the following year. Went to Albright & Wilson in 1969
Dubglas	D916	0-6-0 diesel-mechanical 1956	Went new to Avonmouth. Was sent to Portishead in 1971. Sent to Romford in 1973. Later resold to a Belgian firm
No. 30	D1171	0-6-0 diesel-mechanical 1959	Went new to Avonmouth. Was sent to Portishead in 1972. Subsequently sold to Western Fuels Limited at Wapping Wharf

.c.) indicates outside cylinder

Text: Industrial Railway Society/B. D. Stoyel

APPENDIX I

PBA LOCOMOTIVE FACILITIES AT PORTISHEAD

In 1875, the PBA locomotive *Alexander* was sent to Portishead. It seems likely that sometime after this, probably after 1879 when Portishead Dock was opened, shed facilities for this locomotive were provided. Indeed, reference to a GWR survey of 1885 shows what appears to be a dock authority engine shed near the entrance lock on the Portishead Station side of the dock. Further reference to PBA maps at the turn of the century confirm that this particular location was, in fact, the site for the PBA's original locomotive shed.

The next date of any importance relating to the shed facilities for PBA Portishead, is the spring of 1951 when a contract was placed for the construction of a new locomotive shed, workshop and stores on the south side of the dock. This move had been made necessary by the building of the new Portishead 'B' Power Station. This later shed was a two road affair and was situated near timber sheds one and two. It was closed around 1970, later being used as a canteen. PBA locomotives used at Portishead in the late 1970s were stored in the open once the shed had been closed.

APPENDIX II

TUNNELLING TOPICS

Redcliff (or Bristol Harbour) Tunnel
Double track tunnel brick-lined throughout. Runs under the churchyard of St. Mary Redcliffe for a short distance. Very little cover over the tunnel and in one place in the tunnel you can look up and see a large pipe with the arch carefully built around it. Closed to traffic on 1st January 1964.

Clifton Bridge No. 1. Tunnel
Also known locally as *Suspension Bridge Tunnel*. It is immediately below the bridge. The tunnel itself appears wide enough for two tracks, but the cutting at the Portishead end is only wide enough for one track. Brick lining, but sidewalls left partly unlined.

Clifton Bridge No. 2 Tunnel
Also known locally as *Nightingale Tunnel*, being close to Nightingale Valley. A short section in the middle is brick lined, the rest being unlined. Quite impressive inside.

Sandstone Tunnel
Lining: brick arch, stone sidewalls. Portals are in stone.

Pill Tunnel
Brick lined throughout.

Text: *P. Marshall/The Tunnel Study Society*

APPENDIX III

SIGNALLING SECTION

Additional signalling information: Portishead line

West Loop North Junction — closed 10th May 1936, hereafter controlled from Ashton Junction.

Ashton Junction — 49 levers GWR 5¼in. twist frame.

Clifton Bridge — 27 levers GWR 5¼in. stud frame. The box closed on 4th November 1966.

Oakwood — 18 levers. Opened 14th May 1929; closed 9th September 1960.

Pill — 15 levers GWR 5¼in. stud frame. Frame ordered 2nd August 1918, therefore the box was probably built sometime in 1919. The box closed on 14th April 1964.

Portbury Shipyard — 57 levers GWR 4in. horizontal tappet. Opened: 29th January 1918; closed: 14th April 1964.

Portishead (old box) — 40 levers. Opened: June 1908; closed: 4th January 1954.

Portishead (new box) 83 levers GWR 5 Bar 4in. vertical tappet. Opened: 4th January 1954; closed: 5th April 1965.

Text: *J. D. Francis*

Local Restrictions

Bristol (Temple Meads) to Wapping Wharf (Route colour — red)

Permitted Engines

All classes except ex-GWR 'King' Class, 47XX Class, BR standard Class 8 (4-6-2 and
Gas Turbine locomotives Nos. 18000 and 18100
Trigger Cock Gear Lever to be removed from Class 61XX engines

Stations	Connections and Sidings	Engines Prohibited
Bristol (T.M.) Goods	All waterside and shed roads	BR standard, Classes 6 & 7 (4-6-2), Class 4 (4-6-0) and Class 5 (4-6-0), ex-GWR Classes 78XX, 40XX, 49XX, 59XX, 69XX, 79XX, 47XX, 4073, 50XX, 70XX, 68XX and 10XX
Redcliff Wharf	Nos. 3, 4 & 5 sidings	BR standard, Classes 6 & 7 (4-6-2), Class 4 (4-6-0) and Class 5 (4-6-0), ex-GWR Classes 78XX, 40XX, 49XX, 59XX, 69XX 79XX, 47XX, 4073, 50XX, 70XX, 68XX and 10XX
Wapping Wharf	No. 5 sidirg to Chard's Junction opposite St. Raphael's Church Junction to Coal Road Junction to Quayside Warehouses	BR standard, Classes 6 & 7 (4-6-2), Class 4 (4-6-0) and Class 5 (4-6-0), ex-GWR Classes 78XX, 40XX, 49XX, 59XX, 69XX, 79XX, 47XX, 4073, 50XX, 70XX, 68XX and 10XX
Wapping Wharf	Line adjoining the Quayside	All engines

Wapping Wharf Junction to Ashton Bridge Junction (Route colour — uncoloured)

Permitted Engines

All uncoloured engines, Classes 2251 and 4500 to 4574, 57XX (Yellow), and BR standard
Class 2 (2-6-0)

Stations	Connections and Sidings	Engines Prohibited
Cumberland Sidings	All sidings	Classes 2251 and 57XX
Ashton Swing Bridge	Corporation Cattle Pens	Engines with outside cylinders

Ashton Junction to Canon's Marsh (Route colour — uncoloured)

Permitted Engines

All uncoloured engines, Classes 2251 and 4500 to 4574, 57XX (Yellow), BR standard
Class 2 (2-6-0), and Classes 84XX and 94XX (single, coupled together, or coupled to any other
permitted engine)

Canon's Marsh Dock Side

Class 57XX engines may work into Canon's Marsh Dock Side subject to the following restrictions:-

1) To work with the A.T.C. apparatus clipped up
2) Not to negotiate the curved track at the stopblock
ends of 'A' shed, Shute Road and Oil Road

BRISTOL AND PORTISHEAD

Name of place	Direction of trains		Miles per hour
	From	To	
Portishead Branch	Speed at any point not to exceed		35
Clifton Bridge	Bristol	Portishead	10
Oakwood	At either end of Loop		20
Pill	Bristol	Portishead	10
Portbury Shipyard	Single Line	Up Loop	10
Portbury Shipyard	Up Loop	Single Line	10
Bristol West Depot	West Depot	West Loop North Junction	10
(Goods Running Loop)	West Loop North Junction	West Depot	10

BRISTOL HARBOUR LINE
Temple Meads to Wapping
Wharf Junction

	Either direction	5

Over Bathurst Basin
Bascule Bridge

WAPPING WHARF JUNCTION TO ASHTON SWING BRIDGE

Name of place	Direction of trains		Miles per hour
	From	To	
From Wapping Wharf Junction to New Cut side of Cumberland Road Bridge	Either direction		5
From New Cut side of Cumberland Road Bridge to Level Crossing opposite Underfall Yard	Either direction		10
From Level Crossing opposite Underfall Yard to Ashton Swing Bridge North Junction	Either direction		5

ASHTON JUNCTION TO CANON'S MARSH

Over Ashton Swing Bridge	Either direction	5
Over Junction Lock Swing Bridge	Either direction	5
Over all Level Crossings	Either direction	5
Any other point between Ashton Junction and Canon's Marsh	Either direction	10

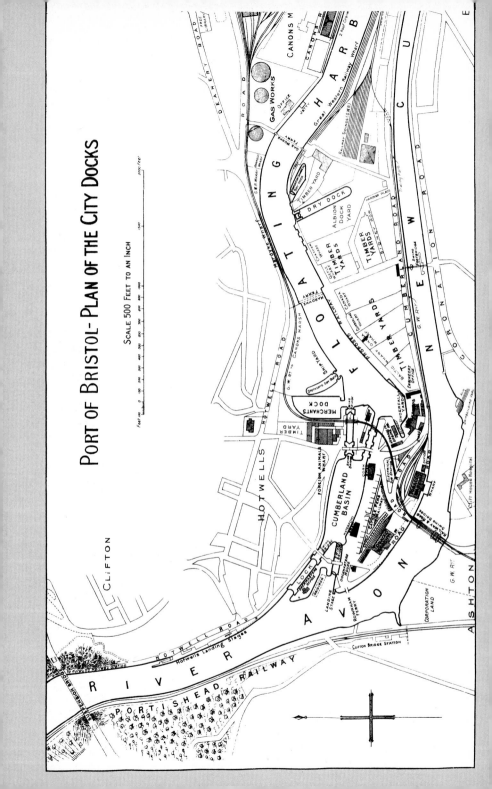

PORT OF BRISTOL - PLAN OF THE CITY DOCKS

SCALE 500 FEET TO AN INCH

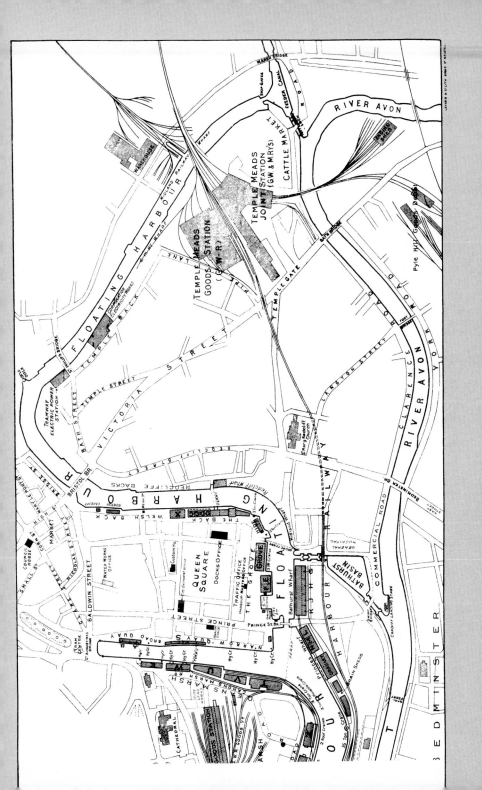

SS Indian (9,121 tons) in Portishead dock, circa 1904. Note the timber seasoning in the dock and the sailors astride the masts of the sailing ship on the right.

Author's Collection

Portishead Dock, circa 1910, showing, in the foreground, part of the goods yard with the line from Bristol sweeping in from the right over an embankment that was slowly replacing the original wooden viaduct that spanned the Pill at Portishead.

M. J. Tozer

No. 7783, nearing Portbury Shipyard crossing loop, with the 1.30 p.m. Bristol to Portishead train, on 17th February 1962.

H. Ballantyne

Tickets: *Michael Wyatt and Photography Steve Smith*

The improvements undertaken in the Bristol area during the early 1930s included the rebuilding of the station at Parson Street. These two photographs show the station in both its original and rebuilt forms.

OPC Collection

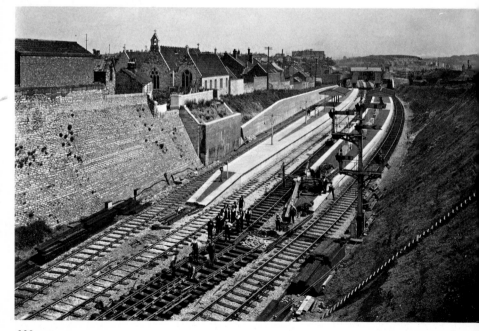

it coils. The goods shed had two platforms, each 600ft in length, fitted with electric cranes and hoist, and altogether 100 wagons could be dealt with under cover. The warehouse, which occupied the upper part of the goods shed, had an area of nearly 4,000 sq. yards and was laid with wood block flooring. It was equipped with electric hoists for rapidly conveying traffic to and from the platforms beneath.

OPC Collection

SELECT BIBLIOGRAPHY

Buchanan R. A. & Cossons N. *The Industrial Archaeology of the Bristol Region* David & Charles (1969)

Clinker C. R. *Closed Stations & Goods Depots* Avon Anglia (1978)

Cooke R. A. *Track Layout Diagrams of the GWR & BR/WR Section 19* (1975)

Cullen E. *Industrial Development by Railways* (Canon's Marsh) GWR Magazine (June 1906)

Fleming D. J. *St. Philip's Marsh* Bradford Barton (1980)

Hateley R. *Industrial Locomotives of South Western England* Industrial Railway Society (1977)

Latimer J. *Annals of Bristol* (all volumes)

Lyons E. *An Historical Survey of Great Western Engine Sheds 1947* OPC (1972)

MacDermott E. T. & Clinker C. R. *History of the Great Western Railway* Ian Allan Limited (1964/1967)

Neale W. G. *At the Port of Bristol* PBA (1970)

Redwood C. *The Weston, Clevedon & Portishead Railway* Sequoia Publishing (1981)

Vincent M. G. *Lines to Avonmouth* OPC (1979)

Warnock D. W. *The Bristol & North Somerset Railway 1863-1884* Temple Cloud (1978)

Warnock D. W. & Parsons R. G. *The Bristol & North Somerset Railway since 1884* Avon Anglia (1979)

Wells C. & Stone G. F. *Bristol & The Great War 1914-1919* Arrowsmith (1920)

Whitley H. S. *The Canon's Marsh Extension, Bristol* GWR Magazine (July 1906)